D0200410

PREFACE

by Abraham H. Foxman
National Director, Anti-Defamation League

One of the great untold stories of the Holocaust was that of the thousands of children who, like me, survived by hiding or being hidden from the Nazis. Many were still emotionally "in hiding" until fifty years later when we at last revealed our stories at the First International Gathering of Children Hidden During World War II in May 1991 in New York City. Some 1,600 of us from around the world together broke the silence about how we survived Hitler's killing machine. We spent three extraordinary days talking . . . with each other and about each other. Jane Marks, the journalist who had first brought these children to the nation's attention with her *New York* magazine article, was at the Gathering to share this moving experience with us.

We exchanged stories about our hiding places: how we lived for months in sewers, closets, barns, and fields; how we joined the partisans and fought the enemy; how we stayed alive. We examined the guilt that continues to haunt us; the pain we felt at losing our loved ones; our anger; our inability to speak of these experiences with our family; our identity crises; and our confused, frightening, lost childhoods.

We had many questions borne out of fear and guilt. Who were we compared to those who faced unspeakable horror and annihilation in the death camps and ghettos? Was it really safe to reveal our Jewish identity to the world? Could anyone but another hidden child really understand how we felt?

Yes, someone could. Jane Marks listened as many of us shared our personal stories with her and we realized that yes, someone else who had not lived through this experience *could* understand.

We came to realize the importance of other people hearing our stories so that they could understand the Holocaust in terms of the living as well as the six million Jews who died. Jane Marks became the keeper of our stories.

It was a weekend of miracles and healing. The barrier was broken at last. No longer would we remain silent, ashamed to speak of our past. Though the war had been over for nearly fifty years, we still had been in hiding . . . and now we could face the dawn of a new day.

Jane Marks's *The Hidden Children: The Secret Survivors of the Holocaust* is an extraordinary contribution to an understanding of the Holocaust. Her collection of first-person accounts, by those who survived the war against Jewish children, preserves for history the courage and resources of the hidden as well as those who rescued them.

For me, these inspiring accounts symbolize the triumph of good over evil. They bear repeating in this age of Holocaust denial.

When I was an infant growing up in German-occupied Poland, I was called Henryk Stanislas Kurpi. To all the world, Bronislawa Kurpi was my mother. Actually, she was my Polish

Catholic nanny who promised my parents she would take care of me. I was baptized and raised as a Catholic. My parents survived the camps and returned to claim me. A custody battle with my nanny ensued but my parents won. Eventually, my family and I moved to the United States.

Imagine the confusion and pain this turn of events inflicted on all involved. There I was, a Jewish child, making the sign of the cross in the home of my parents, who were observant Jews. Slowly I had to reclaim my identity and learn about Judaism and what it meant to be a Jew.

After I graduated from New York University Law School, I joined the staff at the Anti-Defamation League. Ever since, my life's work has been in Jewish advocacy and the defense of human rights for all people. Perhaps this is the legacy of my years as a hidden child.

It is a source of pride for me that ADL helped arrange the first Hidden Child Gathering in 1991. Since then we have joined with the conference organizers to establish the Hidden Child Foundation/ADL, under the auspices of the ADL Braun Center for Holocaust Studies. The Foundation has thrived, thanks to dedicated volunteers. Support groups have sprung up across the United States and Canada, throughout Europe and even as far away as Australia. In July 1993, the Second International Gathering took place in Jerusalem, bringing together even more hidden children from all over the world.

Many thousands of us are still in virtual hiding. Some, particularly in Eastern Europe, are still afraid to admit they are Jews because of rampant anti-Semitism. Others may not even be aware of their true identities because their Jewish families perished during the war and their adoptive parents chose not to reveal their backgrounds.

We should remember that many rescuers were ostracized

by their countrymen for saving Jews during the Holocaust. Today, it is still an uncomfortable subject in some countries.

It is our hope that adoptive families will hear about the work of the Hidden Child Foundation/ADL and understand how important it is to restore their adopted children to their heritage. Only then will their gift of life be made whole.

As you read the stories in Jane Marks's collection, you will be struck by the strength of those who survived by their wits and the grace of God. Many went on to live normal lives, completing college and entering the professions. They became parents and grandparents, doctors, lawyers, therapists, accountants, teachers, writers, artists, social workers, nurses, and business executives.

We can only wonder about the fate of the children who did not survive . . . how many Nobel Prize winners did we lose? These thoughts will always be with me and motivate me to try harder and to reach a little higher.

Jane Marks's book is also a story of hope. Those who survived depended on the goodness and kindness of others. Some had been betrayed, but more often they found those rare men and women with the moral fiber to do what is right. It is ironic that the nightmare and horrors of the Holocaust also became a defining moment for courage and decency.

We need to lift our thoughts beyond the bestiality of that era. Our mission now as hidden children is to focus on the goodness of humankind. We need to bring the message to friends and foes alike that there is hope . . . that there are men and women of good will with the courage to care about others.

My family and I will be eternally grateful to them.

CONTENTS

CONTENTS

THE HIDDEN CHILDREN

The Secret Survivors of the Holocaust

JANE MARKS

Fawcett Columbine

NEW YORK

To a world in which all children are safe

A Fawcett Columbine Book
Published by Ballantine Books

Copyright © 1993 by Jane Marks
Preface copyright © 1993 by Abraham H. Foxman

"A Historical Perspective: Tracing the History of the Hidden-Children Experience," copyright © 1993 by Nechama Tec, Ph.D.

"The Psychology Behind Being a Hidden Child," copyright © 1993 by Eva Fogelman, Ph.D.

Library of Congress Catalog Card Number: 94-94573

ISBN: 0-449-90686-8

Cover design by Georgia Morrissey
Cover photo: Annette Baslaw-Finger, taken by her father, David Szer

Manufactured in the United States of America

First Ballantine Books Trade Paperback Edition: April 1995

10   9   8   7   6   5   4   3   2   1

ACKNOWLEDGMENTS

My first debt of gratitude is to the hidden children, without whose trust and friendship I could never have written this book. It must have seemed as if I was always there: nagging, pestering, probing; and even through tears you never said, "Go away!" or "I don't really want to do this." In fact there were times when it was *your* encouragement that kept me on track. I thank Nicole David, who really launched this project and never left me stranded; and the others: Rosa Sirota, Renee Roth-Hano, Kristine Keren, Richard Rozen, Kim Fendrick, Leon Ginsburg, Lola Kaufman, Sanne Spetter, Marie-Claire Rakowski, Ruth Rubenstein, Joseph Steiner, Clem Loew, Joe Vles, Rina Kantor, Stanley Turecki, Ava Landy, Annette Baslaw-Finger, Astrid Jakubowicz, Carla Lessing, Edward Lessing, Josie Martin, and Ann Shore. You are all wonderful!

There are other voices that appear in the book. I am deeply grateful to Nechama Tec, Ph.D., and Eva Fogelman, Ph.D., for their exceptional chapters; and Abraham H.

Foxman, National Director, Anti-Defamation League, for his important preface. Salka Mandelbaum and Phyllis Wright speak briefly but importantly, adding perspective and truths we might not have seen. In addition there are people who do not speak at all in this book, but whose presence may be felt. I am especially grateful to Dasha H. Rittenberg-Werdygier, Helen Marks, Tom Weisz, Judith Kestenberg, M.D., Esther Perel, Lena Adler, Flora Hogman, Ph.D., Chaya Roth, Ph.D., Lore Baer, Simone Gordon, Joe Erlichster, Elizabeth Trilling-Grotch, Deborah Dwork, Ph.D., and Jacques Szaluta, Ph.D., for talking to me and greatly deepening my understanding of the hidden-child experience.

I thank my editors at Ballantine Books, Joëlle Delbourgo and Sherri Rifkin, for their brilliant editing and their supportiveness—always—through the entire process of putting this book together. I want to give my thanks to Malka Margolies and Teri Henry, also at Ballantine, who were enthusiastic about the book from the beginning and Joan Grant, for her patience, energy, and cheer. In addition I thank my very talented agent, Angela Miller, president of the Miller Agency, for professionalism, savvy, and kind words when I needed them badly. Because this book evolved from an article in *New York* magazine, I thank Executive Editor Deborah Harkins and Assistant to the Editor Fran Kessler, who helped make it happen. I also thank Rochel Berman, principal of Berman Associates, who was always there with her enthusiasm, help, and good ideas. It was she who introduced me to Dennis Klein, Ph.D., director of the Anti-Defamation League's Hidden Child Foundation. Dennis, Mark Edelman, and public relations associate Bonnie Mitelman have nurtured the book in many vital ways, and for that I am most grateful.

I must also acknowledge some other people: friends and relatives who were not directly involved with the book, but

whose excitement over it helped to keep the fire burning: Bob
Steinberg; Roz and Earl Marks; Lise Motherwell; Chris and
Fred Pagnani; Ben and Sarah Steinberg; Barbara Yuan; Mary
Curto; Marje Slavin; Janice Cohn; Virginia DeNyse; Belle
Redman; Philip Jerome; Bob and Jane Abrahams; Dick Mayo;
Katie Hite; Fredrica Beveridge; Arlene Smethurst; Karen,
Leslie, and Chuck Dickinson; Harriet, Tom, and Jim Shapiro;
Pat Rogers; Jan Drucker; Sheila McGayhey; Fran Samuels;
Barbara and Bruce Bean; Edna and Bob Bouchal; M. J. Territo;
Bob and Carrie Hecht; Violet Kiel; Shun-Wah Lung; Phil Diaz;
Bob Nurock; Peter Lehrer; Jane Sharf; Jill Witherell; Carol Per-
kins; Fran Kelly; Charlotte Johnson; Ann Steinberg; Marge
Dunne; and Robert Bear. I am also grateful to three warm sup-
porters of this project, who are no longer here: the late Carol
Rinzler, the late Jim Halpin, and the late Carol Denniston.

Finally I want to say thank you to the three people I love
most in the world: my husband, Robert, and our sons, Christopher and Joshua, who were there for me in every possible
way, with ideas and suggestions, inspiration, good criticism,
patience, humor, and love.

INTRODUCTION

On Memorial Day weekend, 1991, an extraordinary event took place. Sixteen hundred people from all over the world converged on the Marriott Marquis Hotel in New York. These were the secret survivors of World War II, Jews who had managed to keep out of sight during the Nazi Holocaust. Many had never shared their stories before with anyone, including members of their families. Some had only just learned that there were others like themselves.

For the hidden children that weekend was a cathartic experience. For the rest of the world it was an education. We thought we knew all there was to know about the Holocaust, but this was another part that needed to be told. We listened to panels entitled, "To Hide No More" and "The Psychological Impact of Being Hidden as a Child" and "What Motivated the Rescuers?" There was a deeply moving luncheon in tribute to rescuers. There were speeches, lectures, and even after-dinner entertainment and socializing. But for many the most dramatic and enlightening part of the weekend was the work-shops, whose very titles ("Where Was God?" "Who Am I—Catholic or Jew?" "Fear of Relationships," and "I Never Said Good-bye," among others) held promise.

Listening to their stories, we began to learn: how they suffered (while only some lost their families, all were abandoned by the human family and adult world they trusted); how they coped (with the help of family, Christian rescuers, and in some cases all alone); why most of them had kept silent all those years—and why they were ready at last to come out of hiding in another sense. We learned that there was no such thing as a mild case, or only suffering a little. Many former hidden children still minimize their own experiences because they were repeatedly told, "You were safe, you were lucky." But every hidden child suffered in unimaginable ways, during the war, afterward, or both.

My own awareness of the hidden children actually began about seven months earlier, when *New York* magazine offered me the assignment to do an article about this special group. A very grass-roots query had come in from a group in a borrowed apartment-office without even a phone, on the West Side of Manhattan. The magazine wasn't completely committed to the idea, but they were willing to assign it if I was interested. Another writer, a child of survivors, had turned the assignment down. I was second choice. Why me? I was not an expert on any related subject. My editor, Deborah Harkins, remembered from several years earlier that I liked writing what she called "sensitive and thoughtful" stories.

I didn't hesitate to say yes. Little did I know quite how involved and fascinated I would become. What surprised me initially was who the former hidden children were: highly successful, super well educated, upscale—and very charming! Perhaps I'd expected cold people, who would say in effect,

"You don't understand. Leave me alone with my suffering." Instead I found them extraordinarily open. If some were hesitant as they began to tell their stories, it was not because they wanted to shut out the listener but because it was painful to relive what they had been through.

As I listened, I was awed by these people who had shown such ingenuity, tenacity, and grit in their determination to live when the odds had been almost a hundred percent against them. I felt proud to be Jewish in a way that I never had before. When the article appeared, it was hailed as a success. But to me it was just a beginning. Hooked on the subject, I attended the Memorial Day weekend gathering. I listened and wept. I made new friends and grew closer to the ones I had met when I was researching the article and later attending a series of preconference open meetings. One woman hugged me and said, "You're one of us now."

I remember one particularly moving workshop, "The Hidden-Child Experience." At one point a woman who had been speaking stopped suddenly and stared at another woman who had just come in. "Oh, my God!" the one who had been talking cried out as they ran to embrace each other. "I came here for you," the other woman said. They were friends who hadn't seen each other in more than forty years.

For others that workshop was stirring and important in other ways. One man, recounting his own hiding experience, said, "My mother wasn't very maternal—she gave me up."

"Don't you believe it!" another member of that workshop told him earnestly. "Your mother *was* maternal! She saved your life." The man looked startled. "I hadn't thought of it that way," he admitted. Another woman movingly reminisced about her closest childhood friend—whose name was Anne Frank! There was so much emotion in that room. When it was over, I grabbed two of the participants who had spoken with unusual eloquence and insight. I told them that I hoped to write a book, and they both agreed to let me interview them. (They were Kim Fendrick and Annette Baslaw-Finger, both of whose astonishing stories appear in this book.)

Nor was I the only outsider drawn into the world of Hidden Children. At one session I was surprised to see a black couple in the sea of white faces. I sat down next to them and asked the woman if she had been a hidden child. "No!" she said, laughing. She explained that she had read my article in *New York* and been so touched that she had felt a need to be at the gathering, to be part of it. I told Ava Landy, one of the committee members about this lovely woman, Phyllis Wright. "Oh, yes," Ava said, and later she gave me a photocopy of this letter:

2/21/91

To whom it may concern:

I'm Black, a woman, 36 years old. I'm in medical school. I just finished reading "The Hidden Children," New York magazine, Feb. issue. I want to come to the gathering May 26 and 27. I have to be there. I don't know exactly why. I have trouble sorting out and explaining my strong feelings about the Holocaust experience. It's almost as if I were there. Perhaps 36 years of being Black in America has caused me to feel like a survivor too. I identify with what it feels like to be ashamed of who you are, to feel others hate so powerfully that it causes your heart to beat faster. No, there's something more. I, like the others, know that there is something in my soul—a will, a destiny to live, to tell.

I had a patient once, a woman with one leg, and I noticed she had a thin blue line of numbers tattooed on her arm. I knew she was a camp survivor. Her son was a physician. I was still a nuclear medicine technologist. This woman helped change my life.

As fate would have it, she talked freely and at length about her experience. The Germans forced a group of Jews to march in winter snow for more miles than she cared to remember. She was at fifteen the youngest in the group. She was barefoot! She had had her leg amputated after frostbite and gangrene set in.

She was Czech. Her father was a diplomat. Before the Germans, her family was quite wealthy and lived in a beautiful home. The Germans took everything. When she had enough of remembering, she took my hand and made me promise to apply to medical school—to go for it. Well, I did. I'm finishing my second year!! What an inspiration she was for me. I will never forget her.

I used to hear my dad talk about "the six million Jews." When he told me what that meant, something in my soul trembled. From that day on, my world became different. The horror of the pictures he showed me was forever burned into my being. How could people do such things to one another? They were all white!! Somehow this validated my belief that the institution of slavery went far beyond color.

I was profoundly moved by the women's testimonies in the aforementioned article. I know that had I lived in Europe in that era, I would have felt a moral duty to shelter as many Jews as I could.

Please grant my desire to attend the gathering and let me know if there is anything I can contribute to such a worthy cause.

My best regards,
Phyllis A. Wright

After reading this letter I was even more convinced that the hidden children's stories held something of value for anyone struggling to overcome a troubled past of any kind: a traumatic childhood, bigotry, terror. I wanted to write a book to leave a lasting record of how these children lived in hiding; to make the world aware of the exceptional courage and goodness that emerged in the midst of unspeakable tragedy and destruction; and to show how healing can truly begin—even fifty years later.

At the conference and in the months that followed, I met former hidden children and listened to them share their histories and many insights with me. One woman called me and asked if I would listen to her story. "I'm ripe," she explained. "Unless the juices are squeezed, the fruit will be rotten." Her story was unique and important—as were those of the more than sixty other former hidden children I interviewed during the following year. Here were true stories that were stranger than fiction, as each person recounted a miracle of survival—and "miracle" is no exaggeration, since these children survived when thousands of others who did the same things were killed.

But these were more than just interesting—or even mind-boggling—stories of their experiences during the war. The aftermath of the war, the legacy of what they had gone through, and their continuing struggle to heal, were equally compelling.

I was committed to writing this book to record what the hidden children had experienced. The editors and I considered different approaches, but it was clear after a while that the most effective way would be to let the few speak for the many; to focus on a relatively small but varied group—and then let each tell his or her story in a full and candid way. As I listened, certain individual testimonies emerged as the ones that would have to be included. And as I went back to interview those same people again (and often again and again), I began to see the book in four distinct sections: first the ordeal of hiding; second the aftermath; third the legacy, or long-term effects of hiding; and finally the healing. After a certain amount of shuffling, it was clear where each story belonged.

The stories in the first section tell us so much about the hiding ordeal: where children hid, how they spent their days and nights, and what they thought about. We learn what the rescuers were like: some wonderful, some not so wonderful. Also we discover what it took for children to get through each day, beset by constant danger, loss, and often excruciating conditions. Even when rescuers were kind, it was lonely and frightening for children like **Nicole David**, who lost her mother, her childhood, and everything familiar on a Sunday in the Belgian village of Profondeville. (Reading Nicole's story, we understand just why she made an unusual decision as a twelve year-old—and stuck with it.)

We find that contrary to popular belief, the hiding experience was less of a safe harbor than a violent sea of constant menace, uncertainty, and fear. "We were in so much danger," says **Rosa Sirota**, who was hidden in the Ukraine. "That's why people who were hiding were, in some respects, under much more tension and pressure than people who were already caught, because we always had to be on guard." Rosa, who came to understand that survival called for "the mind of an adult in the body of a child," shows us how remarkably she managed to maintain self-control and live a lie that saved her life (and her mother's life too).

Many children, such as **Renee Roth-Hano**, were kept hidden in Catholic convents, but like other hiding solutions, this was far from perfect—with daunting emotional as well as physical hardships. Still other hidden children spent months, even years, in places that humans had never inhabited before, including underground caves—even the sewer. **Kristine Keren** lived under horrifying circumstances; yet she survived not only physically but emotionally and spiritually as well, thanks to wonderful, exceptional adults. Kristine's story is an example of how some hidden children were able to convert horror into extraordinary determination—and success.

Curiously optimism seems to have been a major asset in surviving what can fairly be described as hell. One is struck by the way children like **Richard Rozen** approached each new horror he faced as if it was simply an interesting challenge. Other children, like **Kim Fendrick**, felt safe when in fact they were in grave danger. "I was with my family," Kim explains, "and because of that I never doubted that I would be all right."

Some hidden children, such as **Leon Ginsburg** and **Lola Kaufman**, were orphaned early and had no other adult to take care of them. But somehow these remarkable children were able to find adult strength in themselves—and make it. Like the late author Jerzy Kosinski's young hero in *The Painted Bird*, Leon is one who instinctively made the right split-second decisions that saved his life, not just once but numerous times. Lola, who lived in silence, darkness, and almost complete isolation, managed to summon the amazing forbearance necessary to stay alive.

The second part of the book deals with liberation—the

"happy ending" of the war, which turned out to be neither happy nor an ending, as far as many hidden children were concerned. The years 1944 and 1945 brought official freedom and with it excitement, joy, and relief. But even though the war and Nazi domination were over, the nightmare for most hidden children continued. Many found that their parents and other relatives had been killed. Even children who were lucky enough to emerge with a whole family intact suffered turmoil. Many had to face a disappointing reunion with parents or other family members who had, themselves, suffered greatly and were in no position physically or emotionally to be there in a way that their brave little children desperately needed.

Many children were fostered and even adopted by Gentile families, only to be taken away after the war and returned to birth parents who were, by then, strangers. Ironically for some hidden children such as **Sanne Spetter** and **Marie-Claire Rakowski**, the end of the war was the end of a happy life—and the start of a deeply fragmented one.

The third section of the book deals with the legacy of the hiding experience and why it has, in many cases, had a very profound and lasting effect, even *half a century after the fact*. Earlier we learned that hidden children endured so much yet coped so well. We also know that they have succeeded in the world, professionally and in every other way. We read their stories and we can hardly imagine how anyone could have been so courageous, resourceful, and calm under pressure, so tenacious, so calm in the face of so much horror. But in this section of the book we discover something else—that when childhood ends much too early, this loss takes a toll on the adult, as the very resources that enabled them to survive as children actually became liabilities later in life.

For example, the ability to adapt and live like a chameleon turned into confusion, loss of identity, alienation. The ability to live with anonymity and homelessness became for some an inability to feel safe or close to loved ones. For others there is unresolved bereavement, shame, an inability to remember what happened, and continuing fear. Some hidden children, such as **Ruth Rubenstein**, still bear scars of disorientation, spaciness, and self-doubt as a result of separation that felt like abandonment. The fact that these children were sent away into hiding for their own good made separation no easier to bear. Although she recovered superficially, it wasn't until adulthood and another trauma that Ruth was able to relive, recognize, and finally begin to resolve the earlier grief.

Remaining calm in the face of unspeakable horror and loss without going crazy or falling apart required hidden children such as **Joseph Steiner** and **Clemens Loew** to shut off their feelings in order to survive. But stifling feelings created other problems. Joseph, for example, put all the anger, fear, confusion, and grief on hold—and in effect stopped feeling much of anything. "It was like playing a video game," Joseph says. "I lost my mother, a sister, and many other relatives. I experienced months of extreme danger. But none of it was real to me." Clem is an eminent psychologist and psychoanalyst, a scuba diver, sculptor, photographer, and father. All very impressive, yet there is a part of Clem that is still a small boy, who is not quite sure that he will be accepted and very reluctant to give up the hope that his father (said to have been killed in a concentration camp) may yet return.

The ability to be unobtrusive, to disappear, not to be a burden, left many former hidden children, such as **Joseph Vles**, with problems asserting themselves, negotiating, or even saying, "I have an idea." Joseph, whose hiding experience left him with an unshakable conviction that he couldn't depend on others for security or understanding, has taken an unconventional and often lonely path. (It is only now, in his third marriage, that Joseph is able to enjoy a real sense of intimacy.)

Rina Kantor is the pseudonym chosen by a former hidden child who would not want her therapy patients or her students to know her past. "Rina" has been reflecting uncomfortably on her past. "Because our abilities were stretched to their limits and at times led to miraculous results, we gained a sense of mastery which was greatly needed, considering the circumstances in which we were forced to live," she says. It is only recently that Rina has been able to look beyond her feats of daring to confront—and perhaps heal—the frightened and lonely child she was.

Some hidden children, such as **Stanley Turecki**, see their foolish risk-taking behavior and tendency to end relationships abruptly as results of early years on the run from the Nazis. The inner life was affected too. The heightened sensitivity to danger that was so crucial to avoiding capture left many of the children who survived the hiding experience with fears, gruesome fantasies, and recurring nightmares. Others, such as **Ava Landy,** a former hidden child from Belgium, continue to wrestle with fears left over from the war. Ava's own sense of security is so fragile that she asked me to use her grandmother's last name, Landy, rather than her own. But what troubles Ava as much as the fears is her inability to remember more than a very few fragments of her childhood.

The fourth section of the book is about healing. Remarkably, in spite of everything, the hidden-child story is as much about healing as it is about trauma, grief, and loss. What has enabled them to be resilient? Good nurturing before the war? Loving parents? An intense feeling of gratitude to the rescuers who risked their own lives to save Jews? Is one's own attitude responsible for unusual resilience? And what works best now: a refusal to allow painful memories to intrude in adulthood?

Or is it facing all the rage and sorrow that leads more directly to a resolution? What kinds of therapy, self-help, and sharing work best? And how does some of the best healing occur unexpectedly?

In this section we see hidden children such as **Annette Baslaw-Finger** who have emerged with unbridled energy, love, and gratitude. By making the most of every moment Annette makes amends to herself. "They could force us into hiding, but they couldn't kill our spirit," she declares, refusing to feel like a victim. Other hidden children, such as **Astrid Jakubowicz** (Jakubowicz is her maiden name) are emerging after long years of feeling legitimately sorry for themselves, to come to an altogether new and healing perspective on what happened to them as children.

We also see how the Hidden Child Gathering itself promoted healing. **Carla Lessing** is typical of many children who learned, in hiding, to be inconspicuous—and afraid. However it was the intense year of work on the committee planning the Hidden Child Gathering that gave her new self-confidence. Carla's husband, **Ed**, on the other hand, had no part in the planning—and no clue that the conference would affect him just as profoundly, giving him a new and striking sense of himself, both as an individual and as a Jew.

Josie Martin, who struggled for years to make sense of the past, gives a moving account of the personal crisis in adulthood that led her to an unexpected—and deeply satisfying—reconciliation. And finally **Ann Shore** describes how carefully she kept the facts of her childhood from everyone including her closest friends—until she experienced a deeply personal breakthrough and a compelling need to bring her message to the next generation.

Each individual story stands out on its own as a personal testimony; but just as importantly these stories stand together as a whole, as the many voices form one cohesive and extremely powerful voice. However, as this project continued to evolve, the editors and I decided that one other element would frame—and even further illuminate—the hidden-child stories collected here. We added two more chapters: First, **Nechama Tec, Ph.D.**, a Professor of Sociology at the University of Connecticut, puts the hidden child into historical context. Her essay provides facts and also shows that many exact figures are elusive to this day. It explains why books such as this are so important in the documentation and preservation of history for future generations. The other chapter by **Eva Fogelman, Ph.D.**, the founding director of the Jewish Foundation for Christian Rescuers, ADL, and a social psychologist and psychotherapist, shows the psychological and emotional costs of being hidden and surviving the war.

This has been a deeply involving project, which I've lived and breathed since I conducted my first interview in the early fall of 1990. The first person I interviewed was Nicole David, whom some people call the Mother of the Hidden Children. Nicole told me her story and explained to me that the world needed to know about hidden children, just as the hidden children themselves needed to meet, share their stories, and receive the recognition long denied them. It has been my privilege to listen, to be the keeper of these stories, and now to present them to the world as a real document of what happened to children fifty years ago—and a solemn reminder of what could all too easily happen again if we allow it to.

THE ORDEAL

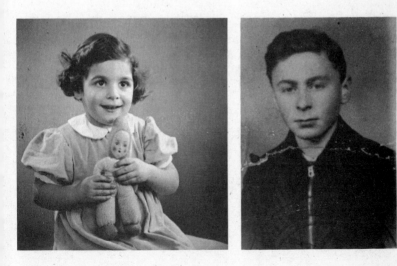

NICOLE DAVID

Nicole David, fifty-five, looks polished and refined in a bright silk print dress. She has expressive dark brown eyes with long lashes, light brown hair, and a certain cool reserve. She becomes animated when she talks about her husband, Ernest, her fledgling career as a couples therapist, and an upcoming hidden-child documentary on English television. Once again at home in London after years in New York, Nicole sits at the antique desk in her creamy-color wallpapered den typing overseas air letters, faxing messages, and (only late at night when the rates go down) phoning friends in the United States. Nicole explains, "I have to feel that I can be in touch with people."

"I was born on September 15, 1936, in Antwerp, Belgium, the only daughter of Chawa Matzner and Munisch Schneider. The Germans invaded Belgium on May 10, 1940. As the bombing began, our family—along with thousands of others—fled to France. At the French border I suddenly saw my father on the Belgian side of a wire fence. It seemed that men of army age with Polish nationality, which he was, were not allowed to cross the border into France. I screamed for him to come with us. Somehow in all the chaos, the crowds, and the noise, he managed to make it through.

"No sooner were we safely in France, when a low-flying

German plane approached. Two minutes later we were in a ditch along with hundreds of others. My parents were on top of me, protecting me. When the bombing stopped and not everyone got up, I thought how lucky I was to have my parents to protect me. I was certain that as long as I had them, nothing bad could ever happen to me.

"In France the Germans occupied part of the country, but they were not yet deporting Jews. Outside a shop one day some German soldiers gave another little girl and me some chocolate. As we ate it, the soldiers stood there, bragging to my father about how strong and well organized their army was: 'With us an order is an order,' one said, 'For example, if we were ordered to shoot these children'—he patted my head—'why, we would do it!'

"After that we returned to Antwerp but had to leave again because of heavy bombing. Then we moved to a small, very beautiful village called Profondeville in the Belgian Ardennes, where my father felt we'd be safer. It was rural and very green with lovely views of the river Meuse. Our small rented house was on the main square with a shared garden in back. I slept in my parents' room, which was cozy, but they didn't get much sleep with my early-morning chatter. My parents often took me rowing on the Meuse and for rides on their tandem bicycle. To me life still felt safe and happy.

"But anti-Semitic decrees were in place, and getting tougher. I wasn't even supposed to go to school, but a nun let me come to kindergarten. One day we were told, 'Christ is everywhere.' I was a bright, inquisitive child. I asked, 'How do we know that if we can't see him?' That afternoon the nun called my mother and said, 'You'd better take her out of here, she doesn't sound anything like a Catholic child. She'll give herself away.' My parents then explained to me how dangerous it was to be Jewish. 'Oh,' I said. Although I'd enjoyed being with the other children, I had known all along that I was different. Leaving school was almost a relief.

"In 1942 the deportation was under way. Jews were required to be registered and wear yellow stars. Deeply concerned, my parents found a secret place for me in a Catholic orphanage. Then they, too, went into hiding in somebody's attic. That separation felt terrible to me. It was very overcrowded in the orphanage. I felt lost. After a while the nuns told my parents that they couldn't keep me anymore because my constant throat infections endangered all the other children.

"My parents decided that I had to have a tonsillectomy. They couldn't get me into a hospital, so my mother decided that we'd go back to Profondeville, where we'd had a very good pediatrician. My father was very much against that idea. He felt it would be much too dangerous. For one thing, as of August 1941, Jews were not even allowed to live outside of Antwerp, Brussels, Liège, or Charleroi. But my mother was very assertive, and she won. I only found that out years later. My father told me that he always had guilt feelings because my mother had said, 'Look, I'm making the decision, and if anything should happen, then I hope it happens to me and not to you. I'm taking the responsibility because I don't want Nicole operated on by just anybody.'

"At the time all I knew then was how thrilled I was to be leaving the orphanage and going home. That made me very happy. October 7, 1942, the day before my operation was a beautiful, sunny day in Profondeville. My father and I went out to buy a newspaper while my mother stayed home to make lunch, which I knew would be something delicious. As we reached the little alley where the paper shop was, we saw two SS men in full uniform with black leather jackboots. They said hello to us as we passed. Puzzled, my father and I looked at each other.

"The Gestapo rarely came to Profondeville. Once, many months earlier, my father and I had come back from a walk to find two Gestapos leaving our house and my mother upset. The officers had come to check my parents' coats to see if they had yellow stars sewn on properly. (As a child under six I didn't need to wear a star.)

"This time we did wonder if something was up, but we continued on to the café on the banks of the Meuse. At the café Daddy ordered an aperitif. He let me have a sip of it, which made me feel grown-up. I can picture the scene before us: the lovely river and the rocks of Lustin on the opposite bank looked so peaceful that I completely forgot about the Gestapo. Then we started walking home. As we approached our corner, we could see three German trucks right outside our house. Suddenly I wanted to run home, to see if my mother was all right. Then a man I'd never seen before intercepted us and warned us not to go home. I started to cry: I was frantic to see my mother. Daddy said, 'Be quiet. The Gestapo might hear you.' That was when I first learned not to cry, a lesson that stayed with me for years and years.

"The man, who was from the Resistance, took us down a narrow road to a 'safe' house, where an Italian woman took us to her attic. We stayed there for the rest of the day. Daddy told me not to go near the window. Members of the SS and soldiers in German uniform passed back and forth all day while they looked for us.

"That evening a non-Jewish friend of my mother's came and tried to reassure me that my mother was all right. She said that my mother had sent a message that I shouldn't worry because my father would look after me. At that moment I got terrible, terrible stomach cramps, but I wasn't allowed to go down to the toilet. Instead a pot was brought up for me. Later that night a man came to take my father back to the attic in Rivières, where he had been with my mother while I was in the orphanage. At the same time a woman came to take me to the family of Mr. and Mrs. Gaston Champagne, Château Saint Servais, Saint Servais, Namur. It was very dark on the way, and I was terribly afraid.

"I found myself living in a large Catholic family with ten children, though only five were still at home. The youngest was sixteen. I didn't know these people! In fact it was through one of the adult sons just two days earlier that my mother had made the arrangements for me. Life seemed strange there. I couldn't go to school. The only regular outing was to church with the family. Most of the time I was by myself and quite lonely. Each day I spent hours and hours making up fantasy stories, the kind my father used to tell me. They always involved Mickey, an imaginary friend, and he could do everything. I had not been a loner by nature. I loved company and loved to talk. But I developed into a very self-sufficient person.

"The house, which looked like a castle, was surrounded by a very large garden. A high wall went all around it, and I could not see the street, except through the gate, which they told me to stay away from. I do not remember any flowers in the garden. There was a small, empty pond, with concrete sides I liked to slide down. Doing that tore my panties, which annoyed Madame Champagne, but it was the only game I had.

"This family was good: they willingly risked their lives, and they never took any money for keeping me. One of the daughters used to say to me, 'Don't forget your Jewish prayers.' Still, it didn't feel like home. I had been a much loved, pampered, and rather willful child. One time, for example, I had eaten thirty sugar cubes. My mother had hidden them, but I'd stood on a chair and then a shelf to get them anyway. That's how I was! However, in the hiding family there were strict rules. The children addressed their parents as *vous* instead of the informal *tu* generally used, and I had never heard such formality in a family. In this thirty-nine-room house that seemed more like a museum, with the large paintings and heavy furniture, we had to be given permission to join the grown-ups in the *salon* (living room).

"I had to learn to do without the hugs and all the special treatment I was used to. For example, my father had always tucked me in with bedtime stories. Now I had to go up two flights alone in the dark in this enormous house. That was torture for me! The windows were covered with black cloth because of the blackout. Everything creaked. Sometimes the two teenage boys in the family would play jokes on me, making strange noises at the top of the stairs. As a result for years afterward I was terrified of the dark. In fact it's only in the last five or six years that I can tolerate it, even in my own house!

"I had been a picky eater at home, and my mother used to run after me with healthy food. She'd lovingly fed me spinach (along with stories of Popeye), fish, and porridge. But the minute I came to the family Champagne, I sat down and ate with everyone else—even though the food was unappealing. It was strictly what we could have on the ration books: mostly boiled potatoes and boiled red cabbage. The bread was so bad that before eating it one had to break the piece in half to see if it formed threads, which meant it could not be eaten. What was hardest for me was having to sit quietly until the meal was finished.

"I was told I had picked up bad manners at the orphanage, so I had to learn to eat my soup without slurping. I learned fast! It wasn't that I feared my rescuers would turn me out, but I understood the need to be a good child and not make trouble. In fact one day I went to mass with a terrible toothache. That, to me, was 'being good.' Later they noticed my swollen cheek and took me to a friend who was a dentist.

"During this time I rarely thought of my mother. I understood that she was gone, and the only way I could cope or make sense of life at that point was to detach myself and just do whatever was required at the time. My father came to visit once. He was hidden at the bottom of a small van, dressed in workman's clothes. I was overjoyed that we got to spend a night together. (That night I had somebody to go up in the dark with me!) When he left in the van the next morning, the Champagnes warned him not to come again because it was too dangerous.

"Instead I was taken to see him once in a while by a woman friend named Ilse Rothschild, who had plain, non-Jewish features and convincing false papers, so she could travel with relative ease. Once, she was coming for me on my birthday. I was standing near the gates waiting for her. I thought I'd be clever and meet her. I went out, but somehow we didn't meet. I ended up at her house, on the other side of town. My hiding family and this woman were terrified! For punishment I had to write 250 times, 'I am not allowed to go out on my own.' That was one birthday I will never forget.

"As kind as the Champagnes were, I still missed my father very much. I was delighted when, after a year at the Champagnes', Daddy arranged for me to hide with him where he was, in the tiny village of Besine. This village had only 150 residents, but at least thirty Jews had been in hiding there at one time or another. Eudor Clobert, the local mayor; and the priest, whose name I can't remember; and Maurice Pochet, who kept the village shop, saved many lives, providing Jews with false papers, food, and communications. The whole village was very good; everyone knew and protected 'Monsieur

Albert' (my father) who was hiding at the Family Jules et Marie Adnet. If anyone saw a suspicious or German-looking car, they would go at once to tell Daddy, who could then go to his hiding place in one of Mr. Pochet's fields.

"One day the Gestapo did come. They started combing the village, looking for tobacco machines. Because of that they didn't see the Jews under their noses! When they came to the house, I jumped into my bed and sort of covered myself up and started coughing. The Germans went through the house, through the stables and everything, but they hardly looked at me. Still, my father felt that was too dangerous and had me placed in another village. But there we were near an ammunition depot. As the war was coming to a climax, we were under horrendous bombing. We weren't hit, but we could see the bombs and certainly hear them. And all the bridges were hit. By then there were rumors that the Americans were coming.

"The rumors were true. The American Army liberated us in September 1944. I could hear tanks going by. We were told that we should go to the main road to greet them. My first contact was with a soldier who jumped off his truck to give me chocolate. I turned around and ran as fast as I could, because I'd been told so often that a uniform was something dangerous! My hiding family then caught up with me and explained that *this* uniform was safe and the chocolate was okay.

"However, that wasn't quite the end of all the horror. For quite a while I couldn't go to my father. We were separated by woods, and there were Germans still hiding in the woods. For weeks we had heard reports of people being killed by snipers. It seemed endless, but finally it was safe to travel. However, by the time I was reunited with my father, the Battle of the Bulge was in full swing. All around us villages were being burned and devastated. By the time we reached Brussels on a cold, snowy day in December 1944, we heard that the Allies had won at Bastogne. But Antwerp was being bombed relentlessly by V-1s and V-2s. It was too dangerous to go back. Now everybody was homeless, and there was no place to go.

"My father met up with some friends. They were willing to take him in, but they were already five to a room. One of the men told my father to put me in the convent where his daughter had been during the war. I was crushed! I was nine years old, and I couldn't understand why I had to be separated from my father again. It was a very, very unhappy time. Nor did he try to explain it to me.

"I hated the convent. The food was dreadful, and we had to eat in silence and quickly even though the soup was so hot it burned my mouth. Each night I had to swallow a big spoonful of cod liver oil, which made me gag. When there was danger of bombing, we slept on mattresses in a freezing cellar. I would have run away from there, but I didn't have any money for the tram.

"Finally, in May 1945, my father and I went back to Antwerp. We lived as lodgers in separate families. After a year and a half my father and I got our own apartment. Now at last we had a semblance of normal life—if it was normal that I never got to see my mother again. I was told nothing about her fate at the time. Later, from records the Germans did not have time to destroy and that were published by Serge Klarsfeld, I learned that my mother was put on the twelfth convoy leaving Maline, the Belgian transit camp, en route to Auschwitz on October 10, 1942. She never came back.

"For years I never spoke about my mother or my grief over losing her. I continued to live with my father and take care of him for the rest of his life. Whenever the subject of the war came up, I minimized what I had gone through. First, I sensed that nobody wanted to listen. Also, we humans have this lovely quality of being able to forget what's bad as soon as something better comes along—a good thing for me, because otherwise I'm sure I would have been a total wreck!

"However, the pain didn't go away. When I was twelve, I made a decision not to have children because of what I had gone through, and the decision stuck. My husband, Ernest, who might or might not have wanted children, accepted how strongly I felt, and so we never did have a child. Do I regret that decision? Not really. I love children. I follow my friends' children's lives with interest and affection. But I know I would have burdened my children with my experiences. I would have been constantly afraid of losing them. And seeing what the world has become, we often say we did the right thing.

"Some skeptics used to challenge me, insisting, 'No *child* could have made that kind of decision. It sounds far too adult for any twelve-year-old.' Then I would have to explain very patiently, 'That's exactly the point! By twelve I *wasn't* a child anymore! I lost my childhood at the age of three and a half.' I felt that the world didn't understand. Perhaps that was why I was so excited when I saw Miriam Abramowicz's film, *Comme Si C'était Hier* (As If It Were Yesterday), about a resistance group of Jews and non-Jews, who saved between three thousand and four thousand Jewish children during the Holocaust.

"I was so moved, I immediately contacted Miriam. She told me that others like me who had been hidden as children had reacted to her film just as I had. Perhaps, she said, we ought to plan some sort of get-together. We began to contact other hidden children. We started out with only four names, then twenty—and then five hundred! It seemed that each one of us had buried our war experiences, unaware that others existed who had had similar experiences—or that our suffering 'mattered.' After all, we had been told so often, we were 'lucky' to have survived and even escaped the camps. So what did *we* have to complain about?

"We had a common bond: We had grown up, but we had lost our childhood—and what we had gone through had not been recognized. Now we would finally get together with all those like us, to recall the past and begin to understand how our experiences had shaped our lives. And we would tell the world! It was more than a year of hard work, getting participants, help with funding, publicity, and all the rest. We had a very dedicated committee. In addition, right from the beginning of the preparations for the gathering, an American friend, Henrietta Schilit, helped me and was an invaluable support. I had met her while auditing a course for advanced social workers at Jewish Family Service during my first year in New York in 1987.

"She was always ready to help, support, and advise. She helped me write the very first letter we sent out in December 1989. A few days before the gathering she offered to read my opening speech and type it out on her computer. When she read what I had written, she told me it was missing something. How, she asked, could I ask people to come out of hiding if I did not tell my hiding experience? She remarked that we had been close friends for nearly four years, and yet I had never told her my story. I said, 'But you never asked!' It was painful, but I did add a short version of my experience to my speech.

"Now it was really happening! As the day arrived, I felt exhilarated, but worried too. What would it do to people's emotions? Here were people who had been hiding—not just during the war, but ever since then too. Many hadn't even shared their stories with husbands and wives, much less strangers. Would they be able to do it now—and cope with the feelings? Were we well enough equipped to help them?

"As the gathering began, people streamed in; there were

unbelievable numbers of people, and yes, many of them did break down. But it wasn't falling apart, this was a form of healing! After almost fifty years the hidden children were coming out of hiding. It was powerful! There was one hidden child from England whom I'd actually discouraged from coming because I was concerned about her. On Monday night, right at the end when the tables had been cleared and long after most people had gone, she was still sitting at a table. I went up to her, and she was beaming. She took one of my hands in both of hers and she said, 'I can't tell you how happy I am!'

"Do you know how that made me feel? Like a mother! The project I had planned and worried over, argued and nagged about, struggled with and nurtured, had become a reality. I shall always feel privileged that I was the one who said to the other hidden children, 'Yes, it's okay. We can do this, and it's time!' "

ROSA SIROTA

Rosa Sirota, fifty-nine, teaches high school Spanish and lives in New Jersey, in a pleasant yellow frame house in a cul-de-sac. On a summer day, with the sounds of birds and a distant mower in the background, Rosa looks trim and relaxed in bright turquoise silk shorts and a matching shirt. Her hair is short, blond, and well styled; her eyeglasses hang on a cord around her neck. On the porch overlooking a garden fragrant with lilies, Rosa talks proudly of her children: Her daughter lives nearby, is married, and works on Wall Street. Her son, who was such a wild little boy, is a doctor and a wonderful athlete. "My husband and I are pretty fortunate!" Rosa concludes.

"I was born in 1933 in Lvov, Poland. When the Germans occupied the country in 1939, they took my grandmother away. Then they sent my father to a forced-labor camp. My mother and I lived in an all-Christian area. When I was eight, they ordered us to move to the ghetto. A Christian neighbor, Janka, said to my mother, 'Clara, don't go to the ghetto. You'll never get out of there.' Janka offered to take us in and hide us by pretending that my mother was her sister. We packed all we could carry and gratefully moved in with Janka.

"Late that first night there was a sudden loud banging on

the door and a lot of screaming: 'Open up,' a man's voice shouted. 'You have Jews in there.' My heart was pounding. To this day I still get goose bumps, remembering that sound! Janka opened the door. Someone from the Gestapo ordered my mother to come with him. He took her outside, but I didn't know what had happened after they left. An hour later there was another knock on the door, softer this time, and that same man was back!

"Now he and Janka chatted in a friendly way, as they proceeded to divide up all our belongings. I realized then that the whole thing had been a setup to take our things from us. I lay awake until morning. Then I told Janka I was leaving. 'Good,' she said. I asked if I could take one very old, frayed jacket with me for my aunt in the ghetto. Janka examined the jacket, decided that it wasn't worth much, and threw it at me. 'Go!' she said. I grabbed the jacket and ran.

"At that point Jews were not allowed to be outside the ghetto. I wasn't sure how to get there, but some angel must have been watching over me, because when I asked a lady for directions, she told me how to get there and didn't turn me in, which she could easily have done. When I arrived, my mother was there—and very relieved to see me. When she saw the jacket, she threw her arms around me and hugged me tight. That shabby jacket was the one in which she had sewn all her jewelry. She explained she could now use that jewelry to buy our escape.

"My mother used the gems to buy a false birth certificate from a man whose wife, named Olga Chrednicka, had died. This was where Marysia came in. Marysia was my aunt's maid, and a wonderful woman, who had gone to her priest and told him that she wanted to save her mistress and the children. The priest had said to her, 'If you can save a few lives, do it.'

'Well, how do you do it in Polish?' I said, 'It's exactly the same, but you speak Polish.'

"I got away with that—and I went to confession. My problem was that I couldn't bring myself to lie to a priest. I told him it was my first confession. I didn't realize at the time that girls had to wear white dresses and be part of a special ceremony when making their first communion. The priest either didn't pay attention to what I said or else he was a wonderful man, but he didn't give me away.

"The complicated lesson I had to learn, was: Be smart, be very, very smart, but don't show it. Sometimes the rules were subtle. One day, for example, my mother and I were walking in the village with a peasant woman, when we heard a plane way up overhead. My mother was holding my hand, and we were wondering about the airplane. I said, 'Oh, it must be an enemy plane because a friendly plane wouldn't have to fly that high.' Suddenly my mother squeezed my hand so hard, I saw stars. I didn't know what I did wrong. Afterward, when we were alone, she said, 'Don't you know that you are not supposed to be smart?' That's how I was trained to know what not to say.

"I remember things from then so clearly, even the smallest details. If I were an artist, I could paint the house and the four-foot-square area behind the stove where my mother and I slept on a clay platform, on which my mother couldn't even stretch her legs when she slept. To make it nice for Sunday, we would spread a fresh layer of red clay that we would have to go and dig in the mountain.

"Good health was a blessing, not a given. I had very bad infections on my skin that festered for months. We tried the local remedy, which was like a round, green leaf, supposed to take the pus out, but that didn't help. I still have scars on my arms and legs. If you were sick and if nature didn't take care of you, nobody else did, because there was just nothing there. The food was poor, but I never felt deprived. Rather I would be excited when my mother came home from work with a stolen piece of bread smeared with sugared butter, which melted a little because she'd had it hidden in her bra. Late at night she'd give it to me quietly and secretly. I can still taste how delicious that was, what a delicacy!

"One late afternoon a Gypsy came into the village telling fortunes. He spotted me, and I must have looked a little different from the other children, though we tried very hard to assimilate. But he found me, and it turned out that he wasn't a Gypsy; he was a Jewish young man sent by my father, who had paid him to bring my mother a letter. The letter was written to 'Olga' as if it was from a girlfriend. It said, 'This is probably the last letter I'm going to be writing to you because my friends have already gone on vacation and I think I will be going in the next week or two.' That was the very last time we heard from my father.

"We lived with Nascia for about a year and a half. About six months into our stay my mother started working in a German laundry. This was a step up from working in the fields. She had only one pair of shoes, so she walked barefoot for about four or five kilometers, and just before she got into the town, she would put her shoes on. Because my mother was bright, hardworking, and German speaking, she was made a supervisor. This aroused the suspicions of an officer's girlfriend, who said, 'This is not your ordinary peasant, she's too smart. This is a Jew!' The following Friday night I waited for my mother to come home, but she never arrived.

"I knew she was in deep trouble, but Nascia didn't. Nascia was somewhat afraid of the Germans. Her husband had been sent to a forced-labor camp in Germany. Still, not knowing we were Jewish, Nascia couldn't understand how terribly frightened I was. She kept assuring me that my mother would be home soon, but I was agonizing! That was the most frightening time of the whole war for me, because I had nobody to talk to and no one to console me.

"On Sunday we were getting ready for church, when suddenly two cars filled with Germans came to our little shack. They started pulling everything apart, hunting for evidence that we were Jewish. Thank goodness, there was nothing to find! As luck would have it, only two weeks earlier Marysia had visited and found that my mother had some family photographs. Marysia had said, 'Are you crazy?' Heeding Marysia's advice, my mother had destroyed every shred of evidence as to who we were except for her false birth certificate.

"Now as the Nazis shredded Nascia's feather quilt, they fired angry questions at me in German. I understood, because I knew some Yiddish, but I kept saying, 'I don't understand.' I hadn't been able to lie to that priest, but I could lie to the Gestapo! Exasperated, they brought somebody from the village to translate for me. Through the interpreter they said, 'We know you're Jewish. If you don't admit it, you'll never see your mother again.' They told me that the one and only thing they respected was the truth. If I told them the truth that I was Jewish, they would let my mother come home.

"I stuck to my guns, insisting that I wasn't Jewish. The point was you couldn't be a child. You had to grow up overnight and to think as a very responsible adult—while you behaved as a child! If you showed that you knew anything, then you were too smart and therefore a Jewish child. The questioning went on for an hour. When they were done with me, I told Nascia I was going to church. As I started walking away across the field, one of the Germans lifted his rifle to hit me on the head. I don't know how I got out of his way, but he brought that rifle down and hit the ground instead of me. I tried not to look too scared, but I was petrified!

"Finally they left. I was still very worried about my mother. A week went by. Two weeks, and I still hadn't heard from her. I cried and pestered Nascia so much, she finally agreed to go to town with me to investigate. We went to the Gestapo, and there was my mother. As soon as she saw me, she put her arms around me and she whispered, 'Did you say anything?' I said no. Then she released me, and that was when she finally smiled.

"She had spent five days in jail, the only woman with four male prisoners. Since then she'd been under house arrest, cleaning and cooking in an officers' club and sleeping on the kitchen floor. Now they told her she could sleep at home, but she had to come back and work in the laundry *and* cook for the officers every day or else they would put her in jail again. It went on like that until the summer of 1944, when we were liberated by the Russians.

"When the front passed through our village and the Russians were securely in power, we came out of our house. There were dead soldiers all over the place. We were sobbing, yet death seemed so natural then. We were finally free to leave the village and assume our real identity, but we were as poor as church rats. My mother and I began a life of the proverbial 'wandering Jew.' First we looked for any surviving relatives among the Jews who were beginning to crawl out of the cellars, forests, and wherever else they had been hidden. It was soon evident that besides one uncle, everyone else in my family had been killed.

"Our greatest wish was to get away as far as possible from Poland and from the people who had betrayed us or didn't lift a finger to help. My mother married my uncle. A year later my brother, Albert, was born. Then we moved to

Budapest, Hungary, where we lived for several months. My stepfather finally located some relatives in the United States. Although they guaranteed that they would be financially responsible for us if we came to the States, the Polish (Jewish?) quota was backed up. It wasn't until seven years later that our quota number finally came up, and we could get a visa to immigrate. In the meantime we moved to Czechoslovakia, and then to France, and from France to Caracas, Venezuela, where we finally knew some semblance of stability—no more living out of suitcases, no makeshift accommodations or hotels.

"I went back to school, which was wonderful, but because my parents often worked twelve hours a day and I had to take care of my new little brother after school, I still had no opportunity to be a carefree child. Even when my brother was five years old, I had to be waiting when the bus brought him home. This kept me from serving on the student council or joining other after-school activities. I had friends, but little time to go out with them, and I found it hard to relate. I was reticent, afraid to tell them my secrets. I was amazed at the intimate things they would tell! Also, much of what they liked to do seemed frivolous to me. I was simply too mature for them.

"All this time our goal was to come to the United States and join my stepfather's family, but we still had to wait for our quota number. In 1951 I came alone on a student visa and went to a girls' boarding school, which was great. At school I had friends and lots of fun. I learned how to swim. I even went to dances. My parents always sent me plenty of money, so I could do what I wanted. On weekends I would visit my aunt in New York.

"To this day I don't know how to ride a bike, and I'm not the only one. None of the people who went through what I went through had the luxury of being children. Because I was almost eighteen when I started having fun, I made sure that didn't happen with my children. When they were growing up, we let them try whatever they wanted: ice-skating, skiing. I found it exciting. It helped make up for what I had missed.

"For all these years there has been so much to relearn and overcome, even in small ways. For example, in the war the police were to be feared. Now I usually see a policeman as somebody I can go to for help. There was also the issue of trust. During the war I lived in constant fear of being found out. Everybody was a potential enemy. Silence was the only weapon we had; it was the only thing we could rely on. It took a lot to change my thinking, but now I have several good friends whom I love and trust, like Esther, whom I've known for over twenty-five years and I feel I can tell her anything.

"Another part of me that goes back to my hiding is that I need to feel in control at all times. I need to have order around me, and to know that everything is taken care of. When I teach, I can't just wing it. I know enough, but I feel uncomfortable unless I'm prepared. That need for control, I think, affected most of us who didn't have any control over our lives.

"Many of the scars have been slow to fade. For years and years I had recurring nightmares where I would lose my voice. Or I had to run away from danger and my legs would not carry me. Or I'd be trying to make a phone call and always making some kind of a mistake, like not being able to make the connection. Or I would want to call my mother because I was in danger, but I couldn't speak and she couldn't hear me. Those nightmares are gone, thank goodness. But they lasted until I was well into my twenties.

"What has helped me to heal? Stability! I married Howard, a very gentle, understanding man who is totally accepting of me, very dependable, and very loving. I know there's nothing I might ask that he wouldn't try to do for me.

"There is also the issue of belonging. The fact that we lost all our roots and were denied all affiliations hurt deeply. For example, after the war I could no longer use the word *cousin*, *granddaughter*, *niece*, because they didn't apply to me anymore. Even now, when people talk about family reunions, I have such a longing. But I've found belonging here! I was elected president of the American Jewish Committee in my town, and I've served on the board of my synagogue. I feel that I belong to this community. When I go someplace, it's a wonderful feeling to be known, which is just the opposite of what we, as hidden children, were striving for before.

"I've also been active in helping resettle Soviet Jews in this area. Again, I know what it is like not to have roots. You can say, 'Well, nobody helped me, so why should I?' I've heard that a lot! Or you can say, as I do, 'Nobody helped me, and I know how it feels; therefore I'm going to help.' I was very involved with the first Russian family adopted by the Bergen County (North Jersey) Federation. A young Russian couple in their twenties with an eight-month-old child arrived penniless, unable to speak English. What started as just helping them get settled developed into a very nice friendship. I taught them English. I taught the woman how to shop and cook and take care of her baby. I also got them the medical help they needed. Speaking some Russian, I interceded with the representative from Federation in negotiating the allowance the family was going to get. Then I helped the couple find jobs. I know I made a difference in their lives, and that makes me feel good.

"Of course the person I felt we should have done everything for but didn't have anything to give her at the time was Marysia, who saved our lives. We never did anything for her, and it hurts me that she took such a big chance and we couldn't repay her somehow. Hopefully the satisfaction of having saved us meant enough to her. I even feel very sorry for Nascia, who didn't know we were Jewish. We took advantage of her, but what can you do when you want to stay alive? People get hurt in many different ways. I hope she didn't have to suffer repercussions for having saved Jews. I have no desire to go to Poland, because all I have are painful memories. But if I were to go, I'd want to find Nascia and thank her in some way, regardless of how she feels about us.

"We went through hell, but the strength that I needed to get me through hiding has also helped me accomplish important things later on. In both my family and my husband, Howard's, family, we were the first college graduates. We have graduate degrees, and so do our children. The Germans were intent on destroying me, but they didn't succeed. That's why I've never wanted to be pitied. I'd rather be perceived as somebody who has made it, who has overcome all kinds of obstacles—and I have!"

KRISTINE KEREN, D.D.S.

Kristine Keren, D.D.S., is petite and has fine features and an elfin hairdo. She is quick to laugh when anyone says that she looks too young to be a dentist, let alone the mother of a dentist, but she is both. Kristine shares an office overlooking Central Park with her elder son, while another son is still in high school. Kristine, who is married to a construction engineer, commutes to work from the North Shore of Long Island. The Kerens' prewar home, with its parquet floors, leather furniture, many books, and treasured objects, is as different as it's possible to get from Kristine's wartime refuge.

"We lived in Poland, in the ghetto of Lvov. My father was always looking for places to hide my little brother, Pavel, and me because the Germans were intent on getting rid of all the Jewish children. One hiding place was a small, empty space, three feet long and one foot deep, below the window, which my father had camouflaged to look like the wall. I remember having to sit in there with Pavel for hours, struggling for air and being so scared! Tears were running down my cheeks, but I didn't dare make a sound for fear the Germans would find us. But silently I'd pray for my father to come and let us out. Each time he came back, I begged him, 'Daddy, *please* let this be the last time.' I didn't think I could take it anymore.

"My parents had to work in the labor camp, so I was often left alone with my brother. Several times when the Germans came, I had to hide Pavel in a suitcase under the bed while I hid in the closet, behind my mother's long, rust-colored satin robe. I was only seven or eight years old at the time, but I could recognize the German footsteps. I had to hide myself and then wait a few more minutes for fear they'd come back again. Then I ran back to let my brother out of the suitcase so he could breathe again.

"He was good! He was only three and a half years old, but he never made a fuss. He understood, as I did, that we just had to be quiet and do what we were told. Life was getting scarier by the day.

"One day I heard a noise—like somebody gasping for air—and I looked out the back window. There I saw some Polish teenagers swinging bats and hitting a Jewish man, who was begging them to stop. But they kept it up until he lay there, dead. I'll never forget that choking sound he made. I was just stunned.

"It was only a few days later that we fled—not through the gates of the ghetto but straight down! My father had been digging a tunnel from the basement of a house near us, right into the sewer. When he broke through, he found himself face-to-face with a sewer worker. Instead of reporting my father, the man said, 'I can help you, but you'll have to pay me—a lot.' My father agreed, and the next day he brought the man all the money we had. It was a risk, but the only real chance we had.

"The next night my father saw some cars with soldiers coming close. He came down to where my brother and I were hidden in the basement, and he whispered, 'This is it!' I cried when he explained that we'd have to go down this very narrow tunnel. He would go first, then me. Then Pavel and my mother.

"I could hear the sound of water in the tunnel down below, and I knew I couldn't do it. I sobbed, 'I don't want to go.' My father said gently but urgently, 'You have to go. Trust me, don't worry.' I watched him go down, and then somebody pushed me. I felt myself falling through the blackness, and then my father caught me and put me on his back. He said, 'Hold tight.'

"I grabbed his neck, and I held on to his hips with my feet. He kept telling me to hold tight. I was shaking. My teeth were chattering so hard, I couldn't talk. Then my mother was behind us, holding Pavel. The walkway was narrow, and we had to be careful not to fall into the water. It seemed like we had to walk forever! I kept asking my father how much longer. He said, 'Don't worry, a few minutes more, a few minutes more.' It was especially frightening when we had to cross from one side of the river to the other.

"Meanwhile, all around us people were dropping down into the sewer through manholes. It was terrifying! Then my father's contact, whose name was Leopold Socha, appeared and took us and several other people to a special tunnel where we wouldn't be seen. He told my father where to find boards we could put across the flowing water, and on which we could sleep. By then I was so tired, I fell asleep leaning on a strange man, who said to me, 'You're little, but you're so heavy.'

"We all stayed there for a few days. Some people couldn't take the stench and the darkness, so they left, but ten of us remained in that sewer—for fourteen months! During that time we never went outside or saw daylight. We lived with webs and moss hanging on the wall. The river not only smelled terrible, but also it was full of diseases. We got dysentery, and I remember Pavel and I were sick with unrelenting diarrhea. There was only enough clean water for each of us to have half a cup a day. My parents didn't even drink theirs; they gave it to Pavel and me so that we wouldn't die from dehydration.

"Mr. Socha and two of his friends very faithfully brought us food. But there were dangers. A few times other sewer workers found us because they had seen our wet shoes hanging up. We had to run to try to escape. I would get so scared, I stopped breathing. But we got away! Another time our little lamp started a fire. We thought we'd be burned, but we survived that too.

"Then there was a heavy rainstorm, and the sewer swelled so that the water was almost up to the ceiling, which was less than five feet high. My parents, who were constantly bent, had to hold us children up high so we could breathe. We were frequently soaking wet.

"The rats were all over us—each one was about a foot long. But we weren't afraid of them; we played with them. We fed them, and they grew even bigger from eating our bread. But they always wanted more, and my father had to stay awake at night to keep them from eating it all.

"All this time nobody had to tell us to be quiet. I felt like an animal, ruled by instinct. I never spoke above a whisper. But after a few months of this life I was very, very depressed, and I didn't want to eat or talk to anybody.

"That was when Leopold Socha picked me up and took me through the tunnels and said, 'Look up.' I saw the daylight, and he said to me, 'You have to be very strong, and one day you will go up there and live a life like other children.' At my father's suggestion Mr. Socha brought books so my father could teach me to read and count. This way, they said, I'd be ready for school when the war was finally over.

"From then on I'd always watch for Mr. Socha when he would come every other day with our food. Always the first thing I'd see was his smile: a radiant smile with perfect teeth. He was such a cheerful man—and thoughtful too! He managed to get my mother candles for the Sabbath, and he'd always share his own lunch with Pavel and me.

"When liberation came, Mr. Socha was the one who came to tell us. We'd heard plenty of Russian bombs exploding nearby, but we didn't know we were free until Mr. Socha banged on the pipe. We all stayed very quiet, unsure of what the banging meant. Then he called our names. He said, 'You can come out now!'

"But even after liberation life was hard. We had no money, and my parents had no jobs. Before the war my father had had his own business, but now he had nothing. It was a freezing winter, and I had no shoes. My father made me shoes out of newspaper and tied them with laces of rope so I could run to keep warm.

"Those shoes embarrassed me. When I went to school, I tried to keep my feet under my chair so nobody would see them. With the first money my parents got they bought me a pair of shiny brown boots. Then I wanted everyone to see my feet! But despite the joy, that was also a sad time for us. Our blond, blue-eyed savior, Leopold Socha, was hit by a drunken driver and killed.

"Soon after that we moved to Krakow, where my parents could earn a living. But even though the war was over, anti-Semitism in Poland was not. My mother and even the school principal, a thoughtful woman named Mrs. Zajac, agreed that I must pose as a Christian. Can you imagine? Even after the war I had to hide my identity! In many ways the anti-Semitism I experienced after the war was more painful than anything that happened in the sewer. I remember how mortified I was when some neighborhood children taunted me and wrote *Kristine, the Jew* in huge letters on a wall. Even when my mother took us for a little vacation in the country, the lady we rented from said, 'Hitler made one mistake: *He* didn't kill *all* the Jews.'

"It was so wonderful, in 1957, when we immigrated to Israel, where we were surrounded only by Jews. Having been a fine student in Poland, I was now enrolled in medical/dental school. But there was a problem: I didn't know Hebrew or English, and I couldn't understand one word of my first lecture! I went outside and sat on the steps, and cried. Then I went home with my new textbooks, which I couldn't understand, and I said to my parents, 'I'll never make it.'

"But my father said, 'You'll make it.' He sounded so convinced! From that night on I would sit down with my books and a dictionary, and I'd look up and translate every single word on the page. Each page took me two or three hours at first, but gradually it got easier as I started to recognize the words that would come up again and again.

"It wasn't easy; I must have studied twenty-four hours a day, but I did make it, just as my father said I would. I remember the first test I took. It was in Chemistry, which was lucky because it's mostly symbols and not that much to write. After the exam my professor congratulated me. He said, 'I don't know how you did it, but you did it.'

"Actually I had a little trick I used then—and used until recently. Whenever anything was difficult, I would imagine myself in a concentration camp with a German soldier standing next to me pointing a gun. If I didn't do whatever I was supposed to do, he would kill me. It was a painful way of motivating myself, but it was effective. It certainly got me through a lot.

"I haven't been able to put everything behind me. Of course the memories come back! Sometimes, when I'm enjoying a beautiful day, I think about the people in my family who died. I had a cousin who was my age, and I'll never forget her face that day I saw her going into the concentration camp. That image will always live with me.

"The experience stays with me in small ways or daily things. All I have to do is smell old fat, and it makes me nauseous—not because it's spoiled but because I remember this as a taste from during the war. When we bought our house fifteen years ago, I noticed that the entrance to the attic was camouflaged in a bookshelf. I thought, What a good place to hide! I also can't stand to see fear in someone's eyes, especially when it's a child. That's why I am an extraordinarily gentle dentist. Believe me, none of my patients are afraid. If anyone shows fear, I have to stop.

"I know I'm different from a lot of survivors in that I've never tried to hide my experiences from my children. My story was featured on a TV documentary in Europe and in a book, *In the Sewers of Lvov: The Last Sanctuary from the Holocaust*, by Robert Marshall (Scribner's, 1991).

"But not so long ago I came across the little sweater I was wearing the night we went into hiding in the sewer. It was green and yellow with short sleeves and a little bow. My grandmother had made it for me. I showed it to my younger son. I said, 'Roger, do you know what this is?' He said, 'I don't know. Something falling apart? Something the bugs ate?' I said, 'This is the sweater that I wore the night we were running.'

"Roger looked shocked. He looked at the sweater again, and he said, 'But, Mom, you were so *little*!' He knew the story, but in his mind's eye, he'd seen me as an adult instead of the small child I was.

"Now I think he sees what I went through in a new light, and this is good. I'd like to think my story can help both my sons when things are difficult for them. I say to them, 'Life is not so easy, and you may feel pretty hopeless and discouraged. But you have to move forward. I believe you can make it through almost anything if you don't give up.' "

RENEE ROTH-HANO

*Renee Roth-Hano, a psychiatric social worker and author, is
tall, expressive, and friendly. Her dark skin and hair are set off
by her clothing—a blend of olive and maroon, with silver and
turquoise earrings, several bracelets, and rings. Renee calls her
apartment "homey" with an elaborate kitchen and warm colors throughout, blending with her pre-Columbian pottery. In
the living room there are figurines, including one of a nun, several large abstract paintings, and on the couch a collection of
dolls (including a Santa Claus), which are Renee's. (She and
her husband, John, have no children.) "It's important to me to
be comfortable and look at things that are pleasurable," Renee
explains with a gesture that seems to embrace it all.*

"It hasn't been easy up to now: whenever we, as a group,
talked about our pasts, some of the people would say, 'Look,
you had it easy, you weren't in a camp, so be happy you're
alive.' But lots of people were very damaged emotionally. For
instance I had a carefree childhood, but it ended abruptly
when I was eight years old and the war broke out.

"I was born in Mulhouse in 1931. Germany, moving fast
after France lost the war, annexed Alsace, where we lived. A
few days later, we were expelled. We took refuge in Paris, but
it wasn't any real sanctuary. Fourteen major anti-Semitic de-

crees were passed between 1940, when we arrived in Paris, and 1942, when we had to go into hiding. The one that bothered me most was the one that said I had to wear the Star of David. I was ten years old. I had always been a very inquisitive, outgoing kid, but wearing the star was like the final straw, the most damaging of all; it made me feel ashamed. I became very withdrawn.

"Six weeks later fourteen thousand Jews were arrested in a roundup. A secret maid's room was found for my parents to hide in. Meanwhile my two sisters and I were sent off to a convent called 'La Chaumière,' or 'The Cottage,' in Flers, a small town in Normandy. I resented the fact that my parents hadn't found another way to hide us. I knew that friends of ours and even relatives had managed to stay together as a family. I really felt abandoned, but I couldn't say so. As the eldest in the family, I understood that it was my job to maintain the family honor and take care of my two little sisters, Denise and Lily. It was a stiff-upper-lip kind of thing: I felt cornered and very burdened, but I had to make the best of it.

"Ours was not the usual kind of hiding: We were not in an attic or underground; we were in plain sight. What we were hiding was our Jewishness. We no longer wore the Star of David. We were passing for Catholics—and steeping ourselves in the Catholic religion. We learned catechism and we breathed the religion every day. Actually I found it comforting. My Jewishness had not been very firmly entrenched. Yes, we'd gone to temple for the holidays, and I hadn't liked the fact that women had to be separate from the men, which meant I couldn't stay with my father. So that was the only real feeling I had about my Jewishness.

"That was why I'd felt so incensed by the decrees, which were telling me, 'You are a Jew,' even though I didn't feel like a Jew and hadn't been raised as one. Still I had some scruples:

I tried not to cross myself often or go in the front door, because if I did, I would have to genuflect. What I loved most was the singing. It made me feel like I belonged, which I needed desperately then. We sang hymns every evening, and I loved that. It wasn't so much God—I didn't believe in God. He was lousy to the Jews! But if you cannot pray to him, who can you pray to? At least when I was singing, there was hope coming from my heart. It was a way of begging God to listen. And as our voices harmonized, I didn't feel so alone or scared.

"On the whole the nuns were very good to us. Sister Pannelay, the Mother Superior, was very strict. One day she scolded my sister and me because my sister was massaging my legs. She was doing it only because I was freezing, but Sister Pannelay saw it as something sexual. She fiercely told us, 'Don't ever do that again!' I felt hurt, embarrassed, and misunderstood. It was only in later years that I could think of Sister Pannelay with real gratitude, understanding that it was she who had taken us into the convent—and saved our lives!

"There was another nun, Sister Madeleine, who was extra nice. We were often hungry, but we children were not supposed to ask for extra food. Sometimes Sister Madeleine would scream to summon my sisters and me to the kitchen. She made it sound as if she were scolding us. Once we were safely out of sight of the others, she would give us special treats, such as eggs. She was wonderful. A couple of times she baked cakes and sent them to my parents!

"Still, I felt sad and frightened. I mostly kept to myself, afraid to make any real friends among the other children, who had no idea that I was Jewish. I didn't want to blow my cover. There was one lady from the town, an old maid named Suzanne, who was always hanging around and asking me questions, like, 'What's your father's name?' and 'What does he do?' He was actually a tailor, but I was afraid that if I said so, she'd know I was Jewish. 'Well,' I said finally, trying to find a way around it, 'he works for a raincoat manufacturer.' She'd persist: 'Well, what would three little kids be doing here at this time with strangers when there's bombing all around and no food?'

"I said, 'There's more food here than in Paris!' I tried to look confident, but one more question, and I wouldn't have known what to say. I leaned down and pulled up my socks to gain some time. I don't know if she was really mean or just nosy. The other children and I made fun of her, calling her 'Capital S' because she had a big bosom and a protruding behind. Secretly I was terrified that this Capital S or one of the others would see through my act and report me.

"When I was depressed, I used to go and sit at the feet of a Virgin Mary statue. She was a mother, I told myself, so she would understand. One time, when I hadn't heard from my real mother for several weeks, I sat on the base of the statue, plucking the petals off a daisy—'She loves me, she loves me not.' A daisy is *marguerite* in French, and that was my mother's name. It seemed symbolic. When my petal-plucking game ended on 'love me not,' I felt terrible.

"During that time at the convent we had very little contact with my parents. Letters had to be perfunctory because all mail was censored. My father looked and sounded too obviously Jewish to risk going anywhere. But he wouldn't even write to us because he was ashamed of his written French. My mother wrote, but during the two years she only came to visit us once. That visit was a disaster for me. She found lice in my hair and cut it all off. I cried so! I wished she hadn't come. I was twelve years old at that time and had a crush on a boy named Marcel. I was so mortified that he would see me looking ugly without my hair. I tried to hide, but he saw me. He was so sweet! He said, 'I really like that haircut.'

"Soon after that I was baptized. The Germans were now in the town, and baptism was meant to make me more like the other children and consequently safer. But I was filled with fear. I thought, Once you're baptized, that's it. I had guilty visions of flying up to heaven without my parents. I was in anguish, but I couldn't tell anyone. I had terrible anxiety attacks, and once I was found sleepwalking in the graveyard. Then I got sick with jaundice for sixty days. I was sure I would die. There was a popular song then about a little boy whose mother was going to die when all the leaves fell. The little boy in the song put the fallen leaves back on the tree to keep his mother alive. While I was sick, I was saying to myself, I'm going to die, too, but nobody will put the leaves back for me.

"Fortunately I recovered. The nuns said it was a miracle. I felt grateful. Three weeks later the Allied troops landed. It was late afternoon. The nun tried to shoo me outside to play with the other children, but I was worried. I wanted to stay near the kitchen to hear the news on the radio. All during supper I was frightened. Afterward I looked outside and I saw this formation of planes come in—like a flock of birds! Then I saw the planes stop, and the bombs fall. I saw it happening! I started to scream: '*Au secours!* Help!' Then the bombing grew more intense. We were bombed for three solid days. Again I thought I was going to die. On D-Day, June 6th, I made a vow: 'God, if you get me out of this one, I promise to become a nun.' From that moment on I was totally committed.

"Shortly after D-Day the police came to the convent to tell us to go and hide in the country. It seemed that the convent was near an ammunition depot targeted by the English. The nuns told us to run and get a change of clothing and a blanket and come right back. Then we left. We hiked six miles to the farm of a lady named Madame Huet, who supplied milk to the convent. There all thirty of us children and the nuns joined a great many other local people, who were also taking refuge. It was something! We had lice, fleas, and worms. We had no towels to dry ourselves. It's a good thing it was summer—June, July, and August. Still, the hygiene was poor. I had twenty-eight infections in one hand, and my feet were bandaged because I had such bad impetigo.

"We had only candlelight, so at night the nuns made us go to the outhouse all together, one after the other. The privy was only a hundred yards away from the barn, but we would sort of dash out and scream to cover our fear. We pretended it was fun, like an adventure, but we were scared stiff.

"Every Sunday we all went to church as a group. One Sunday Sister Madeleine was afraid. The front line of battle was coming close. She said to Sister Pannelay, the Mother Superior, 'Surely you're not going to take the kids to church today!' But Mother Superior said, 'Don't worry. The church is not that far.' She made me go, too, even with my bandaged feet. It was almost as if she didn't see the danger. Nothing stopped Sister Pannelay!

"At first we'd had rations of food, but then we hit bottom. There was nothing left. We didn't even have water. There was a pump, but it was full of rust. German soldiers, who were on the run from the British, would come out of the woods and try to steal the few potatoes still growing, but Madame Huet faced them down, telling them they should be ashamed of themselves for stealing food from children. Toward the end we were so weak, we didn't get up in the morning. Sympathetic, the nuns told us, 'Stay where you are.'

"Finally the war was over. Relieved, we all trekked back to the convent. A real shock awaited us. The entire town was destroyed. Only one wall of the convent and the statue of the Virgin Mary were still standing, nothing else! The nuns declared that that was a miracle too. There was one little five-year-old boy with us named Jean-Jacques whom I liked very much and looked after. He was reckless. I used to kiss his hand when he fell, which happened often. Jean-Jacques was running around as usual, ignoring our pleas to stay put. There were convoys of American trucks en route from Cherbourg to Paris. Before anyone could intervene, little Jean-Jacques was hit by one of the trucks and crushed to death. I was furious about that. I scolded God: 'How can you do that, you dirty God you!' Patiently Sister Madeleine explained to me that it wouldn't have happened if little Jean-Jacques's faith had been intact. For me that was very hard to swallow!

"Soon after that my sisters and I were reunited with our parents. But even though the war was over and I no longer needed to hide my Jewishness, I felt ashamed of being a Jew. For years I told people I was Catholic. Even as I turned eighteen, I lived in terror that they would find out the truth and ridicule me. It was painful keeping that secret; it was always a barrier in my mind that prevented me from getting close to anyone. I felt so conflicted! I had not forgotten my earlier vow to become a nun. For five years I walked around thinking, I don't want to be a nun, but feeling that I was compelled to make good on my promise. Then one day the calling left—and I felt totally empty and depressed, like I had no belief in anything. I didn't know where I belonged either.

"When I was nineteen, I came to the United States by chance, as a governess. One day something amazing happened. I was at Macy's in the early spring—I thought in terms of Easter. There were two ladies at the cosmetics counter, one actually hollering to the other, 'How was your seder last night?' I froze. I thought, 'Wait! You can't talk about a seder here, in public!' I gasped. But nobody minded. I said to myself, 'My God, it's wonderful! Nobody's even ashamed.' The two women went on talking like it was no big thing. I felt something inside me breaking free.

"Since then the process of reaccepting myself has continued. I became a psychiatric social worker. Maybe that was my way of being a nun after all! I found I could relate well to anybody feeling oppressed, and I could help them with real understanding. I'm always very connected with my patients. I sometimes think I'm able to be more loving because I have no kids. I'm sure that energy goes to my patients. I believe in them! I push them, but not in a mean or impatient way. I'm tolerant of the lapses too. I know that's also a part of the healing process. I know how to reach my patients, how to convince them that they have what it takes to recover. And they do recover!

"The fact that many of my professional colleagues are Jewish has helped me feel even less like an outsider. Before Jewish holidays they ask, 'Who's going to be in?' instead of 'Who's going to be out?' That makes me feel mainstream. Now, even when I go back to France, I keep my chin up high.

"Of course that can be a challenge! My sister, Lily, who lives in France, doesn't consider herself Jewish, nor do her kids. One of them actually makes anti-Semitic comments, and she doesn't stop him. Recently she said to me, 'For many French people it's still a calamity to marry a Jew.' I've tried to tell her, 'It's okay to be a Jew—to be anything you are.' But she doesn't know what I'm talking about.

"In the last decade my healing and happiness have grown deeper. I married an accountant named John. We have a wonderful relationship. I also wrote an autobiographical children's book, *Touch Wood: A Girlhood in Occupied France* (Puffin, 1989), which brought many fan letters, including one from Normandy that said, 'Thank you for honoring our town.' In November 1991 the town of Flers held a special event to honor me. There was a dinner, and they presented me with a medal.

"One of my former classmates, named Yvette, was there. She told me that when we were children, she always felt that there was something mysterious about me. She didn't know what it was, but when she saw *The Diary of Anne Frank*, she thought of me. Isn't that amazing? Yvette wrote a wonderful poem for the newspaper about how she wanted to wipe my tears. It was deeply moving to me. It made me realize that there were people in my corner I didn't even know about.

"Now I feel so close to the people of Flers. I'm a special citizen of the town. I almost feel like when I die, I want to be buried there. It's so healing at this point in my life to learn that I can be completely honest and open about myself and still be liked. How strange—and also wonderful—to find that I'm rewarded for the very thing that I had once been made to feel so very much ashamed of!"

RICHARD ROZEN

Richard Rozen, fifty-seven, stocky, smiling, with dark hair brushed back, looks spiffy in a white dinner jacket and red bow tie, as he dances with Rysia, his pretty blond wife, on her fiftieth birthday. The Rozens live in Brighton, a suburb of Melbourne, Australia. They have a second home on the sea, some forty-five miles away. A real estate investor (semiretired), Richard is a grand master in bridge and an active volunteer at the Melbourne Holocaust Center. Richard, whose accent is a hybrid of Polish and Australian, is the father of two twenty-nine-year-old sons, Peter and Mark.

"I was born in Radom, Poland, in 1935. We led a very privileged life in the sense that our family had money, but I didn't get to see much of my father, a doctor who ran a big hospital and had little time to spend at home.

"In 1939 the war began, but it was still remote to me until the Germans actually arrived in our town. We escaped to Luboml, which was on the Russian side of then-divided Poland. In July 1941, when the Germans suddenly invaded Luboml, there was a great hurry to go into hiding. My father had gold coins, and with that he was able to buy us shelter on a farm near Luboml. I don't know how the contact was arranged, but there we stayed in what was actually a cabinet, only sixty or seventy centimeters wide. The length of it would have been a couple of meters, because we could all lie on top of each other comfortably. My parents couldn't stand, but I could, and I sort of walked between them. This cabinet was in a cellar, so it was well hidden. Our presence there was so secret, not even the children of the hiding family knew that we were there. That was where we stayed for thirteen months!

"It was strange at first, but little children can get used to things quickly, and soon it didn't even seem unusual, except for having to be quiet. My father invented all kinds of challenging physical exercises for me to do, and in between, my mother whispered children's stories in my ear. So I was kept occupied most of the time.

"In the middle of the night the farmer would bring us bread and potatoes, and often cold soup and vegetables, a bucket of water for drinking and washing, and a separate bucket to use for a toilet. So we weren't starving; and as horrible as it sounds, I didn't think it was so bad. In fact one great thing about this odd existence was that I got to see so much of my father for the first time in my life! He taught me the alphabet and counting to one hundred by writing on the palm of my hand and silently whispering in my ear. I was challenged and fascinated. I would have loved to get out and go play with the children I could hear in the distance, but when my parents said I couldn't until the war was over, I accepted that.

"After a year we ran out of rent money. The farmer wanted to kick us out. My father begged to stay a little longer. He offered the farmer his French shoes, a great luxury, and that bought us one more month. Seeing my parents pleading and begging to stay longer, I understood that leaving our hiding place while the war was still on would be very dangerous, and I hoped it wouldn't happen.

"One night the farmer told us that we had to leave immediately. We had no choice. As we emerged, I noticed that my parents couldn't stand. They were crouching, and they looked so odd, all I could think of was the monkeys I used to see in the zoo with their long arms, all sort of bent forward. As for me my feet were wrapped in rags because I'd outgrown my shoes. Nevertheless we climbed out and started walking.

"Then something extraordinary happened: The color of the world started changing from pitch black to the pinks, reds, and oranges of a sunrise. I was dazzled! After nearly a quarter of my life in that cabinet I was literally seeing the light. My father warned me not to look at the brightness too quickly, so I wouldn't go blind, but I was enthralled.

"However, the joy of my new discovery soon yielded to fear, as we were captured by two Ukrainian soldiers. They took us to a German officer wearing incredibly tall, shiny boots. My parents told them we were Christians. Skeptical, the officer commanded my father and me to drop our trousers. At that time, in that part of the world, only Jews were circumcised. As soon as we took our pants down, the truth was out. My parents and I were immediately taken away to the Lublin ghetto. There things really changed for the worse. Food was very, very scarce, and children, who were not even classified as people, got nothing to eat. My parents had to share their meager rations with me. My most vivid recollection of that ghetto was the regular sight of dead people being taken away in the morning.

"After four months a new camp was opening—and that was Treblinka. We were slated to go there. My parents, who understood that it was to be a death camp, were very upset. However, it seemed that the Polish partisans were desperate for a doctor. Through the grapevine my father learned that if he could prove that he was a doctor, the Ukrainian guards would smuggle us out. Then we wouldn't have to go to Treblinka.

"Arrangements were made—along with a warning that if my father failed to prove that he was a doctor, we would all be executed on the spot. He certainly didn't look the part after many months of hiding. He had worn the same clothes and hadn't shaved for nearly two years. He looked old, and very dirty and tattered—quite different from his neat, distinguished appearance before the war.

"Luckily he passed the test with flying colors. We were smuggled out of the ghetto, and for the next three or four months while my father worked for the partisans, my mother and I stayed in a village with the family of one of the partisans. This was great: The food was the best we had had in two years, I didn't have to whisper, and I was clean.

"However, I had a special challenge: For my safety I had to masquerade as a girl. My fictional name was Marysia Ulecki. I was supposed to be a distant cousin of the people who were keeping my mother and me. The physical part was easy. After a couple of years in hiding with no haircuts, my hair was very long. The big problem was language. In Polish when a boy says a certain word, it's one way, but when a girl says the same word, you change one or two letters. My mother spent a lot of time teaching me to speak and walk and act like a girl. It was a lot to learn, but the task was simplified slightly by the fact that I was supposed to be a little bit 'backward.' They didn't risk taking me to school, but they took me to church. I remember some kid tried to flirt with me, but the lady we were living with told him not to bother with me because I was retarded. After that the kids left me alone except to make fun of me.

"In order to go to the bathroom like a girl, I had to practice. It wasn't easy! Quite often I used to come back with wet shoes. But since I was supposed to be a little backward, wetting my shoes made my act all the more convincing.

"After a while certain people began to suspect that I wasn't a girl, and it became too dangerous for me to stay in the village. One night the partisans took me to the forest to join my father. We were very glad to see each other. I loved my dad, and the forest itself was warm and inviting. There were all kinds of birds and animals there that I'd never seen. It all looked like fun.

"The hospital where my father worked was half under the ground. I didn't stay with him; I stayed with a group of partisans, some distance from there. We wandered most of the time and often hid ourselves in hollow trees, where we slept because it was safer. I was extremely hungry, as we were fed only once a day, when a couple of partisans who had left the night before would come back in the morning with provisions. One day the two partisans came back very drunk. They hadn't brought any food, but they made up some excuse. There was a big discussion among the partisan leaders. Finally it was decided that these two would be made an example.

"The two were tied to trees, and their throats were cut. I'd seen lots of dead people in the ghetto, but this was the first time I'd seen someone killed right in front of me. It was shocking! After that we still had to go another twenty-four hours without food. It was hard. Grass was not all that tasty, but some of the leaves were reasonably good. If you were lucky, you could catch a rabbit or a mouse, and then whatever you got, you kept quiet about it.

"One day Jorek, the commander, decided it was time for me to become a full-fledged partisan. He gave me a job as the feather boy. He gave me a fairly good-sized feather. He said, Blow on it.' I blew on it. The feather moved. The routine was this: We stayed in hiding until we could isolate one, two, three, or even four German soldiers. Then the partisans would jump them, cut their throats, and take their weapons and their clothes.

"My job was to put my feather under the nose of each soldier and count up to a hundred to see if he was dead. (Luckily I could do that, thanks to my schooling in the cabinet.) Occasionally the Germans used to plead with me and say, 'Frau, frau, kinder . . . my wife, my wife, my children.' But being a very hardened partisan, I had no feeling. Partisans took no prisoners. It was either them or us. For every one of them that lived, it could be one of us who died. I would call over some of the partisans to finish the job. I never did that part. I didn't want to get blood on my hands. I just did the feather business.

"Certainly my existence in the forest was totally different from what I had been used to before, but other than the fact that my shoes were too small and I had to move a lot in order not to freeze, this life seemed okay. The present I got for my ninth birthday was a loaf of bread, the most precious gift I ever got in my life, during the war, before, or since! I kept that bread sitting inside my shirt for about three months. Whenever I was hungry, I would scratch a few crumbs. I started scratching on it in April and I scratched it until it was midsummer. It's impossible to describe how I treasured that bread!

"The winter of 1944 was particularly cold. There was a night of heavy bombing. As usual I stayed up in my tree. We'd been bombed before, and this was nothing unusual. Many of my friends had been killed, which I was used to. But this time was something else: It just rained bombs! When it was finally quiet, I came down from the tree, and I saw many blown-up bodies. I realized how fortunate I was that my tree had not been hit. So many others were. Somebody said that the Germans were retreating and it must have been the Russians who were bombing the forest indiscriminately.

"I looked down, and suddenly I spotted a leg. It was a full-size leg, exactly my height when I stood it up. It was nearly dry. The rest of the body was disintegrated, but that leg was good. I told my officer that I would take the leg to my father because there were a few legs missing at his hospital. I figured someone could use this one because it was perfect.

"My commanding officer didn't say anything. He sort of shook his head, turned around, and just walked away. So I took that leg with me. I was about three hundred meters away from the hospital. The snow was very soft. It took me four to five hours to cover those three hundred meters with that leg! But I worked out a system: I would push the leg in front of me, and the leg would sink and I would sink. I pulled the leg up from the snow. We sort of went up and down like a yo-yo. At times it was very difficult because I would sink in below the surface of the snow. Then I had to crawl out and pull the leg out. But I was determined! I wasn't going to give up.

"When I finally reached the hospital, I asked for my father. He came over and kissed me, and I kissed him. I said, 'There were a lot of bits and pieces blown up there, but this is the best leg I could find.' To my amazement my father didn't pay any attention to it. He muttered something like, 'What has the world come to?' And then he started crying. I couldn't figure out why he wasn't excited about the leg after all the trouble I had bringing it over.

"Then my father snapped out of it, and said, 'Yes, yes. Of course I'll use it on someone.' But he was still crying. It was only a long time afterward that I realized that perhaps this was not the way he'd hoped that his nine-year-old son would be spending a winter's morning. Of course at that time I'd never gone to school or had biology, so I didn't realize that you can't simply sew a leg on someone who needs it. At the time I was certain that I had done a good thing and that somebody was going to be very grateful. That was my very last vivid memory of my father.

"The fighting continued to be severe, and my life with the partisans became very hectic. One night we heard that the hospital had been attacked and everyone in it killed. We went there, and I frantically searched for my father. I couldn't find him. Then someone told me that he had been taken away by the Germans. That was the first time I sat down and really cried.

"Soon after that I was reunited with my mother, whom I hadn't seen in a year and a half. I had known she was well. She was always sending regards and sometimes a bit of clothing or something, another clean handkerchief. (You know how Jewish mothers are. It wouldn't be nice for me to go around without a handkerchief in the forest. Mom did her best!) I was excited to see her, but she seemed strange, really old and very, very depressed over my father's disappearance. In 1944 we returned to our old hometown, but now of course we were no longer affluent; we were extremely poor. I was in rags and I had no shoes.

"My mother decided to visit some of her old friends, other doctors' wives. But the first one took a look at us and slammed the door. As an afterthought she threw some bread out the window. My mother was bewildered. What was going on? The second friend was more explicit. Apparently all the Jews were supposed to be dead. At the third house the reception was identical. The woman there told us that her husband was in charge of the hospital (my father's former job!) and they couldn't help us at all. But she gave us a small handout, so at least we were lucky to get some food, which was the most precious thing then, besides one's life.

"For me this more or less closed a chapter. My father had been a patriotic Pole. He gave his life fighting for that country. Yet this was the reception his wife got from the Poles! As a result I've never considered myself a Pole, and I never will. To them I was always a Jew. I never speak that language, even though I understand it perfectly well. And I will never go back to Poland as long as I live.

"Anyway, at that time I had tuberculosis, and I had to spend three months at Otwock sanitorium. That turned out to be a good place for me. There was plenty of food, a clean bed, and shoes that fit me. In addition I enjoyed the attention from the people who felt sorry for me, and I took full advantage of it. I also learned to play chess from a friend there, who would cheat. As soon as I got close to beating him, he would change the rules. He kept doing this. But, blessed with a good memory, I caught on to all his tricks, and I won my first game. From then on he had to play by my rules, and I kept on winning!

"Three months after I was well, back with my mother again, life was still shaky. Jews in Poland were still under fire. One day we came across a Jewish man who had been shot. He was lying in the street. My mother saw me looking, and she pushed me away. She said, 'You can't see those things. It's not for little children.' I said to her, '*Little children*? I spent a year and a half as a partisan. What's another dead person?' She was horrified. I don't know if she ever quite accepted what took place in the forest. She did ask me what it was like at times. I told her it was cold in winter and hot in summer and other things in between. We didn't talk too much about the morbid things.

"After that we went to a displaced-persons camp in Stuttgart, Germany, sponsored by an American-Jewish organization known as the Joint, which fed and clothed us. For the first time we were well protected. I went to school, which was fun, and I caught up easily. I also learned Hebrew. But the best part was that for the first time in five years I could play with other children my age! We played football after school, which made me really happy.

"While we were there, my mother located her eldest brother, George Blicher, a doctor who lived in Paris with his wife, Fanny, and their daughters, Monique and Evelyn. He spent his money to get us out of Germany and the DP camp. I remember, on our way to France, my mother was telling me that good things were going to be coming for us.

"That first night at my uncle's place they served a dinner like I'd never seen before! There were fifteen people at the table. I was given a seat close to the roast beef, which had already been sliced. Suddenly I started putting slices of meat into my shirt, like the old days when I'd kept my bread in there for scratching. My auntie noticed that some meat was missing from the platter. She looked at me sharply. I felt myself blushing. Getting caught stealing food during the war had meant death. What would happen to me now? I wondered. Auntie took me by the ear and started screaming at me in French. My uncle George came over. He was quite easygoing compared with my auntie. They gave me a few whacks. They didn't hurt. Big boys don't cry. I felt humiliated as I gave back the meat. It was not a very happy reunion.

"The repercussions were even worse: I was instantly branded as a thief, a 'savage,' and was deemed a bad influence on my cousins, two nice little girls. An orphanage was found for me in Drancy (a famous detention camp during the war) near Paris. My mother could not speak French and therefore wasn't able to get enough work in France to support me. Other relatives were too burdened to help us. I stayed in that orphanage for four and a half years. Curiously I was neither outraged nor disappointed that my auntie sent me to the orphanage. To me any place was an improvement over where I had been!

"However, that orphanage turned out to be a pretty tough place. We were all pretty wild, and most arguments were settled with knives and razors. I was careful, but I still got cut a few times, and I have a number of scars even now. At least the schooling was good. In those four and a half years I completed ten grades! At first the schoolchildren at Drancy laughed and teased us because we came from an orphanage, but we took care of them the best way we knew how. I played football and chess at school, to many victories.

"Master Pier, director at the orphanage, ran a very disciplined establishment. We all shared various chores: cooking, cleaning, gathering wood, and so on. The best times were when American ladies from Joint and other Jewish organizations visited us. In return for chocolates, sweets, and chewing gum we told them stories about the war. My stories were the most popular. As the years went by, I had a real fan club.

"Finally, on February 2, 1951, my mother and I boarded an Italian ship, the *Sirena*, headed for Melbourne, Australia. There we were welcomed on March 14 by my uncle and aunt, Berek and Dora Katz, and their sons, Jack, ten, and Alan, three. Since they had a small clothing factory, they worked very long hours. They were paying off their first, very modest, small home.

"I was happy to be there, but having had a bad beginning with the relatives in France, I was cautious this time. That first morning at Uncle Berek and Aunt Dora's the breakfast table was loaded! Everyone was helping themselves. My older cousin, Jack, filled up a glass of milk. My younger one, Alan, took half a glass. Determined to do the right thing this time, I put my hands under my legs and sat quietly, waiting.

"My Aunt Dora noticed that I wasn't eating anything. She said to me, 'Don't you want some breakfast?' I said, 'Can I have some milk?' She said, 'Of course.' I said, 'How much milk can I have?' She said, 'A whole lot.' I suddenly pulled my hands from under my seat. I grabbed the bottle and filled the glass with milk, the first full glass of milk I'd had since 1939—twelve years earlier!

"When I look back, I have to smile. That was one bright moment for a glass of milk back in 1951. But in real life, happy endings are mixed. Twenty-three members of my family perished, including my father. And from approximately twenty-five thousand Jewish children from Radom and its surrounding areas, there are no more than thirty-five known survivors.

"What's the bottom line for me? To survive the war made everything else seem easy. On the positive side I have a lot of willpower, determination to succeed at all cost, the ability to work hard and avoid pitfalls, and also the ability to put on a good act. On the negative side I've had difficulty learning to trust and to love people enough. Have I been successful in my life? Yes! Am I happy? That is still a question mark.

"My mother, who lives nearby in a nursing home, has never spoken about the war. As far as she is concerned, it is a closed chapter with only two witnesses. I have a different agenda. I've become involved with a group called Children Survivors of the Holocaust. I volunteer at the Melbourne Holocaust Center, and lately I've begun going out and giving talks about my war experience. I feel that this time it was us: the Jews. But the same kind of genocide can happen anywhere, anytime, to anyone. Until we finally start to put an end to racism, bigotry, and intolerance, I don't see how any one of us will ever be safe."

KIM FENDRICK

Kim Fendrick is a handsome woman with fine, regular features, light hair, and a fair complexion. A family therapist in Haddonfield, New Jersey, Kim is a divorced mother of two and a new grandmother. With both her parents gone now, Kim feels an enormous sense of loss. "I adore my new little grandson," Kim says. But she resents it when someone suggests that the baby is a replacement for her father. "As much as I love little Josh, he can never be what my father was to me," Kim says with characteristic honesty about her feelings. In her life there is also Walter, whom she met a year ago and calls, "my third child." Walter lives nearby, paints houses, plays guitar—and happens to be the grandson of Jeremkov, the Polish farmer who kept Kim and her family safe from the Nazis.

"I was born in Floceow, in the eastern part of Poland in 1935. The war began with the Russian occupation when I was four, but my own Holocaust began in 1941, when the Nazis took over. When the Germans forced all Jews into the small ghetto, we had to share our apartment with two other families. One of our new boarders, Mr. Kahane, snuffed tobacco. When he sneezed, we all shook! The other family was my grandparents. I loved sharing my room with them. My grandpa was my dearest friend. One morning I climbed into his bed and pinched his earlobes. Laughing, he said, 'Pinch as hard as you want because there are no nerve endings in the lobe.'

"When the pogroms began, my grandfather was one of the first to be taken. He was rounded up in the street with some other men, marched to the *zamuk*, a big stone building in the center of town, and shot. We learned about it later that day, when one man who had managed to escape came and told us the sad news. I was shocked, but as a child I don't think I grasped that he was gone for good.

"A few days later two Nazi soldiers came barging into our apartment, on a search for whatever. My grandmother, who was heartbroken, started to question them: 'Why did you take my husband?' she asked in perfect German. She still had trouble believing that people who spoke the same cultured language as Goethe and Schiller could behave so brutally. Instead of answering, one of the soldiers raised his gun and he shot her, right in the chest. I just stood there, unable to believe what I'd just seen. 'This isn't really happening,' I told myself. Luckily the bullet missed my grandmother's heart. She recovered, but I understood that life was no longer normal or safe.

"Each time there was a roundup, we would all go to hide in the bunker that my father had prepared underneath our house. It was pretty secure down there and well stocked with provisions. One day we learned that the next roundup was to make the town *Judenrind*, or clean of Jews. Now we would have to stay down there in the bunker full-time. However, there was a problem. My cousin, Fela, was a baby. The adults knew that hiding with an infant would be out of the question. One night my mother and my Aunt Adele handed Fela over the barbed-wire fence to a Ukrainian woman named Natalka. I watched without emotion, never doubting that my mother and my aunt were doing what was best.

"That night we moved into the bunker. There were fifteen or twenty of us. Our chief worry wasn't that the Germans would find us and shoot us, but that we wouldn't have enough supplies to last. The food supply was rapidly diminishing. Still, life went on. My mother was always very practical. She taught me to read and write with a Polish elementary primer and many drills and quizzes. My grandmother questioned her, 'Why are you torturing this child? We're all going to die. Why does she need to sit here and do this?' My mother replied, 'If we live, she'll know how to read and write. If we die, she'll have been kept busy.'

"However, my parents were not so optimistic. They didn't want to die at the hands of the Nazis, so they hatched a plan. This was to pin a note on my coat saying, 'Whoever finds this child, please raise her. We have decided to take our lives because we want to die with dignity.' Their plan was then to send me out in the street.

"The hallmark of my existence was always knowing what was going on. My parents didn't keep secrets, and they never lied. So at least the worst was known to me. I didn't have to guess or to worry what was going on. I knew! That didn't mean I accepted what they told me. On the contrary, I turned to them and said, 'If you are going to give me away, why did you ever give birth to me?' I was eight years old then. The thought of my own death was far, far away. My own mortality didn't seem real. What *did* seem very real, very frightening—and totally unacceptable—was to be without my parents.

"I didn't look at it from the perspective of, Wow, if they don't send me out, I may not survive. I only thought, If they don't send me out, I'll be with them. That was what I wanted.

"I was so relieved when they agreed that we would take our chances together. Of course the odds were against us. Out of fifteen to eighteen thousand people from our hometown, no more than eighty to a hundred survived. It was stupid for us to think we *would* survive. But my mother didn't want to be without my father, and I didn't want to be without my parents, so the slim, unlikely chance of surviving was more attractive to us than being separated.

"When our food was really gone, we tunneled our way into the cellar of the hardware store next door. The store was owned by a very nice Ukrainian man named Mandryga, who had allowed Jews he knew to build a shelter there. We had gotten in by removing the cinder blocks that connected the houses. I don't know how we contacted Mr. Mandryga, but he gave us permission.

"The shelter was a hole dug out of rock. It had built-in beds and a garbage can dug into the ground which served as a refrigerator. Best of all, there were provisions there. I ate something there that no one seems to consider a delicacy, but I sure did! It was bread with butter and sugar and an onion sliced on top.

"We stayed there for several weeks with another family. They had a daughter, Clara, who was my age, and we were constantly bickering. There were quite a few rats and mice running around. My father, may he rest in peace, slept with his mouth open. Each morning I would see him picking rodent droppings out of his teeth. I had very vivid nightmares in that place. The dream was always that we were being taken away and killed. Somehow I managed to train myself to wake up when I had a bad dream and say to myself, It's okay, you're only dreaming.

"One day we didn't hear the rolling shade on the store and we knew something was wrong. Then the word came to us that Mr. Mandryga had been taken away by the Germans and shot for hiding Jews in his house. Soon we knew that the Nazis would be searching the area carefully, so we had to get out! We left that night. We had to stop as it got light out. Luckily we were right by a hospital where my father had worked and still knew the director, Dr. Martynowicz. The nuns gave us permission to stay until dark, when it would be safer to travel.

"That was the only day of the entire Holocaust when I was all alone, without either my parents or my aunt and uncle. I was hidden inside in a barrel in the courtyard, while my parents were in another shelter several yards away. I could look through the slats. I couldn't see them, but at least I knew where they were. I also knew they'd be back for me that night, because they told me they would and they never lied. When night fell and it was time for us to set out again, one of the nuns gave my father a Saint Christopher medal to keep us safe on our journey. It was a gift he always kept and treasured.

"That night the nine of us were stopped by Nazi police. They yelled, 'Halt!' Fortunately they couldn't get their lantern or flashlight to shine on us. The police asked us where we were going. Clara's mother answered in Polish, explaining that we were just coming home from a picnic. Bored, the police waved us on. If they had only been able to get their lights on us, they would have seen that we were not Polish folks on a picnic at all, but a bedraggled group of Jews on the run.

"In the forest we had nothing to eat and no means of survival except for dew on the leaves and raw potatoes, which my mother would cut with a knife into paper-thin slices.

"At some point we started back to our own house in the ghetto. I didn't know it at the time, but my parents' idea was we would close the windows and burn the coal and die without the Nazis torturing us. We made the trek back from the woods to the ghetto. However, when we got there, we saw that the windows of our house had been bombed out. Once again, we turned around and headed back to the forest. By some miracle my Uncle Isaac found us. He was still employed in a lumberyard, so he could move about in safety. Now his plan was to take us to a secret loft in the ghetto, where a number of Jews were still alive. We had to be careful as we followed him. He would make hand signals behind his back, telling us when we had to duck into a doorway. It was a dangerous trip, to say the least.

"When we got to the loft, we found it crowded and the people very tense. There was one young woman trying to comfort an infant who was crying. It was just a tiny baby, but he wouldn't go to sleep, and she couldn't stop him from crying. Finally she was given a choice by the other adults: Take your crying baby and leave—or kill the infant. She smothered it. I don't remember if the mother cried, but you didn't have the luxury of weeping. Life was so precious and so cheap at the same time. You did what you could to save yourself.

"Soon the loft became unsafe. Once again we had to go back to the forest. I suppose I should have been very frightened, but I wasn't. It went against all logic and reason to be optimistic, but I was! Because I had loving grown-ups taking care of me, I 'knew' I would be all right. Once more it was Uncle Isaac who came to the rescue. By now he was not allowed to work anymore, but his old boss at the lumberyard, Mr. Jeremkov, had agreed to let my uncle, my aunt, and my uncle's mother take shelter along with another family in a sort of cave under Jeremkov's barn.

"Uncle Isaac wanted to take me there right away. He promised that he would come back for my father, my mother, and my grandmother after the cave had been made a little bigger. I felt fine about going. My uncle was family! I started walking beside him, but I hadn't been eating much, and I was very weak. I said, 'I can't walk.' He picked me up and I sat on his shoulders. I can still feel his shoulders beneath my legs. I remember I kissed his neck. He still remembers it too. That was how he got me back to the cave.

"To enter the cave, we had to go in through a hole in the floor of the barn—a hole about the size of a manhole cover. Then we went down a ladder into a windowless space, about the size of a car. Our access to daylight was a hole smaller than a volleyball, with grass growing in front of it. There were blankets on the dirt floor. Compared with the forest, where I'd been, it seemed to me like the most luxurious, softest, warmest, safest place in the world! My aunt in the meantime had somehow acquired some delicious little tiny pears. When I arrived, she gave me one. I said, 'Auntie, you'll always have little pears for me, won't you?' As an eight-year-old I felt luxuriously safe with these dear and loving relatives of mine.

"By that time my uncle had told Mr. Jeremkov about me and asked for permission to enlarge the cave for my parents and grandmother. Jeremkov said yes. During the day my uncle and the other man hiding down there with us would dig. At night they would cart away the wet rock. A few weeks later my parents and grandmother came and joined us. That was no surprise to me. After all, they'd promised to come, and I had never known them to break their word.

"As a family we stayed in the cave from September 1943 until July 1944. All that time I felt safe and protected. It wasn't perfect. We had serious lice, and I don't ever remember washing. But nobody got sick. Every few weeks we would climb up the little ladder into the barn so that we could move around and see and try to delouse ourselves. I had two books, *Quo Vadis* and a book of poetry by Adam Mickiewicz. I was also drilled on the multiplication tables and the capitals of Europe. (Sofia is the capital of Bulgaria—I'll never forget it!) Listening to the adults, I heard a lot about the facts of life.

"Our main focus was on getting enough to eat, because

there was never quite enough. Every other day we got a bucket of soup, a loaf or two of bread, and baked potatoes. By then there were fourteen of us in the cave. My father devised a method of portion control so that whatever we had would be divided up fairly. We also hungered for news of how the war was going. The farmer and his wife were illiterate, so they couldn't buy a newspaper without arousing suspicion. What they did was, when they bought food, they would ask the shopkeepers to wrap it in newspaper. Once they got home, the Jeremkovs would unwrap the food very carefully and give us the papers to read.

"In April 1944 the Russians entered the town. The first night they were there, a Jewish teenager who had somehow found his way to our cave decided to join the Russian Army. He had lost his whole family, and he wanted to avenge their deaths. The farmer's wife told him not to go, because it wasn't safe yet and the war was still on. The young man insisted on going anyway, and he died.

"That was April. By July the area had been secured by the Russian army. When the Jeremkovs came and told us it was safe to leave, we moved into a little abandoned house on the outskirts of town. I don't know if we got permission or if we just found it, but seven of us moved in: my uncle and aunt, his mother, my parents, my grandmother, and I. My father got a job in a flour mill. He'd bring home sacks of flour, and the women would bake rolls. Then my aunt and I would sell them to the Russian soldiers.

"Eagerly my aunt and uncle went to claim their daughter, Fela, the baby they had given away two years earlier. Apparently her foster parents didn't want to give her up. Nor was three-year-old Fela thrilled about joining us either. I just saw her as a pain in the butt, a little red-headed kid who missed her foster mommy and wouldn't leave my schoolbooks alone.

I was feeling like a very important person! I had just entered school in the third grade, never having gone to any grade.

"A few months later we left Floceow and made our way to western Poland. I entered school toward the end of fourth grade. As the only Jewish child in the class I was horribly persecuted. I had a science teacher who took pride in how well I was doing. He made the mistake of holding me up as an example to the other kids, all of whom were Polish and Christian. He said to them, 'Here's the only Jew in the class. She knows it and you don't.'

"The teachers wouldn't let the other children abuse me physically in school. But the children taunted me anyway. On the way home a girl named Yanka and her brother would throw lighted matches at me. A few weeks of that treatment upset me so much, I quit school. Sometimes I wonder how my parents let me do that. I guess they knew that we would be moving on as soon as we could get exit visas to leave the country. In the meantime I spent my days devouring books. I would go to the library every day and read three books, mostly fairy tales. I just inhaled books. That was how my days went: reading, reading, reading!

"In 1947, when I was twelve, we came to New York, sponsored by the Hebrew Immigrant Aid Society. During our stay at the HIAS residence on Eighth Street, my parents fought constantly. That scared me. One day my father told me he was going to divorce my mother, and I felt like my world was ending. Luckily for me that crisis blew over, though they continued to argue. Eventually I learned to take it in stride and realize that to fight with each other was a luxury for my parents, now that they finally didn't have to fight for their physical survival anymore.

"Once I stopped worrying about them, I got busy Americanizing myself, learning the language and some of the music. And movie stars—I grooved on movie stars! My favorite was Gregory Peck. I got through eighth grade, and then I went to Washington Irving High School, where I graduated second in my class. From there I went on to college and finally a career as a social worker–therapist. This was a logical choice for me. It made perfect sense because in my experience sharing strong feelings always seemed both natural and necessary. My parents had always been open with me before, during, and after the war. I know that many survivors wouldn't talk about their experiences to their children for fear of hurting or intimidating them . . . or not wanting to appear vulnerable in their children's eyes. But in our family talking was important: We always reached in deeply, and we told the truth.

"Now it's forty-four years since we came to this country. My aunt and my uncle are in California, where their daughter, Fela, is a judge! My parents are both gone now; my father died recently. I feel an enormous sense of loss. Now I have nobody here anymore who shares my history. That makes me feel quite unprotected and alone. As much as I could assume the persona of a mother and be one when my kids were growing up, there was always a piece of me that needed to be parented. I feel that acutely now that my parents are dead.

"However, something else happened recently, something very lovely. The Jeremkovs, the Polish family who saved us, had five children. Over the years my mother and my aunt kept in touch with all of them. When one of the sons died, the son of that son wrote to my aunt and said, 'You can stop writing. My father is dead.' My aunt wrote back, 'If your father is gone, then *you must* continue writing!' That grandson, whose name was Walter, did keep up a correspondence with her. Then, quite unexpectedly in the summer of 1990, he was here! He had engaged in anti-Communist activities, and because of that he had been forced to leave Poland.

"My aunt learned that Walter was staying in Vineland, New Jersey, not far from my home. I called him and suggested that we get together. He was so eager!

"When I saw him that Sunday—blond, blue-eyed, and so Polish-looking, like a young Lech Walesa—there was no mistaking who he was! We fell into each other's arms. It was incredible! I took him to a Chinese restaurant for lunch, where we talked as much as my skeletal Polish and his then-faltering English allowed. I handed him an envelope filled with money, a gift from my son and me. Walter shook his head. He didn't even know how much it was, but he refused to take it.

"I told him, 'You must. I never had a chance to thank your grandparents for our lives. That's why you have to take this, because you're my symbol of them.' With some reluctance Walter did take the money, which he clearly needed to get himself established. Since then we've developed a wonderfully warm relationship. I call him my third child! I've helped him get work as a housepainter—he's an excellent craftsman! And now he lives near here.

"Last year Agnes, Walter's Polish fiancée, arrived. When I offered to host their wedding reception, Walter said, 'But I don't have anybody to invite.' I said, 'It's okay, I do!' And sure enough, sixty-five friends showed up to honor the couple and rejoice with them. It was a very low-key affair, nothing lavish, but it was special. It gave me a chance to say thank you, and it really kind of made a circle for me. That was something wonderful for me to experience—and I think, not bad for him either."

LEON GINSBURG

Leon Ginsburg, sixty, is slim and wiry in a neat, dark-gray suit, striped shirt, and flowered tie. An electrical engineer, Leon owns a company that manufactures high-tech dental equipment for which he holds several patents. The home he shares with his wife in Rockland County, New York, is impeccably neat—except for Leon's study, a small room crammed to the gills with stacks of Holocaust-related material, including pictures, maps, books, and his own personal notes. "This is where I go to steal away from everything," he explains. "Sometimes we think of forgetting. Some people want to forget, but I feel more than ever now that we need to remember."

"I was born in 1932 in Maciejow, a small town at the border where Poland ends and Russia begins. Our community was basically Hasidic. We all kept our heads covered, and the older men wore beards. The Ukrainians who ruled that part of Poland were viciously anti-Semitic, but we were unprepared for the Germans and their absolute policy of getting rid of the Jews. I was on the street the day the Germans marched into town. As a gesture of friendship the rabbi was sitting at a little table on the street with bread and salt, the traditional way of saying welcome. Suddenly one of the Germans pushed the table over and told the rabbi to get out of there. I didn't understand what was happening.

"Shortly after that an SS group settled in the town. The first thing they did was to order all the men between sixteen and sixty to report. The SS made it clear that anyone who didn't go could be killed. So most of the people reported. But once they lined up, they couldn't get out; they were covered by machine guns. I was just a little boy, but I saw what was happening, and I got out of that area quickly. Later I heard the shots. All those people had been marched inside the headquarters and killed. After that the killing was at random, but for us Jews normal life was over. We had a six P.M. curfew. If you were caught outside after that, you were shot. I would hear the German patrols marching on the cobblestone streets a block away.

"One night we were all at my grandparents' house on the outskirts of town when they began rounding up Jews. I woke up and saw a light from outside on the ceiling. Yelling in German, the soldiers pounded on the door. My grandfather's name was Yakov, and they were calling his name. 'Yakov, open up!' My brother was afraid to go, but I opened the door, and they came in with flashlights. Right away they asked me where the women were. Almost in a crying way, I said, 'I don't know, they took them away! Maybe *you* can tell *me*!'

"Ignoring me, the soldiers began to search. One of them ran down to the basement. Then he came up and asked me where the attic was. I pointed. He said, 'Anybody up there?' My mother, sister, grandmother, and aunts were all up there, but I said no. Then the soldier took out his gun and put it to my head and cocked it. He said, 'If we find somebody there, you're caput.' He asked me again, 'Anybody there?' I said, 'No.' And you know what? When I think of it now, I feel sorry for that young child I was with my little round red cheeks that all the relatives loved to pinch. Either I didn't understand fear or maybe I didn't think that they would really do anything to me. Luckily the attic was big, and everyone up there was hiding in a corner, blocked off from view so that the Germans never saw them.

"That roundup was over in a week. After that things were quiet until 1942, when Hitler became so maddened and poisoned with his wish to get rid of Jews that he ordered complete annihilation. Our town was one of three in a row. They concentrated first on killing twenty-four thousand Jews in Kovel, one of the other towns. They dug big ditches or graves. They would just take the people there, shoot them on the spot, and push them in. We weren't allowed to move from our town, but a Polish woman who came from Kovel talked about corpses in the street.

"Our turn came in August. There was a feeling in the air that something was going to happen, so my mother arranged for a hiding place in a basement we entered through a tunnel under an outside toilet. We slept there that night. There must have been fifty people in that place. Early the next morning we heard voices. It seemed that the Ukrainians and the Germans were going through all the houses looking for Jews.

"We stayed quiet and were safe that day, but there was one woman with us who had five children, including a little girl who wouldn't stop crying. When that little girl finally fell asleep, her mother carried her up to the house above our hiding place. That was a tremendous decision to make; it was certain death for that little girl. Of course, if she'd stayed below with us, then we'd all have been caught.

"However, the plan backfired. When the little girl woke up, the Ukrainians were in the house and asked where her mother was. The little girl ran to the area where the toilet was, but the soldiers couldn't understand her. They searched inside the house for hours. Finally they realized that this girl was pointing to the toilet, so they touched it and realized it moved. Then they found our place—and that was basically it. We were trapped! People started filing out.

"There was a space boarded up where there had once been a window. As most of the people were going out, my mother suddenly ripped off one piece of board. She whispered for me to get in there and put the board back. When I got in, I had to hold the nail in place with my hand. Then my mother hid under some bedding. By then it was dark, and the police were lighting matches. One had a rifle with a bayonet on it. He was right next to me. Suddenly he took that bayonet and stabbed my mother, who was still hiding under the bedding. She screamed. I didn't know how badly she was hurt, but they took her away. I sat there frozen! They were only inches away from me—so close I had to stop breathing.

"I don't know how long I sat like that. Probably for hours. Then I heard someone speaking Yiddish. I peeked out and I recognized one of the Jews from the town. He said he was looking for a pair of galoshes. He was going into the woods and he was worried about mud! I followed him up to the attic of his house. Then we heard a noise. The man peered down—right into the face of a Ukrainian militiaman with a gun. The militiaman saw the Jew and grabbed him. I stayed hidden as the Jewish man was taken away.

"I sat there stunned, not knowing what to do. I felt like a tiny fish swimming in a sea of danger. Everybody was ready to grab me. Where was I supposed to go? What was I supposed to do? As I sat there, I heard a wagon pull up. Then I realized that soldiers were looting the house, which was the practice. I had to get out. Fortunately I remembered my mother mentioning another hiding place a few houses away, so I went to it, and there I found a little opening, just big enough to crawl through. Suddenly I was dizzy and I almost fainted. Someone hiding in there pulled me in and poured a little whiskey on my lips, which revived me. At last I felt safe! I stayed there for the next few days. These people had a barrel of water, but when we needed more, we had to sneak out to the well, which was the chain type that you crank, and it made a lot of noise squeaking. One of us had to do it very carefully, while someone else watched.

"Soon, however, food became a problem. I volunteered to go get some fruit from the orchard right next to the German headquarters. I chose a Sunday when I knew that most people would be in church. Then I sneaked over there. When the old woman at the orchard saw me, she crossed herself; she couldn't believe any Jewish kid was still alive. She was afraid the Ukrainian workers would see me, so she gave me some fruit and hid me in her attic. She told me to wait until dark, when it would be safe. However, I was scared to wait, so I put the fruit inside my shirt, crept out the window and down to the ground below.

"In order to get back to the hiding place where I had been staying, I had to go through town. Before I knew it, there was somebody in a wagon yelling, 'Jew!' It was a fifteen-year-old boy who lived next door to my grandfather, so I acted casual, not running. Then this teenager jumped off the wagon and started chasing me. As I ran, he grabbed me. He yelled, 'I got you.' A second later I put my hand in my pocket as if I had a gun. I said, 'Are you going to let me go or not?'

"Amazingly he fell for the trick! This kid, who was five years older and so much bigger than I, said in a cringing tone, 'You know I didn't mean anything.' All he had to do was hold me for another thirty seconds, because the other guys were coming around the corner. But I just said, 'I gotta go.' I ran as fast as I could. When I came close to the hiding place, nobody was chasing me anymore, so I dashed back in. A minute later I heard my pursuers running by. They didn't know where I went! We managed to stay in that hiding place another week. Meanwhile the Ukrainians were going around boarding up the houses, convinced that the Jews were gone. They had hatchets and they were hitting the walls.

"When I realized they were about to break into our hiding place, I crawled out a little window. I heard people yelling, 'Jews!' and at first I thought they meant me. I looked down and saw that nobody was paying attention to me, so with a carefully contrived show of nonchalance I walked away. I kept walking, right out of town and all the way to the next village.

"I knew a farmer in that village who had been friendly with my grandfather. I greeted him, but he told me to stay in the bushes because it was dangerous. It seemed that his whole village was collaborating with the Germans. He couldn't take me in, but he advised me to go twenty miles farther, to a town called Luboml, where there was still a Jewish ghetto and where I had some relatives. My uncle, who lived in Luboml, had a big house filled with people who had fled from surrounding areas, including two aunts who had left our town earlier. When I reached his place, I went to sleep exhausted. In the morning, when I tried to get up, my legs were so swollen from all the walking I had done the day before, I couldn't move them.

"A few days later my brother showed up, telling a horrible story. He had been caught and taken to the synagogue in our town, and they were about to shoot him, when he and another boy managed to crawl into a big stove. The police shot into the oven and killed the other boy. My brother was wounded in the leg, but the police didn't see him. When it was dark and the coast was clear, my brother sneaked out and made his way to my uncle's place. That night my brother and

I slept, holding each other, and he said, 'I will never leave you again.'

"We had been there for about a week when I woke up at four A.M. to the sound of gunfire. I knew what was going on: They were rounding up Jews, just as they had done in our town. I looked out, and sure enough I saw the Germans and Ukrainians with guns, bayonets, and dogs. Quickly we all went to hide in a room that was boarded up except for the entrance, through a fireplace that moved. I was packed in there with my father's first cousin, his wife and two children, and other people as well. We stayed there all night.

"It must have been on the second day that one of the cousins wanted some water. He opened up the secret door. That alerted two Ukrainian militiamen, who shot into the wall, right next to me. I realized that this was about to be a repetition of what had happened in the other basement when my mother was taken. But I had gone through it already, so I knew what to do.

"The other people were all saying, 'Close it up!' But my logic said, 'Close up what? They've got us.' I said, 'No,' and started to crawl out. The militiaman pushed me back. He wanted gold. I crawled in again with a hat, to collect everybody's jewelry. Then I crawled out again and I gave the militiaman the hat with everything in it. The soldier's eyes bugged out! He was so excited by the gold, he wasn't pushing me back anymore . . . and I was able to get out of the hole! I pulled my brother behind me. He was petrified; he couldn't move. I actually had to pull him by the hair, and then we were both out. I looked at the soldier, who was still busy with the gold. I inched over to a window. Now I was sitting on the window ledge. I motioned to my brother to get up there with me. Suddenly the militiaman saw us, pointed his rifle, and ordered us down.

"At that moment someone from the hiding place handed them more valuables, and the Ukrainian militiaman got distracted. We ran up some steps to the next floor and dashed into a bedroom and hid under a bed. One of the militiamen ran after us and searched the rooms, but he didn't find us.

"When it seemed safe at last, we headed out the window. My brother went first, to help me down, but we were spotted. We had to run back up a ladder into the attic of the house next door. A militiaman was already in that house! He tried to push open the attic door, but my brother and I were sitting on it, holding on and pushing. The soldier saw it wasn't opening, so he left. We stayed in the attic. Within an hour I heard them leading out the people from our former hiding place at my uncle's. My father's cousin's little girl, who was eight, asked, 'Mommy, are they going to shoot us?' I couldn't hear what her mother answered because so many people were crying.

"That evening my brother and I were hungry. I said I'd go down and get something, but my brother very firmly said, 'You're not going anywhere.' Later I looked around the attic and I didn't see him. Assuming that he had gone to look for food, I decided to go too. I went back to the old hiding place. I couldn't find anything, but while I was looking, I heard voices yelling in German. The Nazis had found the attic—and my brother *was* still in there! I never saw him again.

"That night I met Esther, a cousin of mine who was nineteen and kind of a leader, heading off to the woods with six others, so I followed. It was so dark that I had to hold on to somebody. We had to pass the main railroad area, which was brightly lit up to make sure no Jews got out. When there was a minute between flares, we crossed the tracks. We walked and walked and finally we sat down to rest near a Ukrainian cemetery. The moment I sat down, I fell asleep. When I woke up, everyone was gone.

"Right away my mind started working: What do you do next? I was scared of cemeteries! Kids were always talking about ghosts, and I believed in them. I didn't want to go into the cemetery to look for my companions. I calculated the real risk, and I said to myself, You're afraid, but don't be afraid. Nobody kills people in a cemetery. I climbed the stone wall and dropped down into the cemetery. I was shaking as I searched among the graves. I softly called, 'Isaac,' who was one of the boys with us.

"There was no answer. It was pitch-dark. Then I saw something a little darker, and I went in that direction. When I got a little closer, I saw it was a farm. I looked for the barn and made my way to the stall where a cow slept. I thought, A cow is a nice, friendly animal. So I lay down and slept next to the cow's head. I felt its warm, comforting breath. Just before dawn I woke up and saw a hayloft. It was high up, but I managed to jump up and grab one of the boards and pull myself up—quite an amazing feat for a little boy! Later the farmer's wife came to milk the cow. I coughed to get her attention. She was scared. I said, 'Don't be afraid.' I told her I was lost and I promised I would leave soon.

"She said, 'Don't leave now. Wait until the shepherd comes and takes the cows out.' She brought me a glass of milk and a piece of bread. But while I hid, I heard talk about 'Jews hiding in the graveyard with gold.' I figured those must be my relatives and I'd better warn them. Without a sound I sneaked out to the cemetery, which wasn't far. Sure enough I found my cousins hiding under bushes. Now it seemed our lives were balanced on a hair.

"Our plan was to go to the next town, where there were Jews still in the ghetto. It was a long walk. One night we slept in the woods, and it was so cold, my clothes were frozen stiff. Amazingly I didn't catch cold. Now when I walk without shoes on cold tile, I get sick. But then? Being cold was the least of my problems!

"At one point I volunteered to go into the woods to find one of my cousins. I got lost and walked most of the day. Finally I got back, but I was tired and lagging behind the others. All of a sudden I heard a noise behind me, and when it got closer, I could see it was a guy on a bicycle with a rifle. He passed me and stopped. Then he took off his rifle, shot it in the air, and yelled. I lay down and started crawling away. Elated, I realized that he hadn't even seen me. Then I heard more Nazis coming. I started running, and they started shooting at me. A bullet went through my legs, grazed my shoe, and burned my foot a little bit.

"Wondering what to do, I spotted a drainage pipe that went under the road. I crawled in there. Luckily it didn't go straight, so the Nazis couldn't see me when they looked in. Then I heard them taking my cousins away. I was sitting there in water, afraid to get out. After a while I lifted my head and peeked. There was nobody around. Soaking wet, I climbed out and started walking. By the time I reached a farm, I was so tired, I made a hole in the nearest haystack, burrowed in, and immediately dropped off to sleep.

"I awoke with a start: The woman of the farm was jabbing me with a pitchfork. She was cursing me. Evidently she thought I was some kind of animal! Afraid she'd kill me, I put out my hand. The woman ran screaming for her husband. He was there in a moment, yanking me out and demanding to know who I was. Truthfully I told him, 'Ginsburg from Luboml is my uncle.' The farmer nodded. My uncle, who had owned a bar, had gotten along well with the farmers, who came to town on market day. Now this farmer gave me milk and bread and directions to the home of another farmer named Sliva, who had also known my uncle.

"As I started out, I passed a wagon full of drunk militia with guns. They were rowdy, but I had to play 'You guys don't bother me.' While they were passing, I was paying attention to the other side of the road. It took two days to reach the Sliva farm. When I arrived, the woman there said I couldn't stay. The Slivas had been helping Jews, so they were suspect. They let me stay one night, but advised me to join some other Jews hiding in the woods.

"The next day I found the place they told me to go, but the people were eaten up with all kinds of vermin. It was horrible! As it happened, the Ukrainians found them and killed them with hand grenades. So it was good I didn't stay! Sliva told me that farmers don't always lock the barns. He said, 'Like, for instance, I have a little door that I never lock.' Now I knew there was a place I could sneak in at night and sleep in the hay. When I heard the roosters, that was my alarm clock!

"In this particular farm colony most of the people were not Catholics, but Seventh-Day Adventists. Their philosophy, their mentality, was different. In other words they may still have had anti-Semitism ingrained in them, but they would not betray a Jew. So I was safer. Finally I found a family who said they would keep me if I gave them something. I decided to go to the ghetto of Vlodzimiez Volinsk and see what I could find.

"Mr. Sliva was going in that direction by horse and wagon. Together we left at four A.M. with plans to meet a week later for the trip back. Mr. Sliva dropped me off near the ghetto. He showed me the gate, where they let me walk right in. I saw a Ukrainian militiaman with a gun, and I realized I was in a ghetto surrounded by barbed wire and soldiers. I understood with surprise and dismay that I was trapped, with no way to get out.

"I went to the empty, cleaned-out part of the ghetto in search of clothes. All I could find was a ripped sheepskin. A woman sewed it up for me. I found two shoes—both left feet—lost or abandoned by a Russian soldier. They were too big, but I took them anyway ... and started planning. How would I get out? There seemed to be no way. Finally I had an idea: I put that sheepskin and those big shoes on to make myself look bigger. I waited until the line of people going out to work in the morning all got counted. Then I got in line, and somehow, once outside, I got away.

"That was Tuesday morning. When I got to the meeting place, Sliva wasn't there. I waited a while but knew it would be dangerous to hang around too long. The important thing was not to draw attention to myself, as they were still killing Jews all over the place. Finally I started walking, and eventually I did meet up with Sliva, who took me to the folks who had agreed to keep me. To my surprise those people already had another six Jews hiding in their barn and under the kitchen.

"I spent the whole next winter there. It was the first time since I lost my mother that I felt safe enough to cry. I felt so sorry that I hadn't gotten out to help her. Theoretically there was nothing I could have done, and if I'd tried, I would have just died too. At least I took some comfort from the fact that when my mother went to her death, she knew that they hadn't gotten me. That was a victory for her!

"When spring came, I felt I ought to earn my keep, so I took a job as a shepherd and worked until summer. At this time the Ukrainians decided that the Jews were all gone, and they started attacking Polish villages. Some of these Seventh-Day Adventists believed, as many Jews did, that God would intercede and smite the Germans. Just like the Jews, those Protestants and Catholic Poles were taken to their death—forty thousand of them! Some of them didn't want to run away. I knew of one family that was killed except for one boy who ran away. He saw the Ukrainians kill everyone in his family, bayoneting children to the walls, just like they'd done with the Jews before.

"Where was I to run now? The family I was staying with knew the attack was to come, and they sent me out on the road to watch, like a spy. When I heard shots, they almost left me there, but we ended up hiding on church property. After that there were many close calls. One day that teenager who'd chased me in the city when I got away by pretending that I had a gun appeared. He stared at me and said, 'I know you.' It had only been about a year. I tried to get away, but he followed me. Desperate, I played the game, acting cool. Finally he went away.

"On another occasion two German officers had taken over half the farmhouse where I was working. They took a liking to me. They thought I was Christian. Every time they got their rations, they would give me the candy. When they saw what a hard worker I was, they said that their mother had a farm in Germany and they wanted to send me to her. I got scared because that was all I needed! I knew if I got to Germany, they would give me an inspection and I'd be finished. I had to tell them, 'No, I'm waiting here. My parents may be alive.' Somehow I got out of that.

"Finally the war and my hiding ordeal were over. I was brought to the United States in a group of orphans. I went to live with an aunt. I spoke no English, but always resourceful, I managed to excel in school, earning grades of ninety-five and higher. Later I put myself through college, first with a job selling ice cream and candy in the subways and then with a part-time job in a factory. Now, four decades later, I have a beautiful wife who was also hidden as a child, three successful children, and even a grandchild.

"I'm certainly grateful to the United States, my adopted

country, for the freedom and opportunity I've had to contribute and belong. For example, I'm an electrical engineer. A long while ago I came up with a new and much better way of making a furnace that processes dental porcelain. It was something I figured out. A manufacturer who was the king of the industry at that time looked at my plans and smiled. He said, 'It'll never work.' However, he was wrong: I had virtually revolutionized the process, and I got the patent.

"Fortunately I never lost my wartime ability to size up a situation and know what to do. Not long ago I was at my factory in the Bronx, having just come back from the bank with the payroll. When I walked in the door, there was a big guy ready to hit me with a lead pipe. Bang! He brought the pipe down on my head, but I moved so fast, the blow was cushioned. I fought with him. He must have thought I was crazy. Maybe I *was* at that point! Moments later I had his hat in my hand, and I was chasing him down the street. I ended up with some bruises, but thanks to my very, very fast reaction, I was—once again—the clever little boy outsmarting the bully who wanted me dead.

"When I look back at what happened to me during the war, it all seems so crazy. I've read a great deal about the Holocaust, and I've made a lot of notes. But up until now I've kept my own story to myself. In fact I haven't even shared it fully with my three children, even though my daughter is a psychiatrist. It's still such a soft and vulnerable part of me. When I think about all my relatives who died, I'm afraid I might cry, and that is something I don't allow myself to do.

"However, lately I'm feeling that I can't stay quiet any longer. I was just reading about an organization that's been putting ads in college newspapers, claiming that the Holocaust never happened. In response I wrote an article, giving a little of my background. I sent it to the editor of the Rutgers University newspaper. I felt I had to go on record. I realize that the older survivors are passing away, and I'm getting older myself. When I'm gone, there will be very few people left with any firsthand experience. So what can I do but tell the truth?"

LOLA KAUFMAN

Lola Kaufman is a dainty, upbeat woman with fluffy blond hair, peaches-and-cream coloring, and a warm smile. Lola is a mother of three and grandmother. She works as a bookkeeper in Rockland County, New York. There, she lives with her husband—another former hidden child—in a white ranch house with black shutters and a red door. Lola's favorite room is the den with its wood-paneled walls, rustic furniture, and off-white carpeting. "Our old house in Elmont didn't have a den," Lola explains. "There was a family room in the basement, but I didn't like going down there." Lola loves her present home. "It's neat, it's beautiful, it's just the way I like it," she admits with delight. "I'm always saying to myself, 'I love this place!' "

"I was born on October 4, 1934, in the western Ukraine, in a town called Czortkov. One day when I was a very little girl, I was standing on the street when the Russians came in with tanks and soldiers. Suddenly shooting broke out. Everyone was running. That was scary, but in 1941 when the Germans came in, all the Jews were petrified in general—with good reason!

"It was early that spring, in a Nazi roundup, that I learned just how precarious our lives were. I was living in the ghetto with my widowed mother and my grandmother. There were two adjacent hiding places: one was in a storage area, the other in a room you couldn't see from the outside. As the roundup started, all the Jews in the area started running toward those hiding places. My mother and I were going toward the room you couldn't see. Suddenly she grabbed me. I don't know why she changed her mind, but she pulled me over to the storage area instead.

"We waited, breathless, as the Ukrainian police ran past. Moments later there was shouting and banging next door as the other hiding place was discovered. As the Jews filed out, one man who had just been captured yelled out to the police, 'There are people in there too!' I could see through a crack in the wall that he was pointing to the place where we were hiding.

"Terrified, I would certainly have screamed if my mother hadn't clapped her hand over my mouth. I stood shaking as the police began pounding on the wall—*our* wall! Plaster dust was flying, which made the police cough. But the wall was solid; it didn't give way. Another few minutes and we would have been finished. Luckily for us the police gave up. It was too much trouble! 'That Jew just lied to make us work,' one of the Ukrainian policemen muttered disgustedly as they walked away.

"My knees buckled with relief. We'd made it! But if I felt even a little bit invincible that day, it wasn't to last. Two weeks later it was Purim, a Jewish holiday of joy and celebration. My mother and her cousin and two other women had just left on their way to work when an SS officer with a huge police dog stopped them. He arrested all four of them for no special reason. He took them to the local headquarters, made them undress, and then he shot them to death. That night my grandmother told me what had happened. She hugged me and she said, 'Don't ever forget you were very important to your mother.' That night I lay in bed terrified, wondering what would happen next.

"The roundups continued. Desperate to get me out of harm's way, my grandmother made arrangements with the Ukrainian woman who delivered our milk. For money the woman agreed to keep me, but I would have to sneak out of the ghetto that night and meet her under a bridge. It worried me that I had to go alone. I was so nervous, I don't even remember saying good-bye to my grandmother. Many times I've tried to recapture that moment when I left my grandma, who was all I had in the world. All I can recall is the fear.

"Crouched down and shaking, I made my way along the Seret River, which divided the ghetto at one end from the rest of the town. Cautiously I crawled up and I lay on the bank. I waited, but I couldn't see anyone. Then I crept out onto the bridge. Silently this very round-faced, red-faced Ukrainian woman in a kerchief appeared. I realized that she had been standing in the shadows waiting for me. She held out her hand, and I gave her the tin cup in which my grandmother had hidden the money. Then we set out on our journey through the warm spring evening.

"I was tired by the time we reached her farm. The house was not very big, but there was a room for me in back, just wide enough for the bed. The woman explained to me that when the dog barked, it meant somebody was coming, and I would have to quickly scramble under the bed to hide. One day that alarm system didn't work, and some neighbors walked in. The farm woman introduced me as a deaf-mute relative, who was visiting from another village. This was a good ploy. As a blond, I could 'pass' convincingly, but anyone hearing me speak would have known that I wasn't Ukrainian. As long as I was supposed to be mute, I was fine.

"There was only one problem: The farm woman's son-in-law hated Jews with a passion. He would follow me around muttering, 'You'll only bring us trouble, we don't need you here!' Every day he threatened to turn me in to the Gestapo. 'You're living in my house. You behave and leave that girl alone,' the farm woman scolded him. He ignored her. One day he shouted, 'I don't care what you say, I'm turning her in to the Germans.'

"The farm woman pleaded with him to wait a week. He refused. 'Then one more day,' she begged. 'You can take her tomorrow.' 'All right,' the son-in-law agreed finally. That night the farm woman woke me up. Gesturing for me to be quiet, she sneaked me out of the house. Under a moonless sky we started walking, not on the road but through fields. We were going to a neighboring village, where this farm woman had a sister, who was already hiding a family of Jews. There was complete and total darkness. Luckily the farm woman knew the way. 'You'll be safe there,' the farm woman assured me.

"I realized that she must have been in touch with her sister, because when we got there, we didn't go to the house. We went straight to the barn, where the sister, Mrs. Zacharczak, was waiting. 'Shhh!' was the first thing Mrs. Zacharczak said. I had to be perfectly quiet. I looked around and wondered why. We were far from any other house. In a whisper Mrs. Zacharczak explained that she lived with her son, a policeman who hated Jews so much, he would have killed me with his bare hands if he had known that I was there. For that reason there was no way she could keep me in the house. I would be joining the three other Jews already hiding in a hole under the cellar of the barn. I thought what a brave woman she was to hide us, not only from the Nazis but from her own son! What's more, she did it out of kindness: There was nobody to pay her for keeping me, but she did it anyway.

"Life in that hole was like nothing I had ever experienced.

I crawled into a small tunnel and slid down. Then Mrs. Zacharczak covered the opening. Inside I could not stand up or make a sound. I didn't mind the keeping-quiet part. Silence is unnatural to children, but by that time I was not a child anymore, and silence felt safe. Besides, I had little to say to the family down there in the hole with me. Maybe they resented the fact that they had to share the meager resources, but they were mean! Duzco, the man who was about twenty, seemed to get a kick out of telling me that I was ugly. His sister, Rosia, wasn't any nicer. Nor was her daughter, Betka. I was definitely the outcast.

"Mrs. Zacharczak wasn't able to feed us if her son came home unexpectedly. Sometimes we had to go for two days with nothing to eat. When we heard floorboards creaking overhead, we didn't know if the footsteps were Mrs. Zacharczak coming with food—or her son. I dreamed about food constantly. I felt the hunger pains sharply in my chest, and I would literally tremble with anticipation when Mrs. Zacharczak brought us something. It made me furious when Rosia, who doled out the food, deliberately skimped on my share. I could understand her favoring her own daughter, Betka, but it made me feel deprived and resentful.

"Then there were the bugs! Even though I wasn't eating much, I was *being eaten* unbelievably. The lice down there were very bold. They would walk out onto my face. Everywhere I put my hand, there was another one. Fortunately Rosia had a pair of scissors and cut off all my hair. There were body lice too. They would lay eggs in the seams of our clothing. For the whole six or seven months I was down there in the hole, the only real fun I had was cracking the nits with my thumbnail. It was the only way in which I had even the slightest control over what was going on in my life. Here's the strange part of the whole experience: as bad as things were, I *never seriously doubted that I would survive.* It defies reason, but there it was.

"One glorious day we heard artillery. For us that was a wonderful sound. The Russians had come! Not long afterward Mrs. Zacharczak told us we were liberated. We had to wait until night to leave the hiding place. Mrs. Zacharczak didn't want us to be seen, by her son or anyone else. She was afraid for anyone to know that she had saved Jews. Isn't that amazing?

"Disappointingly I found that even though the war was over, life was still a catastrophe for a Jewish child all alone in the world. In hiding I had hoped that there would be somebody alive and willing to take care of me. However, the Nazis had liquidated the ghetto and killed virtually everyone, including my grandmother. I was only eight years old, but I soon discovered that people were concerned only about themselves and their families, period.

"In the town there was a big empty building where all the Jews who had survived were congregating. Overjoyed, I discovered some very distant relatives, but they said, 'Sorry, we have nothing. You'll just have to go and beg for food.' Crushed, I went to Rosia, hoping maybe she would take pity on me and adopt me. 'Look down there,' she said, pointing to the road, almost clogged with refugees. 'See all those people running?' I saw them. 'You can go with them,' she said, giving me a push. I felt a wave of panic. It was late March and very cold. The people on the road were running. 'Go!' Rosia repeated impatiently. 'Run with those people! Go.' I went. It was late afternoon, just getting dark. I was frightened with no idea where I was going to sleep or where my next meal was going to come from.

"I must have passed out, because the next thing I knew, a man was carrying me. It seemed that he was a friend of my father's who saw me lying in the snow and recognized me. He carried me in his arms for a while, but he, too, was frail and weak after the war, and he couldn't carry me any longer. So he stopped at a peasant's house and asked them to take care of me. 'If you don't, I'll come back and kill you,' he warned them. Before the peasants could respond, a couple of Russian soldiers came in. One of them, a captain who happened to be Jewish, said, 'Don't worry, we'll take care of her,' and they did!

"The soldiers took me to their barracks, where they gave me food and a place to sleep. A few days later they had to move on, so once again, I was all alone, going from house to house and begging for food, homeless and humiliated. Finally, after several months of that, I met another Russian soldier. This one told me he was going to Kiev and he would take me to an orphanage there. Eager to go anywhere that someone would take care of me, I got in his truck. We started out, but we had only gone as far as Gritzef, a little town in the Russian Ukraine, when he received different orders.

"He took me to the mayor of the town. 'I was supposed to take this little girl to an orphanage,' he explained. 'But now I can't get to Kiev, and I don't know what to do with her.' A Jewish man named Serge just happened to overhear that. 'Poor child,' he said in a kind voice. He had lost his own wife and children in the war. He would gladly take me. I lived with Serge, his postwar wife, Dora, and her daughters for a whole year. Life with them was better than anything I could remember. When a judge in the town gave Dora a piece of material to make me a dress, I felt warm, protected, and special.

"Then something even more wonderful happened, as I was reunited with an uncle I didn't even remember I had! Uncle George, who lived in Lvov, had also lost his family—a wife and daughter. But sometime after liberation he had seen a man who looked familiar, and they'd started to talk. The man was from Czortkov, my hometown. He said to my uncle, 'Rumor has it that your sister's child survived.'

"Thrilled, Uncle George began searching for me. He checked every orphanage. At one point as he searched for me, he was arrested and jailed for traveling without the proper papers. Still he persevered, writing letters and making inquiries. Finally he found me. What joy! To this day Uncle George is like a dad to me. I love him. My children consider him their grandfather.

"Through the years I've tried not to waste time regretting anything, like the fact that I don't remember ever having had a toy in my life. I raised myself, and I think I did a pretty good job. I could feel sorry for the fact that I lost so much of my childhood, but I'd rather just enjoy what I have now. I think of my cousins who died in the Holocaust, and many times I have to wonder, Why me? Why was *I* saved and not them? I don't feel guilty about it because I had no control over events at that time. But now that I *am* in charge of what I do, I refuse to waste my time rehashing the past. Isn't that my privilege?

"I went to one workshop at the Hidden Child Gathering, about how we relate with our children. There was one woman there with her two daughters, and you know? My heart was breaking for all of them! The daughters were saying that they had to be honest: Their mother couldn't give love. She was sitting hunched over in such agony, with her eyes closed. I was suffering for her because she went through a lot. But then, I went through a lot too.

"What it comes down to is what you're going to make of the experience. I feel that I paid a dear price, and I don't want all that struggle to be wasted. For example, the experience taught me gratitude. I had so little back then, but now I have so much to be thankful for: my husband, my children, and many good friends. I have people now. I have a home I love, I have everything that I could possibly want. Many times I say to myself, 'I'm dieting again. All that food that I didn't have, and now I have it and I don't even want to eat it.'

"Some people may want to call me Pollyanna, but I don't care. Who has the right to tell me what I feel isn't valid or that I ought to feel bad instead of happy? I'm very, very glad to be alive. I want to make the most of every moment I have. That's the point I keep trying to make to my kids when I say to them, 'Listen, this is *not* a dress rehearsal.' "

THE
AFTERMATH

SANNE SPETTER

Sanne Spetter's eyes are hazel. Her short hair, brushed up, is reddish. "It's dyed," she volunteers with cheerful candor, adding, "It was almost white, but my hiding father was a redhead, and I've always wanted to be one." Sanne is a psychiatric nurse at Montefiore Medical Center in the Bronx. Recently she left her apartment on a seedy crack-infested block near the hospital and bought a garden apartment with a spectacular view of the Hudson River. In this safe, quiet, and comfortable haven filled with books and her stepmother's Wedgwood china, Sanne, forty-nine, feels content. "For the first time in my life," she says, "I have a home of my own."

"I was born in Amsterdam in 1942. Besides being Jewish, my parents were politically active and wanted by the police. So, when I was two months old, they found a safe place for me with a Christian doctor named Drion and his wife, who agreed to keep me in their home in Rotterdam for however long the war would take.

"The Drions were a real family. There was Hanneke, who was born right after I arrived there, and later they had a little boy named Bas. I felt secure and loved and comfortable. I'm sure the Drions didn't tell me who I really was, because you couldn't be sure that a little kid is going to keep her mouth shut.

"My foster mother kept baby books, one on Hanneke and one on me: how we were doing during the first year and the feeding problems. There was no milk, so they used an extract that was made from potatoes. Of course there was very little heat or hot water, which made it hard to wash diapers. For that reason they tried to have us toilet trained. I think the parents were probably more trained than we were. Apparently I was toilet trained and then I wasn't. My foster mom kept a whole book with all of those things! I was very gregarious and would run up to strangers, including SS officers, who said, 'Oh, what a sweet little child,' and jiggled me on their knees. My mother—that is, my hiding mother—told me, 'I used to go crazy. If they'd only known!' But it was probably the smart thing to do.

"How did I learn that all my aunts and uncles, my little brother, my 'twin' sister, Hanneke, and even my parents weren't mine? For years I have racked my brain over that. Even if someone did try to explain it to me then, it would have made no sense. Apparently both my parents had been listed as dead. The Drions were preparing to adopt me when word came that my mother had been killed in Auschwitz, but my father was alive! Sometime after that the Drions were asked to put me in a halfway house until my father could get me. The Drions' job was done, and they were not supposed to have any further contact with me.

"Suddenly I found myself in the halfway house, which was a private home where many children would come to stay for weeks or months while waiting to be sent to Palestine. If I was even told why I was there, it made no sense, for I was far too young to comprehend it anyway.

"I blocked out most of what was happening then. I know

I had a terrible ear infection that needed surgery. I was rushed to the hospital by ambulance in the middle of the night. I was taken to be X-rayed in a dark, cold room, and this icy machine came down on top of me. I was terrified. The next day I was awake when they brought me into the operating room on a stretcher. When I saw all these tools like saws, I said, 'Those are not for me!' It took the whole operating-room staff to hold me down.

"No doubt in my mind, I still assumed that I'd go back to the Drions when I was well. That didn't happen. Instead I went to Amsterdam to live with my father and Ina, his new bride. The Drions were supposed to be well out of my life by then, but I missed them. Even a year later I begged so relentlessly to see them, my father finally allowed Hanneke to come and spend a weekend with us. I looked forward to that visit, but it wasn't fun. It was very awkward. I couldn't figure out why. It was only years later that Hanneke told me how difficult my stepmother had made it for her.

"I understood then that this was where I was going to stay. I also saw that I had to be very, very good. So I learned to follow clues and unspoken messages. In that way I began a very careful relationship with my father. For example, he and my stepmother would say I was too serious. They would do things to make me laugh. After a while I understood that I was supposed to laugh, so I would laugh whether I felt like it or not. That was when I really started hiding, as I hid my real feelings. As I got older, I just got out of the way. If I felt an argument was coming, I'd say, 'I'm going for a walk now.' I never ran away or did anything horrible. I just went for walks.

"In 1951 we were packing to come to the United States. I didn't want to leave! It also meant leaving the Drions in a more final way. I felt—desperately—that Holland was where I belonged. I was only seven and a half, but I figured out a whole elaborate support system of people who would take care of me so that I wouldn't have to go away. But of course adults often don't take children seriously, so that plan went down the tubes.

"I'll never forget how sad I was when we were leaving Holland. We went by train to Cherbourg in France, and the whole time: going to the train, getting on the train, I just kept thinking, Somebody's going to come and take me off this train; I'm not going. But it didn't come true. The French had a rail strike, and we almost missed the boat. I was elated. But my hopes were dashed again as we got on the bus. We were on the last little boat that made it to the *Queen Mary* before it took off. I was groaning. I thought, Couldn't we have been one minute later?

"Later on I felt so many times, Why didn't they leave me where I was? I would have been better off! So much of the crap that I hated wouldn't have been happening. For example, as I was growing up, my stepmother told me things about the Drions that weren't true. She said, 'They took you only because we paid them money,' and 'We gave you beautiful clothes, but they gave them to Hanneke and you wore rags.' I can't believe that my stepmother lied on a conscious level. I'd rather think she just had a very strong wish to make things right somehow.

"On occasion I tried to discuss the past with my father, but that was no help. Whenever we'd talk about it, he'd say *my* perceptions were wrong, *my* recollections were not correct. I believe he saw my loving the Drions as a negative reflection on him—and it felt to me that I could never convince him that it wasn't so. It was much easier to hide my feelings than argue.

"One of my earliest memories of living with my parents was my father's having lots and lots of bookcases and books, just like I have now. On the very bottom shelf there was a series of small books with pictures. I was a curious child. If there was a cranny to get into, I would go and investigate it. I looked at those books. I haven't seen them since or dared to ask about them, but I'm sure they were part of the documentation for the Nuremberg trials. There were a lot of pictures of the crematoria, the bodies, the clothing and shoes, the gold crowns and rings. My father had been a witness at the Nuremberg trials. I think that was part of the reason why I never questioned him. I knew that it was too much to ask.

"So I also kept a secret, a question: Why was I spared? What would make me different? What did I come up with? Nothing! Just luck, which doesn't seem like a very good answer. I knew he went through some very horrible situations during the war, including losing my mother. I do look very much like her. When I was in my twenties, I looked exactly like a picture I have that was taken of her when she was twenty-one. My father tells me that I have some of my mother's mannerisms. How is that possible? I have no idea, but I think that I was always a reminder to him.

"On some level there has been that continual reproach—and that's cost me a lot; it's made me feel at times that there were pieces of me missing. In my thirties, when my marriage wasn't going well, my husband and I went into couples therapy. It didn't work. I decided then that I'd better figure out who the hell I was because I felt that I had so many unresolved questions. I decided to go to Holland. I hadn't seen the Drions since we left Holland in March 1951. Now seeing them again was exactly what I needed! It gave me a sense of where some of my strengths stemmed from, and it proved to me that whatever is really stable in me comes from there.

"Still, my marriage ended. For a long time I believed that it was all my fault. However, that was not true. As a kid I'd dreamed of having twelve kids, animals, growing things, blah,

blah, blah. But none of that happened. In fact I actually refused to have kids because I had very strong feelings that I couldn't be a good mother after what I had gone through. Proof to me was the way I had felt about my half brother and half sister after they were born. I'd had to be caretaker of them a lot of the time, and I used to get furious. I would get so enraged with them that I'd lock myself in my room—away from them, because I wanted to kill them. It wasn't subtle. It was very clear! Even later I knew that I was still angry, that the rage hadn't gone away.

"I know a piece of this anger has to do with my father and my old compulsion to please him, regardless of how I felt inside. For years I thought that if only I did the right thing, then things would be better. I'm only now starting to learn that the more I can keep my own feelings separate from whatever I think my father expects of me, the better we do. Thank God, I'm finally breaking free of that! Since I was about forty, I've come to accept that maybe I do know something, and that if I have an opinion, I can voice it and not have to hold back. Now I don't try to be so pleasant, to be so good, to be whatever you want anymore.

"For years I think I was pretty resentful. Then at some point I decided, Jesus, life is very short, and keeping grievances takes so much energy, it's not worth it. If you don't make something positive for yourself at least, what you have is wasted, gone, and you can't get it back. One thing I've always felt good about is my career. It's funny: I'm a nurse because nursing seemed interesting to me. I had no idea until recently that my hiding mother was a nurse! I didn't know that, because by the time I knew her, she was home with the children.

"Why did nursing attract me? I thought that because I had pain, I could hear pain. On the wards I have a reputation with the adolescents for being very tough. I've heard that they call me the General. But they also respect me because I'm fair. I've always been good with the older patients, with immigrants, with people who have gone through the camps. And I'm one of the few people who can work with the really depressed patients and the ones who get angry and act out.

"My philosophy is, first of all, I'm not living with them, so that's a big relief. Secondly I'm only there for eight hours. I can do anything for eight hours. I compartmentalize things. I think, Okay, if I can get through this little piece, then I have it made. Then we'll see about the next piece. In a way a lot of my life has been like that. 'Okay, I've gotten through this trauma, take a deep breath, maybe there is another one, maybe not. At least, this one is over for now.'

"Right now I think I'm beginning to question more seriously how come I don't remember so much. Certainly a lot of my reading over the last ten years shows I've been growing more interested. Why now? Part of it has to do with the process of maturing and being better able to handle it. Before this there were very few times that I ever, ever spoke about it outside the family. Sometimes I'd mention that my father had been in the camps, but nothing else. Or if I said that I had been in hiding, nobody seemed particularly interested. In fairness I'm sure I gave the message 'I don't want you to ask.' After all, it was such a forbidden subject for so long. That first time I went back to Holland when I was in my twenties, my father was very much against it. In fact, I feel that he still gets upset when I go there.

"But I do it anyway! Since that first time I reconnected with the Drions, I've been going back to see them regularly. In 1978 my foster mother had cancer. When she was really sick, they called me. I said, 'I'm coming over.' Then I said, 'Is that okay?' They said, 'Yes of course! That's why we're calling you.' I said, 'Good!' and I called up my job and said, 'Look,

I need a leave of absence without pay, I don't care. I need to have it. I'm leaving immediately.' I was prepared to resign if they said no. I went to Holland and stayed there for five weeks. We biked to the hospital every day. Even if we said nothing, I was there, to be part of what was going on and part of the family. I stayed until she was back home again, and then I was able to say good-bye. A month later she died.

"After that I was pretty much alone with my feelings until May 1991, when I attended the Hidden Child Gathering. Since then I've joined a local hidden-child support group right nearby. Both have helped me so much. You say to yourself, Nobody wants to hear it, and it stays inside. This kind of sharing opens it up and lets the air in. That's the relief: that I'm not crazy, I'm not out of my mind. I'm not out of my skull, I'm not weird. I'm not all kinds of ungrateful. This is a real thing and it's validated. That's so important to me. Now I feel like some of the healing can finally start."

MARIE-CLAIRE RAKOWSKI

Describing herself as "artsy and European-looking," Marie-Claire Rakowski, forty-eight, wears a black leather miniskirt with a cream-colored silk blouse. Her brown hair is naturally curly, with the crimped look that chic women pay a fortune to emulate. Marie-Claire recently resigned from her job, managing—among other things—an international boutique in Trump Tower. Since then she has stayed home, sleeping late, making chicken soup with fresh bok choy, and working out at her health club on Manhattan's Upper West Side. Over Christmas Marie-Claire sold jewelry at Tiffany's. What's next? She's not sure. "It has to be fun," she says. Marie-Claire—also known as Miriam—is full of fun. Nevertheless her smile is often ironic, and sometimes—even when she's laughing—her eyes look sad.

"For me the hell began after the war. I was born in Belgium in 1943, when the Germans were in control. Afraid we were going to be captured, my mother sent my sister to a convent. Because I was just a baby, I was placed with a Catholic couple named Hicket, who couldn't have children. I felt safe and much loved in their home. I was especially attached to the husband, a jolly, big teddy bear of a pharmacist I called Poppy. His shop seemed very big, with dark wood and mirrors and a huge candy jar on the counter that was full of gumdrops. My absolute delight was when he'd lift me up so I could reach in the jar and grab a handful of candy.

"The Hickets loved animals, so I learned to love animals. We had several dogs, a cat, and a pet donkey. Since I had no other children to play with, the animals were my playmates. I spent happy afternoons under the table with one of the dogs, a collie. The tablecloth hung down almost to the floor all around us, so I pretended that we were in our own little house.

"All that changed abruptly in 1947, when I was taken away from the Hickets in the middle of the night. All I remember is a red-headed man with a red beard, holding tightly to my hand as we walked across railroad tracks in pitch darkness. As a four-year-old I was very, very perplexed. I didn't know this man. When I started to whimper, he gave me candy: strange, iridescent hard candy, which I didn't like. It was nothing like the delicious gumdrops in my Poppy's jar. Moments later we boarded a train. I felt very uncomfortable and very confused. 'This will be over and he'll take me home soon,' I told myself over and over.

"I was wrong. I was never to see Monsieur or Madame Hicket again. That night I didn't know what was happening. What I learned later was that my mother had tried to get me back earlier, but my hiding family had not wanted to let me go. In fact the war had ended in 1945 when I was two, but my mother, just coming out of Auschwitz, was so ill then that I was allowed to stay with the Hickets for another couple of years while she recuperated. Now, however, she had authorized a Jewish organization to take me back.

"Apparently this organization was committed to saving Jewish children, but their so-called idealism ruined my life. At least that's the way I see it. That red-headed man with the red beard kidnapped me, turning my peaceful, happy life into chaos.

"The train took us to Switzerland, where I was reunited with my sister. She had contracted typhus in the convent and lost most of her hair. She could see right away that I was a more glowing, happy child in many ways, and she resented it. The first thing she did when she met me was to grab the doll I'd brought and rip it apart. From then on she took every possible opportunity to make me miserable.

"The worst part for me was still the shock of missing the Hickets, as my sister and I were sent to one foster home after another: a whole succession of strangers who didn't know me or care about me. For quite a few years I didn't know what the hell happened. I kept expecting things to get 'back to normal.' They never did! I hated my life. As we were shuttled around, the only constant was my sister, who was, as we would say today, mentally disturbed, as she had every right to be. But she was beating me up a lot!

"I don't remember much about Switzerland, except the alpine view of a white icecap and a lake. When my mother came to visit us, we went to the baths, which was what you did for recreation. I refused to believe that this flabby, unattractive person who kept pawing me was my real mother. I felt disgusted. She told me that someday soon we'd be living together. I was delighted that it wasn't to happen—at least not right away. After two years in Switzerland my sister and I were brought to the United States. It seemed that we had Belgian passports and could get visas, whereas my mother, who had been born in Poland, had to wait because the Polish quota was filled.

"We arrived at Ellis Island, which was crowded with people. There we were taught the Pledge of Allegiance. We were each given a bag with a toothbrush and other things, such as a notebook, pencils, and crayons. By this time I was so accustomed to moving, I was eager to find out what was coming next.

"We were placed with a family in New York City, and though we'd been with Jews in Switzerland, this was my first exposure to real religious people. These folks were Satmar Hasidim, a Hungarian sect that wears the fur hats, the black satin coats, and white socks. I was now called Miriam, instead of Marie-Claire. And the rules were endless! It was a whole new discipline, almost military. I was taught to cover my legs and my elbows. On the Sabbath I wasn't allowed to turn on lights, carry anything outside, or do much of anything. I was flooded with new information—including the rule that once you've said your prayers at night, you're not allowed to touch your body afterward. One agonizing night I was itchy. I tossed and turned for hours, not daring to scratch. That was torture!

"What I did like in that household was that they served food family style. After living in Europe where food was scarce, the freedom of being allowed to serve ourselves and take as much as we wanted was exciting.

"After two weeks, for reasons unclear to me, we left there and went to stay with a family in Detroit, who were not Satmars. This was Rabbi and Mrs. Wasserman, a wonderful couple. We stayed there for two years, and I think they would have kept us even longer. They finally gave us up because they couldn't stand our constant fighting, as my sister attacked me and I tried to defend myself. She was savage; there was no containing her.

"So it was back to New York, to another family and then another. This one was a nightmare for me. The children in the neighborhood called me a 'mockie,' a foreigner. I felt different and unacceptable. My sister continued to beat me up. Far from having anyone there to comfort or protect me, the father of this family, a rabbi, abused me sexually. Feeling miserable, I came down with whooping cough. I was very sick! That was when I finally felt the full impact of what had happened to me: I had lost my hiding parents (the only people I could ever think of as my real parents). I understood now that there would be no going back.

"The only relief was summertime. Regardless of what family we were with, we spent each summer at a camp run by the Jewish organization that was in charge of us. In fact this camp used my picture on their letterhead as a symbol of Jewish children saved from the war. A lot of other kids at camp were homesick for their families, but I felt so lucky to have gotten away! The only thing I dreaded was the last day of camp, when we would have to leave.

"The summer I was ten, something very dramatic happened: My mother arrived at camp. This was planned, expected, and a big deal to everyone else. In fact the whole camp was planning a *simcha*, or party, to celebrate my mother's arrival. I felt out of it and very uncomfortable. I had already had so many new families and so many upsets and changes, there was no way that some mythical person called my mother was going to come and solve my problems. It was too late.

"Everyone else rejoiced as the chosen day arrived. Excited, my sister went to the bus station to meet our mother. I stayed in camp. I was at lunch when the door opened and she walked into the dining hall. Everyone in the camp was there. Someone pushed me up to the front, where she was standing. I looked at her shyly and tried to smile. She was a big woman. She grabbed me and hugged me very hard against her stomach. I felt smothered. I was actually gagging because I didn't like the way she smelled; she smelled like decay and death to me. I was her daughter, and she was very happy to see me, but to me she wasn't anyone I liked or loved. I felt very awkward. The whole camp was singing joyful songs in Hebrew. Everyone was laughing, crying, hugging each other. I could see that they were all getting off on this whole experience. I just felt trapped.

"At the same time I felt guilty. I'd been told that when my mother was saved by the soldiers, she weighed only seventy or eighty pounds. She had been in Auschwitz with my father, who died there. The Nazis had done crazy experiments on her. She really needed us. Still, she wasn't what I had in mind as a mother. I ran off to be by myself, but a counselor brought me back, reminding me again how my mother had suffered and waited all these years to see me and felt hurt that I wasn't responding to her. Of course I went back and tried to be more understanding. I have to get to know her, I told myself. I knew that she was going to be my next family.

"The next day my mother left camp to find an apartment in Brooklyn. When the summer was over, my sister and I would join her. Everyone regarded this as a happily-ever-after ending to the war for our family. As it turned out, it was anything but happy! She never was what I wanted in a mother, but she was what I had: a woman whose life was still very much dominated by her war experiences. She sometimes hallucinated and would often scream at me and hit me—for anything, for nothing. She was also very paranoid and locked up all her things, believing that I wanted to steal from her.

"I wasn't allowed to have a key to the apartment. I'd come home from school starving for a snack, but I'd have to wait outside until she and my sister got home from work. Even then I was often hungry. Yes, we were poor, but not that poor! My mother was simply the cheapest person I can ever remember knowing. She wouldn't even buy toilet paper or sanitary napkins. If any food spoiled, she ate it and expected us to do the same. There was no such thing as throwing out even a blackened, wet lettuce leaf.

"In the evenings my mother and sister loved to discuss the war. My sister wanted to know all about the family and the past. I had no interest in any of that. I distanced myself; I just turned off. To me these were just people I was living with, not my real family. Emotional distance did not make me safe, however. Quite often my mother got angry and forced me out of the apartment. Sometimes I found refuge with my friend, Lois Fineberg, who was also having family problems, so we kind of banded together. But that didn't always work out, and there were many times I had to sleep outside our apartment in the hallway.

"My sister was always trying to turn my mother against me. She often succeeded, and then they'd both hit me. As I got older, I started to feel that maybe I didn't have to take it anymore. One night when I was sixteen, my mother took a frying pan to me. I responded by picking up a knife. I said, 'If you hit me with that, I'll kill you.' She was terrified and called the police. When they came, she told them that she didn't want me anymore. The police contacted the Federation of Jewish Philanthropies, and one of their social workers placed me in a group home called the Girls Club. That was when I left my family, and I never moved back.

"In the beginning it was very frightening for me, a protected, religious Jewish girl. (I *was* a girl who covered her elbows!) Suddenly I was in a different neighborhood with girls who were so different from anything I'd ever come close to. Everything I'd heard of as being dangerous and bad was comfortable for these girls, who cursed like sailors, shoplifted, drank, took drugs, slept with men, and slept with women. I was not only scared, I was desperately homesick for my mother and sister. As bad as all that had been, at least it was familiar!

"Gradually I realized that the Girls Club did offer certain freedoms and supports I'd never had before. For example, the rooms were comfortable. I could come home right after school and study. They also had a bowl of fruit right out where you could help yourself any time you felt like an apple, a peach, or a banana. That was bliss! At meals you could eat as much as you wanted. After a while I stopped worrying about my next meal, as I had been doing for years at my mother's house. This took a lot of pressure off me, and I started to relax at last.

"One night at supper, a bad girl with a lot of makeup who intimidated most of the other girls was talking about World War II. She said, 'Maybe Hitler had the right idea.' She was doing this for my benefit. To her surprise I stood up to her and told her, 'That is the stupidest remark I've ever heard.' Everyone was impressed.

"I stayed in the group home and finished high school. That was a touch-and-go situation, as I was beginning to become quite rebellious and somewhat self-destructive. As a preteen at home the worst thing I'd ever done was to wear slacks and talk to a boy—for which I was slapped by the rabbi and kicked out of the Jewish parochial school. Now I was somewhat more incorrigible: hanging out with drug addicts and staying out all night. Why did I behave that way? Why not! At that point in my life I found it hard to believe that anyone was on my side or would be good to me.

"Underneath I must have had some hope. While I was hanging out with drug addicts and around drugs constantly, I never touched the stuff. What protected me was the solid foundation of love that I'd had up to the age of four. That was something I was able to hold on to in a private place. It helped me to endure the bad parts because I knew there was something better, even if I didn't have it anymore, even if I'd never find it again. That of course was what my sister was always so jealous of and couldn't forgive me for. She understood that I had had love and security, which she had never had. That drove her crazy.

"Around this time I made up with my mother. I even ended up taking care of her until she died in 1970. However there was no reconciling with my sister. I haven't spoken to her in twenty years, and I have no desire to do so. When I was eighteen, I took an apartment with Barbara Baer, a friend from the Girls Club, and worked as a bookkeeper. I was also seeing a psychiatrist, Dr. Charles Konia, and he really saved my life!

"I was still staying out nights and doing crazy stuff, but eventually, with my therapist's help, I started getting myself together. I decided to go to college. Toward that goal I invested the small amount of money I inherited from my mother. I made enough to stop work and put myself through college and even two years of grad school in finance. The whole motivation for getting a financial degree was security, but over the years I've gradually begun to realize that money isn't everything. Now for the first time I want to find work that is satisfying for me, rather than just a big salary.

"I know I still have a lot of problems that go back to my traumatic childhood. For example, I've lived in my apartment for ten years, but I can't bring myself to decorate—or even unpack. I like antiques a lot and I'm very visually oriented, but I can't seem to make my home beautiful. Perhaps it's because I still half expect to be taken away or moved or kidnapped. I don't dare get too comfortable. But I'm beginning to make myself a home. Better late than never.

"Another problem I've had has been in maintaining relationships with men. In part, I know, it relates to the fact that

I never got over losing my father, that is, my hiding father. Four is when all little girls fall in love with their daddies, but while most people get to outgrow the attachment, I never did, so I'm totally unresolved in that area. That's held me back. I have a tendency to chase away good, wonderful men because it's too frightening to think of falling in love and then losing that person. It's almost as if a very hurt and scared four-year-old is still inside me, directing my love life. Not a great situation! Sometimes it's like I want to grow up, but I don't know how the hell to do it. It's a real dilemma.

"My Catholic parents are dead now. I feel frustrated that I can't show them the gratitude and love I feel. I did write to them, but for years I was too involved in the ongoing nightmare to really appreciate all they did for me. In therapy and life I've worked hard on myself. All in all, I consider myself to be relatively healthy, compared with a lot of other people. I know that in some ways I'm an overachiever, and in other ways I can't get it together. But if you look at my history, I should be crazy! I should have killed myself at twenty-one. But I'm beyond that, which says a lot about the human spirit and a person's recuperative powers.

"I never spoke about my experiences around my family. I felt they'd suffered more, and that my suffering was unimportant compared with my mother's and my sister's, so I didn't have a right to speak about it. I thought there are the Holocaust survivors, and then there's me. I never imagined that there had been other children hidden by Catholic families and then taken away.

"One day, about three years ago, I happened to attend a meeting of a child survivors' group, at which Miriam Abramowicz was the key speaker. She presented her film, in which I saw so much that applied to me and my life, I couldn't believe it! I introduced myself to Miriam, and she invited me for coffee with a dozen others, including Nicole David. Nicole and Miriam said they were planning to do something for the hidden child. They didn't even have the term *hidden child* yet; it hadn't evolved. It was 'the Jewish children and babies who had been hidden during the war.'

"I loved the idea and immersed myself in the planning. By the end we were meeting several times a week. It was a very emotional process. I felt some ambivalence about going public. For example, I was in the article in *New York* magazine. However, I was the only one of the seven people in it who refused to be photographed. Then came the conference itself: the culmination of the whole effort. It was quite an event. At the end I stood up before the sixteen hundred people who had come. I told them, 'By coming here, you have validated your experience and the experience of all children.' Then I said, 'I would like to give you a homework assignment for the next thirty years: Tell your story! Tell your story to someone, and you will begin the process of healing.'

"I really hope they took that to heart. I'm convinced that it's time for us to share our stories with the world. If we don't speak up while we have the chance, there will be nothing to stop future generations of people from saying, 'Those children were so young then, and it was so long ago. How could it ever really matter anymore?' "

THE LEGACY

RUTH RUBENSTEIN

Ruth Rubenstein is a petite woman with fine features, dark eyes, and dark curly hair. Ruth is a divorced mother of two adult daughters. She lives with a man named Philip in a cozy and pleasantly cluttered house surrounded by trees in the New York suburb of Hastings-on-Hudson. There Ruth is a psycho-therapist in private practice. On weekends she is usually in her tennis gear complete with a knee brace and a tennis-elbow splint. She and Philip are always game to play, even if the court needs a little work first with a leaf rake or a snow shovel. Ruth's demeanor is very upbeat. One would never guess the private hell Ruth went through as a child—and again just a few years ago. "This is the first time I'm feeling emotion telling this story," she admits. "Usually I feel detached, but the conference broke something open a little more, so that I'm closer to feelings."

"My life began in Koenigsberg, East Prussia, but we fled from there to Belgium in 1939 when I was one and a half. Shortly after that my father was picked up and sent to a detention camp. I was distraught. I kept asking for him, but all my mother could think of to say was, 'He went to buy bread,' or 'He went to the butcher shop.' The camp was a horrifying, filthy place. When he escaped and came home a year later, I didn't even recognize him. I called him the uncle. I said to my mother, 'The uncle brought me chocolate.' I don't know if I truly didn't know that he was the beloved papa I'd missed so much—or if, even then, I had the concept that you just blot out the picture of a loved one who's left in order not to hurt so much.

"By 1942 life was more precarious. My father was almost arrested, but he jumped off of a balcony and escaped. However, the Gestapo had his papers, so from then on we had to keep a very low profile. Because I spoke German, my parents were always shushing me in the street. I noticed they both had stricken, angry looks on their faces, and I wondered what I'd said that was bad. In the evenings they'd often snap at me. Not understanding the pressure they were under, I felt responsible. At night I slept between them. My father tossed and turned and talked in his sleep. Once, my mother's crying woke me up. I tried to stroke her cheek and her soft curly hair, but that just made her cry harder.

"Too frightened to go on as we were any longer, my parents decided to find a safe place for me. They'd heard that convents were taking in Jewish children. Still, the decision to place me was hard. To this day my parents tell me that the worst part of the whole war experience was letting me go. All *I* felt was intense surprise on that gray, damp morning when my mother dressed me to go out. We hadn't gone anywhere in a long time. I was wearing a little brown hat that tied under my chin. My mother told me in a cheerful voice that I was going to a boarding school. Not understanding that she was actually going to leave me in that strange place, I was startled when she hugged me and said good-bye. I thought that maybe she and my father were coming back for me later in the day. Then we'd all take the tram together and I'd have my cocoa and my supper. I planned to be very good and very quiet in bed that night.

"My parents did not come back for me. The nuns, strange ladies in black who spoke French, a language I didn't understand, took me to a room with colored windows and wooden benches. I could see candles burning, but it was still dark. One of the nuns showed me how to get on my knees on the floor. Then she took my hand and tried to get me to make an odd sign across my chest. I was confused. I wanted my mother. Moments later I felt a chill down my back when the nun took my hand and dipped it into a small bowl of water.

"My parents didn't come the next night either, nor the next. My eyes burned. I felt cold all the time. At breakfast I was supposed to eat watery gruel, but I couldn't do it. A nun named Sister Louise slapped my face, but I still couldn't eat. That night I woke up in a crib in a large room with other cribs. I felt like I was burning up. I had itchy blotches on my face, and I was coughing. It sounded too loud, so I tried to muffle the sound in my pillow. I had the measles.

"After six weeks my parents were allowed to see me. Of course they had it better than some parents who didn't know where their children were. But when they came to see me, I was a wreck! I was practically mute and I kept crossing myself. I wasn't sure who they were. I had lice, impetigo, and bronchitis. I also must have been very angry. When they asked me if I wanted to come home, I said no. My father said, 'This is impossible! No matter what, we're taking her home.' Ironically the Nazis were beginning to raid the convents at that time. After I left, some children from that convent were taken; so, for me it was a close escape.

"At home I sat very still and looked in the mirror while my father cut my hair and carefully removed the lice. But home was only temporary. My parents had located a Belgian couple named DeMarneff, who had no children and were eager to take me into their home. I don't remember saying good-bye to my parents as I went off with Madame and Monsieur DeMarneff. She played with me—something about fingers and pretending they weren't there. We laughed together.

"I recovered very quickly, at least on the surface. The couple lived in a villa in a suburb of Brussels, and they were very, very kind to me. The DeMarneffs passed me off as a niece from Italy. Later I learned that the whole village knew I was Jewish and they all protected me. Madame DeMarneff—Mami—was very nurturing and roly-poly and always making wonderful butter cookies and overfeeding me. I became a fat little girl, which is where I get my obsession with fat.

"As it turned out, this was my first normal childhood experience. I had children to play with, including two best friends, Raimonde and Jacques. We used to play in the meadow and do a lot of handstands. I would hang from my knees and try to walk on my hands like Janeen, one little girl I admired greatly for that feat! My hiding father, Papi, made me little dolls out of chestnuts and matchsticks. Once he brought me home a pair of little magnetized dogs.

"My parents, who spent the war hiding in a series of different places in Brussels, visited me once a month. Apparently that was the only time they got to eat. Strangely I cannot remember a single one of their visits! There was one time I wasn't there when they came, and my mother left a chocolate hen. When I saw that chocolate hen, I just cried and cried. It was such a breakthrough of grief! Underneath the outward composure I must have been brimming with sadness and longing.

"I stayed there for two and a half years. When the war was over, Mami and Papi DeMarneff didn't want to part with me. Once again I don't remember any good-byes. Years later I asked my mother, 'Wasn't I upset to leave them?' She said, 'No, I don't think so, I think you were eager to come home.'

My mother admits that I was very quiet and it was hard to re-connect. I just felt fat, lonely, and boring. (I still get these periods of feeling fat and boring!) I had problems with my hand-writing, crocheting, and knitting. I felt very mediocre. I was convinced that everybody else was better than I was.

"I was lonely at that time, especially on Sunday after-noons. Again, on the surface everything seemed sort of nor-mal, but there was an underside of sadness and confusion. I remember crying as I tried to knit a yellow sock on three needles and it wasn't coming out right: I couldn't knit the holes together. That was probably a perfect metaphor for my life!

"We came to America when I was eleven. I was pretty ex-cited about it. The man who gave us our affidavit put us up in an apartment house he owned in New York City. It was very swank. My mother covered the rug with newspapers—this gor-geous blue rug! I went to the neighborhood school and I was put in a class for non-English-speaking kids. Compared with the rest of them, I was brilliant. However, the first day I tried to come home for lunch, and I got lost. I wandered for a long time and finally found my way home and went upstairs, and I was all alone in the place. Suddenly I heard a siren from a fire engine, and I got very frightened. I was sure it was a bombing raid.

"My father was a doctor, but since he knew no English and therefore couldn't take his boards to practice medicine in the United States, my mother went out working—cleaning people's houses. She had come from a very wealthy family, so it was quite a switch. But she took to it very well. Meanwhile I was just this fat little girl. My parents made me carry a big briefcase to school, which made me feel weird and uncomfort-able. There was one incident when some little girl made fun of me in the playground for the organdy dress I was wearing. I hauled off and slammed her. I was so pleased! Basically I was this very well-behaved little kid with no self-esteem at all. Whenever anybody wanted to be with me or chose me, I was amazed.

"Even later, when I went to college, I was delighted—and so surprised—when friends I wanted to room with wanted to room with me. After college I went to Belgium and visited the DeMarneffs, but it was terrible. We didn't get along at all. They had been so wonderful to me—even selling rugs to get me eggs and other luxuries during the war, and I don't remember that they ever scolded me. But I didn't feel any special gratitude. I was defensive on the visit, afraid they would treat me like a child. I think I must have been very angry at them: first because they weren't my parents, and second because they'd let me go. We never did reconnect emotionally. When I got back to the United States, my mother said, 'You should know better by now.' It's painful to admit this, but later on, when the DeMarneffs died, I felt nothing. It wasn't lack of feeling. On the contrary I think that was just the measure of how really angry, hurt, and confused I must have been!

"When I was twenty-three, I got married to a younger man, an American. I was very, very happy. We had an extremely close marriage, a little cocoon for two. He was tender and nurturing and so focused on me. In part I think I married him because I felt he wouldn't hurt me. I think we both felt that he *had* to stay with me forever to make up for what I had gone through. But there was a price: I couldn't get angry, I couldn't complain, and I had to adore him, no matter what. That was the unwritten bargain. Eventually that deal broke down. After eleven years of marriage and two children he began an affair with another woman. I was devastated, but I covered up my hurt so he wouldn't leave me, and it seemed to work. Everybody still thought we had the perfect marriage.

Friends said he adored me. On our twenty-fifth anniversary my daughter made a toast, saying, 'To the only happily married couple I know.' Famous last words! At that point my husband was involved with one of his students. I was crushed: I'd trusted him with my life, and he'd betrayed me.

"This time the affair did not blow over. My husband left me. That was so painful! I found I was reliving my earlier abandonment when I had felt that I must be bad because my mother didn't want me. This time I was hysterical—howling and screaming and wanting to vomit—all out of character for me. The loss of control terrified me. I was really afraid that my anger would smack up the whole world and make everything explode. Fortunately I was in analysis all this time, which helped, but it was hard work, reliving that early experience of being abandoned and wanting my mother so desperately. I even thought of killing myself, but I couldn't.

"Nor was I the only one suffering. My older daughter picked up some fear of abandonment too. After my husband left, she kept getting into relationships with men who were totally unavailable. She told me how she would wake up in the night and look at a man she was madly in love with and say, 'I've got to look at him because I may never see him again.' I felt as badly for her as I felt for myself.

"Eventually, in the midst of all the misery, I had this tremendous high, when I started to believe in myself. I became very active. I started doing things on my own, like mountain climbing and skiing. I felt wonderful knowing I was able to meet these challenges. It was exhilarating, and a huge relief. There is another man in my life now, and this is a good relationship for me. But sometimes I have this fear that he's going to die on me because he smokes. So the thing with abandonment is there—whether it's the war, infidelity, or even smoking. It's there! And I have to live with it.

"My experience convinced me that healing has to do with reenacting trauma. In that sense my husband's leaving was a great help to me because I had it right there: I was drowning in it. Still I find it's very hard to reach out to that little girl I was. There are still so many defenses against it. When you have such early trauma, you numb out. It lessens the pain to a level you can live with, but there is a whole part of the self that stays frozen—for years and years.

"That can get to feel familiar and safe, but it keeps you locked in the past because you are not allowing any kind of closure, which is so helpful in healing. So the experience stays with you. Details may be forgotten, but the feelings are alive, unacknowledged but still very potent. There's all that anger, for instance, and that saps your liveliness and your spontaneity. Even now I have to fight to feel more alive, to feel joy and even appropriate anger, and to get rid of that old dullness. I lost the ability to play, the ability to be silly, to have fights, to deal with competition. I don't know how to play! Tennis, for example, is a deadly serious business for me. And I have all these feelings about being the worst one in the group and losing, even when I'm playing with somebody who isn't as good as I am.

"I know I've underachieved professionally—massively! Early on so much of my energy was engaged in being nurtured and saved; getting what I didn't get before or feeling safe. But the other thing that hampers me is just not being aggressive enough. In hiding, aggression was really taboo. It's not that I'm shy, quite the contrary! I remember those early days in hiding when I had to be shushed. Now I have great impulses to shoot my mouth off—in meetings, for example. I annoy people terribly because I can never shut up, and then I get enraged if anybody tries to quiet me. Perhaps I have a wish to be somewhat exhibitionistic because that was so thwarted.

"I simply have trouble being aggressive enough in terms of promoting myself and my career. Aggression is still very frightening to me. I suspect that I'm afraid that it will make everybody go away. I have this crazy idea that you can't be loved and successful at the same time. You can have one or the other, but not both. So if you get out there and make money, then you're going to lose the person who would take care of you. When you have been abandoned, you need to have someone there for you and to care about you, someone who's not going to leave you. It is so very powerful and so overdetermined that it's hard to take a chance. It's really, *really* hard for me to take a chance.

"There's a syndrome of feeling left out and feeling different, and not fitting in, which is very powerful. Lately I feel more ordinary, and it's a very great relief. People ask me directions, and I find I'm still surprised that they would see me as someone who would know!

"There are other symptoms too. When you've been left so young, it's very hard *not* to feel that you're bad and that you're rotten and that if anybody ever gets to know you, they're going to run away from you because you are such a rotten and bad person. And that's compounded by the rage that you feel, just under the surface. As a child you're angry at the mother and father who left you. You're also afraid that your angry thoughts are dangerous to others. Later on you may actually start to do things that will send a person away. Or you pick people who will leave you. But you don't know you're doing it. It's very unconscious.

"Another legacy of my past is a kind of spaciness. I'm so busy processing my inner life that I get lost sometimes. I live in this town, but I can actually get lost in it! Feeling lost is a metaphor for not knowing where you belong and wandering all over the place. I can lose myself in time too. There are days when I'm not sure what day of the week it is. My man, Philip, complains that I don't listen—and in a way it's true; I don't listen when he's talking about concrete, technical things about the world. I don't have the energy. I'm gone! I don't even hear it.

"I do listen, but only when people talk about their inner lives. In a similar way I never read essays, only novels—and then I get buried in them. It's one of the ways I've gotten through life, even as a child. It's partly to escape, but it also feeds me. That same searching probably led me into becoming a therapist. For example, the anger and guilt that I mentioned before are true for a vast multitude of people I work with. One of the things that I get out of working with them is that we end up working on some of my own stuff. I can vicariously feel for them more easily than I can feel for myself sometimes.

"I consider it my job to bring people, or at least their emotions, back to life. This isn't limited to my professional life. For a long time I felt like my friendships were based only on that and that nobody would want to be my friend unless I was nurturing and rescuing and healing them in some way. Whether it's a patient or a friend, I can't bear it when someone is hopeless and wants to give up. It makes me furious. I want to shake them and I want to tell them, 'How dare you give up? How dare you want to commit suicide? How can you give up? You've got to try, you've got to live.' I get very irrational about it.

"I have a patient who's been trying to wear me down for months, telling me that she's hopeless and it's a waste of time and I should give up and you can't water a dying tree. The whole thing. I realize that my anger at her has to do with how hopeless I must have felt at some point and how much I don't want to feel that.

"My parents are still living. I recognize some protective

feelings I have toward them that haven't gone away. They were always gentle, but I've turned myself into a pretzel trying not to make them angry. The theory is: They suffered enough, so you can't be mean, you can't be nasty; you've got to be tactful and polite and good—super good. I have to be super good because a part of me still feels so bad, and there it is once more, that sense that if I'm not very, very good, people will leave me all over again.

"Finally I've had to face difficult issues of abandonment with my adult children. When my husband left, I remember those first days when I was alone in the house. My God, it was so strange, there was nobody in bed with me!

"My elder daughter moved in then. At first it was very stormy. She couldn't bear my pain, and she'd get furious at me and furious with her father. She'd call him up and berate him. One night we were running around the house screaming at each other. Then I had to have surgery, and that was the last straw. She didn't want to take on this responsibility at all. She even got furious about having to go to the drugstore to pick something up for me. I think it was just that we were very close—too close!

"Both my daughters still have a tendency to worry about me. I think they sense my vulnerability, and it scares them. When I went to the Hidden Child conference, there was a workshop on parents and children, and there was a lot of pain in the room. One young girl was talking about her mother who was not speaking to her because she moved out and her mother's pain and loss. I stood up and told my own daughter that I wanted her to stop worrying about me and to live her life. I wanted to set her free and I wanted her to know that I was very, very tough.

"She was embarrassed, but it meant something to both of us. Afterward we saw the other young girl in the hallway. She said, 'I was jealous when you said what you said to your daughter.' I told her, 'Well, I said it for you too.' Some time ago I asked my daughter to move out of the house. She's twenty-five and very messy. I'm not very neat, but she's a disaster! So that was very hard for me. I felt so incredibly guilty! I was sure that she was going to hate me. Shortly after that she went to Germany. Her notes sounded cold. I was convinced that she was going to forget my birthday. But guess what! She didn't forget my birthday! In fact she told me she was thinking about me all day. It's funny, but we've been getting along better since I told her she needed to move out. Maybe that was just what she needed to hear all along."

JOSEPH STEINER

Joseph Steiner, fifty-eight, is a brisk, friendly man with reddish hair, aviator-style glasses, and just the hint of a Polish accent. Sales manager for a printing company, Joe lives in an upscale New York City high-rise building with his wife, Marilyn; their eight-year-old daughter, Jenny; and a Persian cat. On a Sunday Joe is wearing shorts and a purple T-shirt with the logo of a helicopter-skiing center. An apartment on the thirtieth floor of their building is designated as a residents' lounge. There Jenny sprawls on a soft gray couch, listening to tapes on her Walkman, while Joe reads The New York Times *and drinks his tea from a Styrofoam cup.*

"I was born in 1934 in Warsaw, but it was only by chance that we were still there when the war began. In 1939, when the war broke out, my father went to Vilna. He made arrangements for the whole family to join him, and he even sent a car for us. But my mother said, 'No, how can I leave this beautiful house?' She was certain that the war would be over in a few months. Some neighbors from downstairs took our places and ended up safe in Australia.

"We were not so lucky. In 1941 the Nazis forced all seven hundred thousand Warsaw Jews into the ghetto. By Yom Kippur of 1942 most of them had been sent to the death camps;

only about ten thousand Warsaw Jews were left. My mother and my sisters, Ania and Nusia, and I were among those remaining. As far as the Germans were concerned, all the children were officially gone. I was still there because we were hiding out in a huge warehouse with a group of rag collectors.

"The warehouse covered a whole square block. It was completely filled with bales of rags. During roundups the Germans brought sniffing dogs inside the warehouse. Fortunately there were so many bales—hundreds of them, corridors of bales—they never found us there. Those dreaded roundups took place in cycles. It would be quiet for several weeks, then they would hunt Jews nonstop for two weeks or so. Then it would be quiet again.

"Once, during a quiet phase the night before Yom Kippur, I was filthy and covered with lice. My mother remarked that it was a miracle I hadn't died of typhoid. She said to my older sister, Ania, 'Why don't you take Jurek (my Polish name) and give him a bath?' Ania agreed. A couple of her friends, Ted and Stenia, who were hiding with us, decided to come too. Where did we find a bath? Very simple! You could just walk into any house in the ghetto. (Remember, you had an area of maybe two hundred square blocks, and not a person there.) If you walked into an apartment, you could even see food on the table that the family was eating when the Germans took them away!

"In the apartment we went into there was no hot water, but the plumbing was still connected. So was the gas. All we had to do was heat water in pots and take our bath. Our plan was to sleep there, wake up at four A.M., and then sneak back to our hiding place behind the bales of rags. That night we had our baths and quickly fell asleep. When we awoke, however, we were shocked to find that it was ten A.M.! One of my sister's friends had made tea and forgotten to turn off the gas.

Someone staggered to the window and opened it. We were groggy, but not too groggy to realize that we'd missed our chance. It was daylight. Now we would have to sit there until dusk before we could make a move.

"While we waited, we heard the Germans and the Polish police going by. I couldn't help wondering who they were taking this time, who they would find. Later, when it seemed safe, my sister sneaked out to see if the roundup was over. A little while later she came back and said, 'The Germans took quite a few people.' Then, in a very soft voice, she said, 'Mother and Nusia are gone.' Neither one of us cried. We just sat there on some deported and possibly dead stranger's sofa and looked at each other. You might wonder why we didn't cry. After all, I was just a little boy of seven or eight! But by then I was already numb! I had lost so many people: an aunt one day, a cousin the next. My only conscious thoughts were, This is the way it is. You were born a Jew, and Jews are meant to be hunted and killed. However, I wasn't going to give up! If anything, I felt more determined than ever to survive.

"Following that roundup it became very quiet in the ghetto. Ania and I moved into an apartment with Ted and Stenia and Ted's parents, Frances and Henry. Stenia was engaged to Ted. My sister, Ania, was engaged to Ted's brother, Wladek, who had escaped to Russia sometime earlier. In a way we were a family. That winter of 1942 to 1943 was freezing. When we needed wood, we went to another apartment and took a door. We cannibalized everything we saw. Nobody bothered us anymore. As long as we kept a low profile and stayed inside the apartment, the Germans never showed up.

"Finally spring came—along with another roundup of Jews. This time the Germans intended to leave no survivors. It seemed that the only way to stay alive was to find a way out. It was just before Passover when the first shots were fired. This was it! Ted, who looked Aryan, had sneaked out through a hole in the wall one night and made connections for a hiding place. Naturally I wanted very much to be taken away to safety, but I had competition: Frances and Henry had two nieces about my age. There were long, tense deliberations. Finally they decided that the girls, who looked very Jewish, were too much of a risk. I was chosen.

"What luck! I thought happily when they told me I was going. Looking back now as an adult, I can say that was selfish and callous that I didn't give a thought to the nieces. At the time all I felt was relief, which turned to excitement the next night when we all followed Ted through an unguarded open place in the fence—and out of the ghetto for good.

"This was mere hours before the infamous Warsaw ghetto uprising. Just as we got to our first Aryan hiding place, I heard a machine gun burst. The next day we heard more shooting and we could see smoke curling up over the ghetto wall. When it got dark that night, I went up on the roof. I could see the entire ghetto in flames. But I wasn't even thinking about people dying. For a kid my age it was an interesting sight, that was all it was. My thoughts were simply, I'm glad I'm on this side, not that side.

"After two days the Pole whom Ted had paid to hide us got nervous and told us we had to leave. Fortunately Ted had arranged another hiding place. This is what you had to do: hide here, but always know where you're going next. We had to be prepared in all sorts of ways. My sister, Ania, looked very Semitic by Polish standards. Whenever we traveled from one hiding place to another, she wore a black veil and carried flowers, as if she were coming from a funeral. That's a Polish custom. She walked very slowly and demurely.

"Unlike Ania I was blond. With the help of a little peroxide I became even blonder. When we left one hiding place to go to the next one, I never went *with* Ania, but always ten yards behind her. The theory was, if she was caught, why should I be caught too? One time I lost her! Confused, I went back to the hiding place where we had just been. Just as I arrived there, I saw a German truck pull up and park right in front. The police jumped out and began arresting the other Jews who had been hiding in the same apartment complex we had just left. What timing! As I watched the Jewish people getting in the truck, I knew that I shouldn't run. I stood there and watched as they took away two or three families, including kids my age.

"Meanwhile there were all these other Polish kids yelling, 'Dirty Jew, dirty Jew!' I started yelling, 'Dirty Jew, dirty Jew!' as well, so I wouldn't stand out and arouse suspicion. The truck left. I was still standing there wondering what to do when all of a sudden I saw my sister! She must have realized that she'd lost me—all this had taken maybe fifteen or twenty minutes. She had come back for me, and there she was, a block away, waiting with her veil and flowers.

"I followed her, and we made it safely to the next hiding place. Amazing, wasn't it? The reason I brought up this particular experience is that I was eight years old, which is my daughter, Jenny's, age. Under no circumstances could she think like that today. But you have to remember that I had been in the ghetto for three years already. I was conditioned. I was tough. What feelings did I have, all that time they were rounding up the other Jews? Only, I'm glad it was them this time, and not me.

"Here's the strange thing: I was never really scared! Going from hiding place to hiding place was a game of hide-and-seek. To summarize my odyssey, I hid in twenty-two places. Half the time we all stayed together, but sometimes I lost my sister for a day or a week and hid out by myself. I grew up in a hurry! I taught myself to read and write, and I even carried a map so I could plot the advance of the Russian armies. There was another element of danger: Out of those twenty-two hiding places I was in, at least sixteen of them were with members of the Polish resistance, who used me as a courier. Naturally this magnified the danger.

"The Pole would say, 'Do me a favor, Jurek. I want you to go to this place and carry these papers of onion-tissue-written orders.' The theory was, the Germans wouldn't spot a kid. I was eight or nine years old, hopping and skipping along! Not only was I Jewish, I was also carrying underground messages. Still, to me it was a game. I knew how to be careful. When I delivered a message, I had to watch myself coming back so that no one trailed me to our hideout. I moved quickly and I never took the same route back. Soon I knew Warsaw like the palm of my hand, as I climbed over garden walls and cemetery fences, always looking around.

"There was one very close call. As usual I was walking behind my sister when this guy in a leather coat with a Doberman pinscher on a leash started following her. I knew that he had to be either a Pole working for the Germans or a German in plain clothes. As I was trying to figure out what to do, he turned around and inexplicably started running toward me.

"At that moment I was standing next to a church. I knew that every church in Poland had a graveyard, and that every graveyard had a wall around it. If I jumped the wall, I would be in a completely different neighborhood. With no time to spare I dashed through that church, darted through the graveyard, and scrambled right over the wall. I cut my hands. Every wall in Warsaw had jagged glass on top. But so what? I was safe! And here was the child in me: A month later, when once again I was going from one hiding place to another, I saw that same church. I couldn't resist popping into that church's graveyard, just to find out how high I'd jumped. I stood there and gawked. It was so high! I said to myself, *Never!* I was impressed. It just shows what you can do when you're really under the gun.

"Our final hiding place, from the winter of 1943 until August 1944, was out in the suburbs with a young Polish fellow and his wife and mother-in-law. To get there, we had to take a train from the main station of Warsaw. The ride itself was less than an hour, but I had no shoes, only a pair of white sandals. This created a big problem. As bad as the Poles had it, they still had shoes. Maybe they didn't have leather shoes, but they all had something on their feet. If I'd gotten on the train in sandals, someone would have noticed. To avoid attracting attention, we put cardboard in the sandals and painted the whole thing black. Could you imagine? It was December, so I needed this disguise. I wore the painted black cardboard, and I made it. As for Ania, there were no flowers in December, so she carried a branch of an evergreen.

"The family we stayed with was nice. The only trouble was the man got roaring drunk every night. He had enough guns and machine guns there to start a war of his own. At last we were liberated by the Russians in August 1944. We were taken to Lublin, where I had my first bite of chicken, my first glass of milk, and my first chocolate in five years! Accustomed to a near-starvation diet of rotten potatoes, onions, and hot water, I got violently sick to my stomach for three days. Besides having food, another thing that seemed weird now was being able to talk. In hiding we only whispered. It took me two or three months to speak in a normal tone. Another habit that I still haven't lost is holding my nose when I sneeze, to stifle the sound.

"As soon as the war was over, Jewish agencies began springing up. My sister ran around to register with all of them, in hopes of finding her fiancé, Wladek. Then Henry, Wladek's father, took her aside and told her, 'Don't bother looking for Wladek, he's dead.' Ania was shocked. 'What do you mean?' she cried. 'He went to Russia.' Henry shook his head. 'No, believe me,' he said. 'I know! I dug his grave myself.' Even before we'd left the ghetto, Henry knew that Wladek had been killed. He'd had no obligation at all to save Ania and me, and yet he'd done it anyway.

"After that Ania, her new husband, and I wound up in a DP camp in West Berlin. Everyone wanted to go to America, which was the promised land. But you had to be registered in a DP camp in order to go. We stayed in the camp from 1945 to 1947. Everyone there was engaged in the black market. You bought anything American soldiers wanted to sell—whether it was truckloads of cigarettes or truckloads of canned peaches—and you resold it. I was eleven and peddling, stealing, selling, like everyone else. It was wild! It was beyond comprehension. I went to the movies twice a day. There were plenty of kids; there were soccer teams. I even went to Hebrew school there. My sister was looking out for me, but most of the time she was involved in the black market also. She went back to Poland, bought what the Russians stole, and sold it back to the Germans. Then the Germans sold it back to the French. It just went around in circles.

"I came to the United States in May 1948. I went to high school. Though my English was very poor, I graduated from high school with honors in math and later went to City College at night. Then I joined the army, but even my life in the army wasn't normal. I wound up working for the Military Intelligence Detachment (MID, a forerunner of the CIA) in West Berlin from '55 to '56. More hiding, more subterfuge, more games.

"After the army I went back to school, but I had trouble making the transition, so I went to a psychiatrist for about three years. That was when I realized what my problem was:

The war was not a reality to me. I had no feelings about it. Yes, people were killed. My mother and sister were killed, but I could never feel it. For example, there was one incident in the war when I was on a balcony, and there was a German soldier no more than a hundred yards away from me. I saw him lift up the rifle, aim at me, and shoot. Actually the bullet hit the wall a foot away from me, but I just stood there. I had no sense of reality. *It was like a video game!*

"I never discuss it: not with my sister, my son, my wife, or my stepchildren. This is the very first time I've talked about it at length. Sure, I've tried to tell a few stories, but there's no understanding. How can I expect a young person to relate to the time, for example, when my sister and I were hiding out in a small apartment facing a courtyard. During the day we sat in a corner the whole time and at night we moved around a little. If we went to the bathroom, we didn't flush the water. Every two or three days the Polish person who owned the apartment came in to bring us food, flush the water, and tell us what was new—how much longer we had to stay there.

"One night we looked outside and saw fifty Germans armed to the teeth with machine guns! We knew that they weren't looking for two young Jews. We opened the window, and we heard them talking. We learned that we were right in the den of the Polish Resistance!

"The German officers ordered the men to round up everyone and shoot on sight. They were ordered to search every single apartment: not to knock, just break the doors down and beat people up. Very quietly Ania and I made our way up to the attic. It was dark up there, but we saw that we were inside an apartment. In the next room someone was asleep, snoring like there was no tomorrow. I saw a uniform and a sword. Then we heard the Germans outside the door say they wouldn't come in because this was the apartment of the Japanese military attaché. Finally the Germans left the building. We sneaked back to our apartment and hid for two more days until the resistance person came—and we begged her to get us out of there.

"Is *this* a nice story to tell my family over a beer? How can they comprehend it when I have trouble understanding it myself? When I think about my life, what I miss is belonging. No doctors came from my family, no professional men. We were refugees, and my father, who got to New York in 1949, was a poor, broken-down Jew out of a Japanese concentration camp. Naturally I'm hoping that my own son will make it. I've been married twice, to Jewish American women, and each time I thought their families represented stability. I thought a country club meant stability. But Jewish nouveau riche is not real belonging at all.

"In so many ways I'm still hiding. I go helicopter skiing. I have a medal that says I have one million vertical feet skiing out of a helicopter. Half the people who go helicopter skiing in Canada are Austrian or German. I look at them and I think, If you only knew that I was in the ghetto forty years ago!

"Right now I'm not afraid of getting cancer. I'm not afraid of being run over by a truck. What I'm *terrified* of is that I'll be fired any day. I'm sales manager for a printing company, and I'm doing a hell of a job for them. But it's this fear! It's a great job and I'm happy there. Still, I'm looking for another or to start a business. I suppose I'm just looking for another hiding place. I had worked for another company for thirty years and then I lost my job because of the recession. There's a lot of misery in New York. You see the homeless. I have pity for everyone who's not working. But I never say to myself, I had it worse in the ghetto. It was a big game. That's all it was. I try to treat it cavalierly. If you ask me what's better, losing a job or going back to the ghetto, I'll take the ghetto. Of course it's ridiculous. The ghetto started out, as I told you, with hundreds of thousands of people, and by the time it was annihilated, who was left? Only a thousand!

"In general I'm still playing a game, still hiding. With me it's always the expensive suit, the designer tie, the Rolex watch. I am never myself because I spent all those years being someone else: peroxide hair and genuflecting everytime I passed the church. I knew the Latin prayers inside out. Even in the army I had two phony passports because of my work with the MID. Routinely I lie about my age. I tell people that I was an infant in the war. That way I can claim I don't remember anything.

"At least I am authentic as a father. My son, Perry, is twenty-six, and it hurts me that he goes his own way. My wife, Marilyn, and I have an adopted daughter, Jenny, a foundling from the Philippines. We're close. She loves me, I know. She gives me little cards, and so on. I am also the stepfather of two children, Tom and Pam. The kids are a reality—and I care so much! If anything, I worry too much about them. In other words, to me an accident is not just breaking your pinky. To me an accident is fatal.

"I still have bad dreams about the war, but they're very strange. In my dreams I'm always observing; I am never, never speaking. I'm always looking. The bad things are happening to other people. When I was unemployed, I had a dream that I was standing on a wooden platform at the railroad yards and they were sending the people to Treblinka. But in my dream I saw the Germans executing *American executives in business suits!* One of them was my director of manufacturing. I have only one or two of these dreams a year. God forbid if I had them every day. I would be in the insane asylum.

"In my dreams I always have the mind of an adult. And I'm always in short pants. Like in the ghetto and the ghetto is burning, but I always manage to escape. I'm always the outsider. That's the association I have. I'm a runner. One friend I run with is a psychiatrist, so I get free analysis. I tell him all my dreams, and he must know me very well. He says, 'Joe, you're a survivor, and you know why? It's because you're always on the outside looking in. Don't you get it? You're never really *there*.' "

CLEM LOEW, PH.D.

Clemens Loew, Ph. D., is tall and slender. He has a mustache, curly brown hair that is gray at the temples, brown eyes, and a substantial nose. Looking like a young, athletic Albert Einstein, Clem paces around his office—one wall of which is completely covered with framed degrees and honors. In a modest, almost boyish way Clem explains that in addition to being a psychologist and psychoanalyst, he teaches, writes books, and is a director of the National Institute of Psychotherapy, an analytic training institute of twenty therapists and forty graduate students. Clem is also a sculptor and photographer. A lot of success, he concedes. But still not enough to chase away some of the demons from childhood that continue to lurk.

"I was born in Stanislawów, which is Russia now, but was part of Poland in 1937. The war broke out in 1939 when the Russians invaded our country. However, things were still fine for us. My father was a bank manager, so we were comfortable. I was an only child. When my father carried me on his shoulders, I held on to his straight blond hair and I felt like I was on top of the world. My father seemed so very tall! He even protected me from my mother when she tried to make me eat something I didn't want, like eggs.

"But those innocent days were soon over. In 1941 the

Germans invaded Poland, took away our house, and put us in a ghetto. To me that was a drastic change, much as if a hurricane had struck. As a four-year-old I felt naked, exposed, vulnerable, deprived, angry, and confused. I'd just been literally stripped of all my toys and possessions. My room, my things, my order, and my friends were all gone! The most painful part of all, though, was seeing how helpless my father had become. Up to that point my dad, and my grandfather, too, had seemed so powerful and protective. But the Germans didn't respect them. Now suddenly life seemed dangerous.

"My father got hold of some false papers certified by the church, which was the best kind. There were only three sets: for my mother, my grandmother, and me. We three would go to another town and live as Christians, while my father and my grandfather stayed in the ghetto. Of course I would have liked it better if we'd all been together, but I wasn't worried when we said good-bye. I understood that this was only a temporary separation. It never crossed my mind that I might never see my dad again.

"With our papers my mother got a job in another town, and we rented a room from a Polish family. Each day while my mother was at work, I stayed with my grandmother, a tall, handsome woman. I have an image of my grandmother always smelling sweet, cooking something good like chicken-barley soup, while I stood beside her, hugging her legs. Late one afternoon we heard a noise and looked out the window. The Gestapo were coming! Without a second's pause my grandmother grabbed me by the hand and pulled me out a back window. We were able to intercept my mother, who was just coming home from work. Afraid to go back to our room, we spent that night hiding with Jewish friends. But those friends were frightened too. They made it clear that we could only stay there for one night.

"My mother and my grandmother had a more immediate concern: whatever jewelry or money that remained was in our rented room. There was a lot of discussion then about who would sneak back to get our valuables and who would stay with me. Finally it was my grandmother who insisted on going. 'Don't worry, I'll be fine,' she said, setting out. That night she was betrayed by the Polish landlady and then arrested and subsequently taken to a camp, where she was killed.

"It's amazing. My mother was only in her mid-twenties when all this happened. I look at my daughter, who is twenty-one, and it's incredible what my mother was faced with: losing her mother, hiding, having no money, and not knowing what to do with a son or where to go. My mother didn't give up; she pressed on with me to the next town, where we rented an apartment and she got a job. I liked the new place. There were other children in that building. I would play soccer with them. I was just like the others on the outside—noisy and playful— but inside I did feel self-conscious. My mother had warned me repeatedly, 'Don't yell too much, or you might get carried away and forget yourself.'

"Our landlady was a large, robust, and rather intimidating woman. One day my mother was working and I was playing soccer in the courtyard with the other boys. Suddenly the landlady appeared and walked toward us. It was like the sea parting as she walked right up to me. My heart was beating double-time. She said, 'Take down your pants.' I was terrified, immobilized. Somehow the pants came down. 'Take down your underwear,' she commanded. Somehow the underwear came down. I stood there, shaking with fear and shame, as she looked at my private parts. I could tell from her frown that she wasn't pleased with what she saw. Then she just walked away. None of the other boys said a word about what she had done.

'Hey, where's the ball?' one boy shouted, eager to get back to our soccer game.

"That evening, when my mother got home, the landlady asked her, 'Is he really your son?' My mother (who could have passed for Polish with her light hair and eyes and her small pug nose) was very smart. She knew something must be up. She said, 'I'm glad you brought that up. It's quite important, and you're right: Klemak *is* my son, but he is adopted!' 'Ah,' the landlady said, apparently satisfied. In private my mother scolded me, not because I'd pulled my pants down but because I hadn't told her what happened. Wearily she explained that we simply couldn't take this kind of risk anymore; stronger measures would be needed to protect me.

"The next day my mother went to a bishop and told him we were Jews. She promised to donate a lot of money to the Catholic church if he would take care of me. The bishop agreed, and he arranged for me to stay in a convent in a town called Olsztyn, outside of Warsaw. Great! We went by train. It wasn't cold, but I was wrapped up in a scarf and hat so that my curly, dark hair and big nose wouldn't show and give us away.

"When we arrived at the convent, a nun named Sister Leonia showed us around the clean three-story building with its large and friendly looking dormitory for the children. Suddenly my mother started crying. 'What's the matter, don't you like it?' the nun asked, troubled. My mother quickly explained, 'It's wonderful! I'm crying only because I'm so grateful.' That was where I ended up staying for the next three years. Emotionally I was numb. They treated me well, but I was just going through the motions of doing what I was supposed to do. I learned all the prayers very quickly, but I was aware of being different. Sure, those thirty Christian children at the convent also missed their parents just as I missed mine. But at least the Gestapo didn't come looking for *them*!

"I had several close calls. One time I was outside playing in the sandbox when a nun rushed over to me, grabbed me, and dragged me inside. She slid me under a bed, whispering, 'The Gestapo are coming to search for Jews.' I lay there terrified until the coast was clear. Another time the Gestapo did find me. The officers were actually dragging me away! One was yanking me out the door when a retired bishop living in the convent hobbled down the wide steps and yelled, 'If you take him, then you have to take me too.' He put his life on the line for me! The Nazis could easily have taken both of us, but for whatever reason they left me alone.

"Not long after that the Allies started shelling the convent with big guns because they thought it was a Nazi-occupied building. We all moved down to the basement. For months we had almost nothing to eat. We used to eat hard noodles in lukewarm water, which was all the cooking they could manage in the basement because it was too dangerous to go up to the kitchen on the main floor. The windows were covered with bricks, but one day a shell hit the window smack dead on. There was a red flash and the smell of gunpowder. I was thrown across the basement. It was pretty frightening!

"At the same time Warsaw was burning. We could actually see the fire. I cried, so afraid that my mother would be killed. One of the nuns tried to console me. I said, 'How do we know whose parents will survive and whose won't?'

"Finally the war ended. Parents started trickling in to pick up their children. As soon as someone came in, the news of 'a parent out there' spread like wildfire. We all made a beeline for the front door, hoping. Each time someone came, my hopes went up. Each time it wasn't my mother, I felt the shock of losing her all over again. If she was dead, who would ever come to pick me up? Nobody else knew I was there! I felt like my entire existence depended on my mother coming back for me. Luckily she did! She walked a hundred miles. When I saw her, I ran to her and we both cried. I just held on to her, and it was wonderful.

"My father, on the other hand, was gone. We heard that he died in a concentration camp. He actually broke out of a train en route to the camp. He and another man jumped off the train at high speed and they survived the fall, but then they went to see a friend, who subsequently betrayed them, and so they were sent back to the camp and killed.

"My life seemed to be taking many zigzags and turns. I had a tough time trying to make sense of the fact that one day I'd been a Catholic child—angry at the barber who suggested that I might be Jewish—and seven months later I was a Jewish boy in Munich, going to Hebrew school and waiting for a visa to come to the United States. I adjusted. One of the prominent characteristics of survivors is a chameleonlike ability to adapt to situations. I definitely had that.

"However, such radical shifts in identity do leave a mark. Maybe nobody sees it on the surface, but in my 'bedroom,' so to speak, where most people don't see me, another life goes on. That's what I struggle with, even today, almost fifty years later. Here's an example: I think if someone meets me, they would never guess my history. People may recognize a slight accent if they're sensitive to it. Most do not. One day I was in New Jersey. A Jewish organization had invited me to teach the Holocaust in public schools. As I was telling the kids about my experiences, there was this knock on the door.

"I was startled! I associated that knock with the Nazis coming to look for me. It was fleeting, it was a flash, and of course right away I told myself, Nazis aren't here, I'm safe. The children and the teacher would never have that kind of re-action. Of course there was no *real* danger, and yet my heart was pounding.

"That's not my only scar of psychological damage from the war. I know, for example, that I might feel anxious with strangers, especially if someone isn't Jewish. Is that surprising? After all, I had to literally hide my physical appearance and even my emotions for the first eight years of my life. I could not say my real name. I had to be careful what I said and who I spoke to. The word was mum: the less you said, the better. That's why I still have trouble revealing myself as freely as somebody else might.

"I also tend to be a little paranoid. I get a chip on my shoulder when I feel the remotest possibility that someone might be taking advantage of me. If I ask about a car rental and they quote the wrong price, I tend to take it personally as if they did it on purpose because I'm a Jew. I often overreact. I have a sensitive, raw spot about being mistreated, being lied to, not being accepted.

"Then there's alienation. I'm definitely not a hermit. I have colleagues and many friends. I have two great kids, and I'm even friends with my ex-wife. But in a gathering I often feel distant and separate from others. It's hard to let myself be vulnerable. It's hard not to confuse the vulnerability one needs in a relationship with helplessness.

"In part I've converted the old fear of helplessness into a demand for perfection in my children. I put pressure on them to be strong and successful, not in any specific way but just to develop themselves. That comes from my wanting to protect them (or maybe to protect myself *through* them) so that they won't have to experience problems, losses, disappointments, hurts. I'm sure that a lot of my childhood feelings of abandonment and anger have spilled over onto my children. If you don't get treated well as a child, it's hard to treat your children well when you grow up. I had a very disastrous and troubled childhood. That has made it hard for me to see at times who my children are and what they need. I wish I had had more compassion for them!

"It goes back to the fact that our parents themselves were stretched to the limit; they didn't have enough energy or know-how to help *us* get over the trauma. My mother was never able to help me deal with what happened emotionally. I don't recall that she ever talked to me about my father or asked me, 'How do you feel about not having a father?' Or, 'How is it for you?' I wish she had. She felt that I was just a kid, and kids don't remember anyway, so what's the big god-damned deal?

"We were just kids, but we had the pain! Nowadays if you're a cop and you kill somebody, you go for counseling, to be debriefed psychologically—and you should. On the other hand, we went through hell, and nobody provided any psychological counseling. We just had to deal with it. Children were ignored, and as a result a lot of us pushed our feelings under the rug. Maybe this is one reason why it's taken so long to 'come out' with those feelings in a public way.

"About six years ago I went to my first gathering of child Holocaust survivors. I walked in and sat down there in a very arrogant way. I felt above the others, convinced that I had more money and more professional credentials. I also felt I was more emotionally intact. I was putting up a wall of superiority to distance myself from the others. Then, as they started talking, I felt that wall come down. Suddenly I was with brothers and sisters! It was a powerful connection. Since then I've been to several similar gatherings, and I've even run workshops.

"I'm a scuba-diving enthusiast. Going to these meetings is a little like going diving. It's great to immerse yourself in the depth, but you can't stay there too long. If I do, the painful, vulnerable feelings from the past come up, threatening to overwhelm the successful adult I am now. Since I've been going,

I've begun to look at my childhood in a different light. I went through hell, but life is for learning. I believe that every experience has some value. I don't recommend what I went through as a way of developing a positive outlook, but I have it! I may feel doomed in the world, but a part of me knows that there is always another window to open, and that's a big help in overcoming a disappointment or a failure. No matter how dire a situation seems, I know in my heart that I can get through it and go on to something else.

"This year, for the first time, my son joined a group of other kids whose parents are like me, and afterward he said, 'Dad, I have to tell you one thing. I've been afraid to tell you this for a long time.' I kind of braced myself. Then he said, 'I'm angry at you for being a survivor.' He said, 'I know it's like saying I'm angry with you because you have brown hair. It's that silly. But I have to say to you that I am.' I said, 'Well, you know what? I am too!' I told him, 'I wish I was some guy that grew up in Connecticut and had fifty acres of land and a couple of servants, you know. Then I wouldn't have to talk to you or myself about this f—— trauma.' It brought us even closer than we were before.

"My own father is dead of course. I did have my Uncle Andrew, who survived the war in the Polish underground, disguised as a Catholic. Andrew was something of a substitute father. I always enjoyed calling him Uncle, because I didn't have someone to call Dad. Still, not having my dad was painful. I do love to talk about my father. If I get some emotional connection to him that way, I feel stronger for it. Over the years I've thought about him often. I've imagined the things we would have done together if he had lived longer. My mother and I came to this country when I was twelve. When I was in high school, we would have assemblies with an invited speaker, and I would always have this wonderful fantasy that the speaker would be my father. I imagined we would see each other and run down the aisle to embrace.

"I may never get through mourning my father. I've been to all kinds of workshops about saying good-bye to him and so on—but I still have this magical faith he may still be alive. I don't think I want to lose that! At these child-survivor meetings there's a bulletin board of missing people. I put up a notice about my father. Sure, I know it's probably futile, but I still do it, and I want to do it, because you just never know."

JOSEPH VLES

Joe Vles, fifty-two, is a friendly, compact man with curly hair and glasses, who likes to wear a tennis sweater and jeans. He has just moved from a New York suburb to a 1907 Victorian house in San Francisco with a view of the Golden Gate Bridge. Joe's daily exercise is walking the fifty-six steps up to his house from the street. Joe is director of Management Information Systems for the Computerland Corporation. "The title is fancier than the job," he says with a self-deprecating chuckle. At other times Joe has moonlighted as a flight instructor and an aerial photographer. He also wrote a self-published book of thoughts called Snow Clinging to the Window Panes. *Joe enjoys California, especially now that his wife, Deborah, has just been able to transfer her own career to the West Coast and join him.*

"I was born in Holland in 1939. By the time I was three and a half years old, the Germans were coming in the middle of the night and taking Jews away. My parents were grateful to be offered a hiding place. There was no room for the children, so very quickly they had to find other places for my brother and me. I was taken to a family named Dagnelie, who owned a plant nursery in a small farm community called Amerongen.

My parents didn't know where I was and vice versa. But the family treated me well, and several events stand out.

"One was a very sad occasion. The Dagnelies had a pig that roamed around the nursery, and everyone liked him. One day we had these little cubes of meat, cut up real small. We never had meat because food was very scarce. From the winter of 1944 to 1945 there was just no food at all. People ate whatever they could get their hands on: flower bulbs and tulips or nothing. Many people were starving. But we had this meat one night. I remarked about that. I said, 'Gee, this is very nice.' Then it came out that this was our lovely pig, our friend.

"The second event was terrifying. Because Mr. Dagnelie was in the Resistance movement, he was under suspicion. The Germans showed up at the house quite often, and when they did, I was hidden either in the basement or upstairs in the tiny, secret room that Mr. Dagnelie had made for me, with chests in the hall covering the doorway so it didn't even look like a room was there. I'm not sure I knew I was a Jew. I'd never even been in a synagogue. I did realize that the soldiers were coming to look for people they wanted to take away with them, and somehow I understood that I was one of those people. In that sense I was very much aware of what could happen.

"It was four or five in the morning when two German soldiers entered the house. They came upstairs and found my room. I was in bed of course when they shoved the door open. They were both standing there, pointing guns at me! I tried to shrink down, very consciously so that they would think I was pitifully small. It worked! The two soldiers stood there for a while looking at me. Then one of them said, 'Ah, leave him be, he's such a small kid.' I couldn't speak German at the time, but the words in Dutch were similar enough, so I understood.

"They lowered their guns and went back downstairs and

out into the night. I was lucky, I knew that! I also knew at that moment that the world was dangerous, and nobody, not even the Dagnelies, could protect me. In the months that followed, there were several more incidents with Germans coming into the house. One day five or six of them were down in the living room. We had drinking water stored in the bathtub upstairs because the water supply was not constant. You got water once a week if you were lucky.

"One of the soldiers was cleaning his gun when it suddenly went off, shooting a bullet right through the wood-beamed ceiling, into the tub. The water started dripping right on his head. I thought it was very funny, but even as a little boy I understood the psychological implications of this thing: It was a humiliating experience for the German. Obviously I couldn't laugh. If this German thought he was being made fun of, he could have killed us all right there on the spot. It took all my willpower not to smirk or giggle. I was very quiet. Finally he left. I felt enormous relief that we had all survived.

"The Dagnelies' house was on a hill. It had a big red cross painted on the roof so that bomber pilots would think it was a hospital. But bombs fell all around us anyway. Toward the end of the war it was mostly Allied planes, dropping bombs wherever they thought the Germans were. Each time we heard the sirens, I would run to the basement, thinking, This time, they're going to kill us for sure. The bombs made a very eerie whistling sound as they fell. Then for a fraction of a second there'd be total silence. Then, bang! An enormous explosion. After it was over, I'd go outside. There would be huge craters in the garden where bombs had landed. I loved to play in them. Those holes were probably only four or five feet, but to a little kid they looked much deeper.

"Finally we were liberated. Canadian troops were throwing loaves of bread and chocolate bars right out of their tanks.

I had never seen bread that white before. It seemed so special. Not long after that my parents came to pick me up. That was very upsetting for me, because I didn't even know who they were. Why were these two strangers telling me that we were going home? I didn't understand. I thought I was home. They said, 'No, we are your parents.' I didn't like it. I was wearing a short little brown pair of pants and a blue sweater. Holding my hand, they walked me out to somebody's car, an old Citroën. I felt very strange, sitting between these people who *claimed* they were my parents as we drove away from what I'd always believed was home. I cried, and my mother cried too—but for totally opposite reasons.

"My parents told me that my aunt and my grandfather had died in the war and that many other relatives had suffered horribly in the camps. They also told me that my brother, who had been hidden not far from where I was, had died of some illness because there was no medical attention at all and certainly not for a little Jewish kid who was in hiding. This was all news to me. I didn't even remember that I had a brother! After that I never went back to see the Dagnelies. I don't know why. I was only a child, but I don't know why I didn't at least ask to see them again. Now of course they are dead.

"I didn't stay long with my parents either. In 1947 I had to leave home to go to a Dutch sanitorium-school in Glion, Switzerland, because I had severe asthma. I saw my parents in the summertime, but I didn't *really* get home to stay until I was ten. However I don't remember missing anyone or feeling lonely. I told myself I didn't need my parents, that I could take care of myself. I taught myself to be pretty independent, and my mother reinforced it, telling me that I was a very wise young boy who could take care of myself. Even today she says, 'I thought you were a grown-up. *I* learned from *you*.' To cope on my own was exactly what I wanted to do! As soon as I turned sixteen, I left home and I never went back.

"That was a young age, but I learned very quickly how to stay out of harm's way. I developed a sixth sense, so that I always knew when I wasn't wanted in a certain place. You can feel it by how people look. For example, once I was in a shop where an obviously Jewish woman was pushing ahead. My feeling was, Don't do that, because that's very bad for all of us. When I looked at the shopkeeper, I could tell that he agreed with me.

"Today I'm still on guard, protecting myself. As a Jew I don't think I could ever get involved with the spontaneous, backslapping male bonding that goes on in bars where guys get together to watch football games. I wouldn't be able to let down my guard enough to have that kind of fun. I always need to know exactly what's going on. I have to be in control. Sometimes I think that's why it took me three marriages before I could feel at all relaxed or trusting.

"By the same token I know that my very practical, independent survival philosophy made life difficult for my four children. I'm close to them now, but I wasn't when they were younger. I didn't have the patience for their little problems. I often thought, Well, this is a tiny little problem in the scope of things, so why don't you get over this so we can concern ourselves with the larger picture? I was looking at the larger picture. I stood back and decided the trees weren't important, that what was important was the forest. You can't get emotionally or fully attached to this one tree, it just is not important enough.

"Now I'm finally realizing that this attitude is not so good, that people need to look at one tree—or one tiny child's problem. You need to spend time. That's hard for me. I have a tendency to distance myself quickly, not let my emotions totally attach to something—or someone. It's based on thinking: Why bother if I'm going to lose it anyway?

"It's been hard for me to develop a real, real intimate relationship. I've been married to Deborah, my third wife, for eighteen years now. I have the feeling that, yes, I can be myself. It's the first time! Deborah, by the way, is not Jewish. She is black. Sometimes I wonder if that was what I was unconsciously looking for. My first two wives were white Anglo-Saxons. Deborah is the only woman who has ever really understood me. She and I are extremely close. When I tell her what I went through, she often says, 'I understand that because I've gone through similar things.' She grew up fast also. In another sense we've grown up together. If you compare us now to, let's say, ten years ago, there's quite a difference.

"I'm still detached in the sense that I don't have any real buddies who say, 'Let's go play cards or go out drinking.' I don't do that. I feel that might be nice, but it's something I can't get into.

"Another way in which my personal life reflects what happened to me as a kid is the way I've approached education. In high school I didn't ask anyone for guidance, and nobody offered me any. I remember thinking to myself, Algebra will never keep me alive, so it's useless. I gave up algebra. I did learn languages because I felt that the study of language *had* the potential to save my life. Finally I dropped out of high school altogether, convinced that formal education was basically frivolous, offering nothing that I really needed.

"Now I'm fifty-two. I really wish I had a Ph.D. It's like a badge that gives you immediate recognition so that you don't have to keep proving that you're bright or that you know things. Still, I've done okay without even a high school diploma! I got into the computer field twenty years ago when it was new and nobody knew anything. There was no such thing as computer science and no school that taught it. I knew what I was doing. I even wrote a book on computers for the American Management Association.

"Some people ask if I'm bitter about the war and its aftermath. I'm not! In effect there are no hard feelings because I never had that much trust in other people in the first place. That's why I don't get mad. I think that's my legacy from the war, that I'm not an angry person. Sometimes I've felt that I'm a less than complete human being because I would never think of saying to someone, 'I trusted you and you disappointed me and I'm angry.' Instead I'm much more likely to say, 'Ah! You've changed your mind! I understand. That's only human, and that's okay. And have a nice day.' It's like, 'If I can please you and you're happy with me, then you won't kill me.' That approach has helped me survive and get along well with people.

"Of course, on the other hand, it's kept me from becoming a very good negotiator. That can hurt. In almost any job situation there's a certain point where you want to say, 'Okay, I will do this if you do that.' Instead my tendency is to say, 'I'll do it, I'll do it!' As a result I have colleagues I have worked with in the past who have negotiated much better deals for themselves than I've been able to do. I'm still cautious, but recently I've started forcing myself to negotiate instead of automatically giving in. Not long ago I was very surprised—and pleased—when, after a first round of negotiations, the other person said, 'Yes, you have a good point. Let's talk about that.'

"I know I was damaged by all that happened to me. Certainly having to leave the Dagnelies was the worst. Had my parents died during the war, I would have probably been quite okay. I would have been told at some point, and I would have said, 'Well, these people died, and that's how it is.' I don't know if I would have even been that upset. I never did feel close to them. My father and I were never friends. My mother's still alive in Holland, and we get along. We spar on intellectual issues, which is what she likes to do. In that way we're friends. Still, it's not a very loving relationship. We never hug or kiss.

"Sometimes I compare my situation to that of the people who experienced the earthquake in San Francisco. It happened two years ago. It was devastating then, but now it isn't a problem anymore. That's how I look at my own childhood trauma. The Germans terrified me, the bombs fell, and my parents took me away from the only family I knew and loved. And yet I survived it all! It's like a cork that you push under the water. You push it down, but it comes back up, and it floats again until somebody pushes it down again. Let go and it comes up. No matter how deeply it's been down, it still comes up. It's resilient—like me!"

RINA KANTOR, PH.D.

Rina Kantor, Ph.D., fifty-seven, looks more like forty-seven, with intense black eyes, a straight nose, and wavy, dark hair framing her round face. Tall and slim and wearing a turtleneck and slacks, Rina practices therapy and teaches social science at a prestigious midwestern university. Awaiting a student, Rina sits in her office at a huge desk with books and piles of what she calls her 'organized papers' and her 'not-so-organized papers.' At first glance the office seems devoid of personal items, but this is not so. Rina points out a little Indian box, a cowl from Barbados, a huge seashell from Israel, and large, colorful prints of a sunset and flowers. "These are all personal items," she explains with a smile. "But I'm the only one who knows that they are!"

"I was born in Berlin, Germany, in 1934. When I was five, my father was beaten to death in a concentration camp. Almost immediately after that my mother sent my sister, Tova, and me away to Belgium to stay with some of my father's relatives. She told us that she would join us there later. I'm not sure that I understood then that my father was dead, but I was frightened and very upset to be going away without either parent for the first time in my life. What's more, these relatives were total strangers. The first day there I held on to my sister for dear life and tried not to mind the scratchy wool knee socks my mother had put on me the morning we left Berlin.

"I felt timid, but my father's relatives were so warm and caring that I adapted quickly. They responded with even more affection. For example, they loved to hug, so I went around hugging everyone. I even taught them how to kiss 'properly,' which meant on the lips, as I had learned at home. To the outside world I was a cheerful child, avidly receptive to the loving kindness our relatives showered on me. In reality the double loss of my father and then my mother was more than I could deal with, so I buried my feelings so well that not even I knew how sad and bewildered I really was.

"Tova, four years older, was more reserved. I'm sure that she was suffering deeply, but the relatives soon tired of her reticence in the face of their attempts to draw her out. Sometimes Tova looked over at me, and I could see she was disgusted. Here I was, an adorable child getting all this attention when I was supposed to be the scared little *younger* sister, not the star of the show.

"A few months later our mother, Hanna, joined us in Belgium, just three weeks before the Germans invaded. My mother was savvy and realized that we had no time to lose, that one had to flee or go under cover. By nature a resourceful woman, she had saved some money. With it she was able to get us false papers. Believing strongly that there would be no safety in numbers, my mother moved us away from my father's large orthodox family. I didn't want that separation, but my mother was adamant.

"Shortly before we left the relatives, the Germans decreed that all Jews must wear yellow stars for easy identification. My mother received a number of these stars to sew on our coats. One afternoon she was sitting with our coats bunched up at her feet, ready to begin the sewing. Suddenly she dropped the needle and the whole sewing kit. In a quietly determined voice, she declared, 'I cannot do this.' She told us that wearing stars for all to see was like walking into the enemy's fire, *asking* to be deported!

"She said, 'Your father would not leave Berlin because he did not believe the Germans would ever harm us. Because of that misplaced trust, he was picked up as sure as if he had given himself up to the Gestapo of his own free will.' My mother continued, 'This must never happen to us again. We will never give ourselves up willingly. Instead we'll live like the goyim, talk like them, walk like them, and live in their midst. Only between ourselves will we know who we are, you hear me?' Yes, I had heard her. I was impressed by her determination, but I also felt a keen sense of loss.

"By accident, or so it seemed, we moved into a house occupied by German soldiers of the Wehrmacht. My mother saw this as a real advantage. She said that if we behaved properly, the soldiers could make us safer. First the Wehrmacht was not involved in the roundups of Jews, and second wasn't it unthinkable that *Jews* would look for safety so close to German soldiers?

"We lived there for about a year. During that time we *were* safe, just as my mother had predicted! Tova and I went to public school, where we learned Flemish and French. Tova was a whizz at numbers, had beautiful penmanship, and enjoyed reading, but I was a terrible student. I could neither read nor write nor understand the simplest arithmetic. I was humiliated when the teacher drew red lines through my work. At the end of the year she told my mother that I was sweet enough, well behaved, and that I sang pretty songs and recited little poems. However, I would have to repeat first grade because my schoolwork was '*tres, tres mal*' (very, very bad).

"That same year my mother was remarried to a man named Leon. Just as I was trying to adjust to that big change, the roundup of Jews intensified. It was no longer safe for us to remain in Belgium. My mother and Leon decided that we must flee to France. In preparation for leaving, my mother made us memorize all the information on each other's false identity cards and passports, including parents' and grandparents' false names, dates, and places of birth, addresses, dates of entry, and so on. As the youngest I had to learn the information especially well. The theory was that if anyone was taken in for questioning, it would be the little child. If the adults were lying, a child could be counted on to trip herself up.

"I sat down to learn it all, and I did it! It was a job not unlike the task of memorizing poems and songs, which I was so good at. (In fact it was the only thing I had been good at!) The night before we left, everyone was hiding jewels in clothing, including mine, and also hiding diamonds in condoms, which they would stuff in their rectums. I was so happy that I didn't have to do that; I felt sure that I had the easy job.

"The next day we were stopped at the border for a control check. Everyone was questioned, but just as my mother had predicted, I was the one who was taken away. A tall, heavyset officer led me to a large office with dark wood on the walls, a huge, heavy round desk and a red rug. There I was seated in a big chair and questioned. The interrogation seemed to last forever, but finally the officer told my mother that I had done well, and the family could go. Then he winked at me, as if to say, 'I know you're Jewish, but since you were so brave and withstood my test, I won't tell on you.'

"I was stunned. To my family I was a big hero. I alone had saved us all. Privately I felt ashamed that I hadn't done a good enough job. I hadn't fooled the officer; he had merely taken pity on me because I was the smallest one! But at the same time I did feel a certain excitement from having been helpful. That good feeling almost covered up the shame, but not quite!

"Crossing the border into France, we headed for Nice, where Jews still lived in relative freedom under the Italian occupation. My mother went to work as a broker for a *maison de haute couture*, while Tova and I were sent to a private boarding school in the city, for our security as well as our education. Two important things happened in Nice. First my mother decided that Tova and I should learn to swim. I never understood the reason for this seemingly whimsical notion. I can only assume that our mother was trying to prepare us for some unforeseen emergency, when we might have to escape through a waterway. We were taken to a pool. Tova went in first. The teacher put a belt around her waist and guided her in the water with a pole connected to the belt. He showed her how to move her arms and legs, and by the time Tova's lesson was over, she could swim!

"Now it was my turn. As soon as the teacher put the belt around my waist and lowered me into the water, I screamed in panic. I begged him to save me from drowning. There were faces looking down at me from the side of the pool, and they all seemed to be laughing. Humiliated, I promised to teach myself to swim. And I did! A few days later I tied myself to the stakes of a pier that jutted out into the Mediterranean. I hated it, but at least this time I was in control, and somehow I managed. I felt proud and vindicated, but again, not quite enough to cover the shame of having failed that day Tova learned to swim.

"The other significant event for me in Nice took place in the summer of 1943, when Leon and I were apprehended in one of the first large roundups of the Jews of Nice. The Italians had retreated from the south of France. The Vichy French, in compliance with strict Nazi rule, began the intensive roundups of Jews in the city. My mother—in anticipation of what was to come—had already prepared a secret second apartment where we could go to hide if necessary. Incidentally it, too, was located across the street from the authorities, in this case the French police. But I knew none of this.

"One day my mother and Tova were out doing errands. Leon was in our family's 'official' apartment. I was outside playing in the street. A gendarme came by and asked me where I lived. Oblivious to the change from Italian to Vichy French government that had taken place in the last few days, I pointed up to our apartment. When the gendarme asked me to bring him up to the apartment, I did.

"The next thing I knew, Leon and I were being taken downstairs and put into a car with a siren and a blue light on top. We were taken to a roundup place that looked like a very big police station, and we were kept there overnight. For years I have puzzled over this and tried to remember: Did Leon abandon me, or did I walk away from him? Did he tell me to leave him, or did I want to rid myself of him because he looked so Jewish and spoke with such a heavy Yiddish accent? I think he must have told me to let go of his hand and tell the gendarmes that they made a mistake, that I did not belong to him, that he was not my father, that I was not Jewish, and that my name was Helene Daveaux (the name on my current false papers).

"I cried nonstop for hours, in a panic, in a wail. I marched up and down the long hallways. To my right were offices; to my left, ugly gray shiny walls and large windows. I screamed at the police, 'My name is Helene Daveaux; I am all alone; this is a big mistake! You must take me home because my mother will be sick with worry if I don't come home immediately!'

"Eventually, after many hours of wailing and pacing up and down those horrid corridors, the gendarme in charge said if I was telling the truth, he'd take me home when he finished his paperwork. In the meantime I would have to be quiet because my screaming was getting on everyone's nerves. Several more hours passed, and I did remain quiet this time, but I still kept walking back and forth in front of his office, to remind him that I was still there and still waiting.

"Finally at the end of the day the gendarme took my hand and walked me to his car. He asked me where home was. I gave him my stepfather's cousin's address. I figured that as a French Jew, her name and address would arouse no suspicion. I wasn't going to make the mistake of giving our address again! The gendarme drove me where I said we lived. I thanked him and started to get out, assuring him that I could manage from there on and didn't need to be escorted to my door.

"He did not insist on crossing the street with me. I suspected that he, like the Customs official at the Belgian-French border, knew that I was Jewish but decided to give me back my freedom. I'm not sure what happened next. I know that I entered the house across the street from where the gendarme had let me off. I walked up the stairs to the apartment. But then, whether or not the woman let me in, whether she was at home ... or whether she closed the door in my face, whether she ushered me in, fed me, and then told me where my mother and sister were (in hiding by now), I do not remember.

"No sooner had I come back down into the street than I literally bumped into my sister, who had been sent to look for me. We fell into each other's arms. Then she led me to that secret backup apartment my mother had rented in case we needed to hide. When we got there, to 13 bis Rue Trachel, the green shutters were closed. It was all dark inside, but I could see my mother as well as a number of relatives and friends.

My mother held me close to her. We both cried. Then Tova told how she had found me.

"Everyone wanted to know what had happened to me and to my stepfather, Leon. I told them the whole story. Naturally they were terribly concerned for Leon, who was still in custody. But I was the child of the hour. Once again I was hailed as a hero, a brave little girl who had misled her abductors. The fact that Leon was still detained and the fact that it was I who'd been responsible for our capture in the first place were never mentioned. Inside, my guilt was enormous!

"To this day I am tormented, trying to figure out what actually took place. Did I really bring that gendarme into our apartment? *Had* I been playing outside? Or is it possible that we were captured in the apartment together, and only later, after I was released and Leon stayed behind, my mind distorted what had happened, so that I felt guilty for the beginning of our ordeal instead of the outcome? The fact was, Leon never did come home. He was shipped to Drancy and shortly thereafter transported in one of the boxcars destined for Auschwitz. But he never arrived there. In an attempt to save himself, he and two other Jews jumped off the train at a bend in the track. The other two men escaped, but Leon was shot. When they returned to Nice, one of the men told my mother the sad news. Then and there, as my mother would remind us later on, her hair stood on end and turned completely gray.

"From that point on there was no respite for the Jews of Nice. Roundups were becoming more frequent. Our hiding apartment was across the street from the police station. We saw the Jews being brought in each day. Clearly, it was time to flee. On September 8, 1943, we fled from Saint Martin, a nearby town at the foothills of the French Alps, into Italy.

"I don't know how this flight was organized. On the

morning we set out, there were eight hundred of us. In the evening, when we arrived at the *col delle finestre*, which was the plateau at the foot of the mountain range we were about to cross, many had already turned back. Tired but determined to go on, we bedded down to sleep under the open skies. I felt warm, happy, and safe under the stars as a small boy sang Yiddish songs. It doesn't take much for a young child to recuperate, if she has the resources!

"We were up again before daybreak, led by a guide. The paths were very narrow, and the slopes extremely steep. I remember the guide pointing out stones along the slope, marking the places where mountain climbers had fallen and died. That night many people turned back. In the morning, when there was just one huge stone mountain to cross, a pregnant woman ahead of me fell down on the path. Suddenly an avalanche of stones tumbled down in front of me. I was down on all fours, hanging on for dear life, with my mother behind me and my sister somewhere nearby.

"Finally to our relief we reached the top. Down in front of us we could actually see the Italian frontier! My God, I said to myself, I really did it! I was elated, and convinced this was the happy ending. As a child I was sure that each obstacle we overcame was *it*; there would be no more. It was dark as we descended into the little town of Valdieri. The guide took us to some empty Italian army barracks, where hot soup was ladled out of a huge vat. We all bedded down on straw, and I had no trouble falling asleep.

"Suddenly in the middle of the night I was awakened by my mother, who frantically told us that she'd had a *vorgefuehl*, or premonition, that something terrible would happen to us if we stayed in the barracks. Once again she felt unsafe with so many Jews in one big place. We had learned to respect her instincts, so we didn't argue. Heart pounding, I hurried out silently with the others. Exhausted and cold in our summer sandals, we walked for hours back up the mountain, our fear propelling us onward. At least we were hopeful. We were saving ourselves!

"In the morning when we looked down, we realized that we'd spent the night climbing and walking in a circle! Right there below us we could see the town of Valdieri and the army barracks we had left just hours earlier. Then we saw something else: There was a convoy of German soldiers below. The Jewish refugees who had been in the barracks were now being herded into German trucks. Some tried to escape—only to be caught again. We heard gunfire.

"Now we knew there was no turning back. Our only hope was to find someone willing to hide us. We stopped at one small weathered house with ropes of garlic hanging outside, apparently to keep bad spirits away. A fierce-looking Italian man with a big mustache came to the door. He seemed scared of us. In French my mother begged him to let us rest and give us some food, at least for the children. She would pay him, she assured him; she wasn't asking for charity.

"The man frowned. He went into his kitchen and came back with a shotgun. Muttering angrily in Italian, he pointed the gun at my mother. He shoved her away from the door. My heart sank. What would happen now? We trudged for quite a while, numb with hunger and exhaustion. Eventually we found a woman who understood my mother's offer to pay and took us to her little hut in the mountains. It was primitive. The fireplace had no flue, so the ceiling was black and the room was filled with smoke. We walked bent over, because since smoke rises, the only air we could breathe was from waist level down to the floor. This was where my mother cooked. Thank God, we had plenty to eat. We hid there for several months, sleeping in the barn next door. At first we froze, but slowly we acquired some winter clothes and wooden clogs. At night we slept in the barn with carcasses of little slaughtered lambs hanging over us.

"As spring approached, we had to find a new hiding place. There were bands of Sicilian marauders about. Some were deserters and others ordinary bandits who had heard that there were refugees hiding in the mountains. Some families in the area had already been raided and robbed. My mother felt that our best bet was to get to Rome, where we could hide in a convent. Our first attempt failed. We got as far as Bologna, but we were bombed out at the train station. The fighting between the Germans and the Americans was fierce. By sheer luck we managed to make it back to the mountains above Valdieri again.

"Several days later we tried leaving again. There was no choice now: The snows were melting, and the shepherds were coming back into the mountains to let the cows and sheep graze on the slopes. In part on foot, in part by train, and last by hitchhiking, we made it to Rome. Now my assumed name was no longer Helene Daveaux, but Elena Swenson. My mother claimed that she was Hungarian, married to a Swedish businessman. She went to the Swedish embassy and, with the special permission of the Swedish consul, placed Tova and me in the ultraorthodox Convent of the Order of the Dorothean Nuns, who were directly under the jurisdiction and supervision of the Vatican.

"At the convent nobody knew that we were Jewish. Believing we were Protestant, the nuns put a great deal of energy into teaching us the ways of Catholicism. We prayed in the chapel three or four times a day, often kneeling for hours on end. Tova's knees were swollen. I'm sure that my knees were swollen, too, but I felt that she was suffering more. I felt that as a younger child I was able to adjust better to new situations.

"I learned the catechism very quickly. I was fluent in Italian by then, and I found real solace in the church rituals. I even traded holy-saints cards, much like trading baseball cards, with a little Italian friend. I was a very good student and apparently a nice little girl, so the nuns decided that I should be confirmed in the upcoming children's communion ceremony. My mother, who visited us weekly from her own distant hiding place, didn't think this was such a great idea. She told the Mother Superior, 'No, Elena would be the oldest and tallest of all the children, and she would stick out like a sore thumb.'

"The Mother Superior was not so easily dissuaded. She wanted her Elena in the procession! So instead of making me into a communicant, she simply made me into an angel, who would lead the procession to the altar. There I, too, would partake of the wafer, the body of Christ, and be blessed by the Holy Father. I was very, very excited! I was dressed up in a long light-blue satin dress. One of the novice nuns put my hair up in curls with a hot curling iron. Finally a pair of real white feather wings was placed around my shoulders.

"Then, lice and all, I led the communicants up the aisle, where I took the wafer, was blessed by the Father Superior, recited the prayer, and sang the hymns. All the while I knew that my mother was watching from the balcony. This was a sheer heroic act on my part. I was living this double life and enjoying both parts. The nuns were friendly, and I was like their little mascot. Once again I felt a kind of charge.

"When it was all over, I ran up to my mother, kissed her, and whispered in her ear, 'Don't worry, Mommy, I am Catholic only on the outside. On the inside I will always be Jewish!' I think now of what it must have cost the child I was to do that kind of acting. I don't think I could have done it unless a part of me, deep inside, really wanted to be Catholic.

"When Rome was liberated in June 1944, we left the convent and joined our mother and an uncle in the apartment where they had been hiding on Via Bradano. Even then we didn't tell the nuns that we were Jewish. My mother had given this a lot of thought and decided not to risk offending their Catholic sensibilities. After all, helping Protestant children was one thing, but saving Jews was quite another! We told the Mother Superior that we were simply going on summer vacation and would return in the fall. Of course we did not return. Instead we went to an Italian public school, where now I finally had my real Jewish name back again: Rina Kantor. I was a dazzling student! I spoke Italian fluently and knew both northern and southern dialects. On top of that I sang Italian folk songs and would eagerly put on little shows for anyone who would pay attention.

"More mastery! Once again I felt I had it made. I was not at all prepared for what was yet to come: Shortly before Passover in 1945 my mother decided to send Tova and me to Palestine. The war in Europe was still raging, and bombs were falling over Belgium. Through contacts my mother was able to get us two very precious places on a ship to leave from Bari, a city at the southern tip of Italy's boot. Off we went, along with five hundred orphaned Jewish children aboard.

"I didn't want to go. My mother had told us that while we were gone, she would try to return to Belgium with our uncle to seek any other survivors in the family and retrieve whatever valuables she'd left with non-Jewish acquaintances. Even with her explanations this separation was unbearably painful for me. Tova and I were seasick from the moment our ship left the harbor. Neither of us recovered until we reached the shores of Cyprus, where we were quarantined by the British for health reasons. We were placed in barracks with long halls and many offices. There were British soldiers everywhere. The refugee children stood in line for everything: health examinations, soap, toothpaste and toothbrushes, for delousing, for little tiny combs that caught the lice in one's hair when one combed it wet, for food and drink, and for sheets for the cots. I thought back to the roundup place in Nice. I wondered if this was what a concentration camp was like.

"Finally I was taken in for official identification. This was the last queue. 'My name is Rina,' I told the British soldier. Now I could drop all my Christian aliases. No more Hella, Helene, or Elena. I vowed that from now on I would be known by my Hebrew name only, and I've never changed that, not many years later, when we came to the United States.

"Tova and I were pretty frightened. At least we had each other, and we were inseparable. Then the day came when we were shipped off to Palestine, to Ben-Shemen, a fine agricultural youth village, which had agreed to accept a certain number of Jewish refugee children. Now we were separated for the very first time since the war had begun. As an eleven-year-old I was taken to the children's village. Tova, who was fifteen, was taken to the adolescents' village.

"These places were less than a mile apart, but to me I felt as bad as if we'd been sent to different continents. I had to undergo a second delousing, followed by a welcoming address by the houseparents. That was when I lost control. I began to cry and didn't stop until they got Tova to come and calm me down. I was overjoyed to see her. As soon as I stopped crying, they took her away. I was in tears all over again, inconsolable this time, but this time they wouldn't bring my sister back.

"Eventually I fell asleep. In the morning I wouldn't speak to anyone. I refused to eat. Luckily my houseparents were very patient. My housemother, Betty, invited me into her little house each day and let me admire the pretty objects that stood on the bookcases. Her husband would sit with me for hours

170

after the official mealtime was over, encouraging me to eat. More than once he even fed me himself, which was definitely against his better judgment as a professional educator.

"At last I did eat. I also went to school. I was in fifth grade now, and I learned Hebrew, English, and some Arabic. I got involved in class projects, too, and made a lot of friends. In fact by 1947, when my mother received permission from the prime minister of Belgium to bring her children back, Tova and I were somewhat reluctant to leave! The story goes on and on. Life had its ordinary pleasures and common miseries, and we thrived more or less. But for me it was always of utmost importance to remain a star. I made it my business to excel in everything I did, but with a certain self-deprecating smile and a secret feeling that nothing was really that important anyway.

"Through the years I was never reticent to talk about my hiding experiences. As a mother I made sure my children knew about the Holocaust from the time they were three or four— just able to listen and understand. They learned of their mommy's 'heroic' feats, as I told them stories of hiding and rescue with fervor and imagination, at bath or bedtime, or when I was driving them to nursery school.

"But that was several years ago, and now you're catching me at a time in my life when I'm reviewing things for myself, and I don't feel particularly like a hotshot. For years I only celebrated the mastery and I covered up the pain. It is only very recently that I have allowed myself to discover the painful and terrifying feelings that lay buried within those feats of daring.

"The fact was I'd become virtually addicted to the feeling of excitement which came from being a winner in difficult situations. It not only felt good, it covered up the pain! Take the Leon story, for example. It's still hard for me to remember that I allowed myself to enjoy the applause when I felt so guilty about having left Leon behind. I realize that as a child I was in no position to examine my feelings—or even feel them. I was too busy coping. You push it all down, and you don't look at what you're losing.

"Now I see my own experiences from the age of five through ten as a series of heroic feats. Because my abilities were stretched to their limits and at times led to miraculous results, I gained a sense of mastery which was greatly needed in the life-and-death circumstances we were in. I came away from the war feeling larger than life, with an illusion that others depended on me for survival.

"I know that even today I have a sense that my importance derives only from what others can get out of me, for the function I can serve for them. I guess it's not surprising that I became both a teacher and a therapist. It's also a characteristic of my personal life. Take the recent episode that occurred at my sister's pool. Her grandchildren wanted to learn to dive. Tova said to one of the girls, 'Ask your Auntie Rina, she'll teach you.'

"It was true, I'd learned to dive in Palestine and I'd even won some dive-and-swim races. But that was forty-three years ago! I declined. Still, the children wanted to dive but were scared to try it. Their father was egging them on, telling them that there was nothing to be afraid of. So for their sakes—as well as the sake of the child I still was—I taught them how. I hated it! I'd really never overcome my old fear of water. But I did it for the children. I also felt a certain exhilaration! I had to smile, too, because at the age of fifty-six it still mattered very much to me that I had good posture, the kind required for race-diving from the side of a pool.

"Clearly I am still doing everything I can to be a hero. I want to save the day! Deep down I am often very sad, and sometimes I don't even care if I live or die. I'm haunted by the contradictions and my own doubts: *Was* I heroic—or was I just lucky that people were kind to me? I only hope that in time I will gradually learn to accept the somewhat competent, certainly not heroic, and also not-so-perfect little girl I was—and remember how frightened and lonely and needy I was."

STANLEY TURECKI, M.D.

Stanley Turecki, fifty-five, is a handsome and rather debonair-looking New Yorker with dark hair, dark eyes, and a British accent. His real-life demeanor is far friendlier than what one might expect after having seen the rather brooding photograph on the flap of his best-selling book, The Difficult Child. *Stan, a psychiatrist, founded and directs the Difficult Child Center in New York. He is a renowned expert on children's feelings. Yet he has so little recollection of his own feelings as a pre-schooler hiding in Poland that he asked his charming older cousin, Salka Mandelbaum, to listen and fill in the gaps. Salka agreed, and it was on a summer evening in her apartment that the story of Stan's hiding emerged—not in one voice but in two.*

STAN: "When I was born in 1938, the family lived in Suwalki, near the border of Germany. When the war broke out, we moved to Vilna, choosing to be under Russian rather than German occupation."

SALKA: "We had already left. We escaped just before the war started, but I do remember you as a baby in a carriage in the summer of '39. You were a beautiful baby—and so good too! Everybody was very proud and made a fuss over you. Then I didn't see you again until 1945. I only know what happened to you from your mother's stories."

STAN: "Well, that's what I know as well. My knowledge begins from the time that the Germans attacked Russia in 1941 and occupied Vilna. All the Jews were forced into the ghetto. We lived in a small apartment with lots of other families. One night the police were rounding up children to be killed. I was a toddler then. My parents hid me in a closet. I don't think I was especially scared. I was a kid who could be very happy on my own, pretending, dreaming, humming to myself. I also trusted my parents completely. If they said, 'You have to stay in there and be quiet,' I did that.

"It worked! The police never did find me. It wasn't long before they came for the men, and that time they took my father away to be shot. At that point a lot of other men would have given up, but not my father! He took off his gold watch and slipped it to the guard who was walking the men to the shooting place. This bought my father enough time to break away, down an alley. When the other guards noticed that my father had escaped and started shooting at him, he was over a wall and out of sight, gone!

"He jumped over the wall, and then he came back for us. Sometimes I've wondered, Was he really a great, courageous man? I'm not sure about that. I think he liked gambling, and he was physically adventurous. He seized that opportunity to escape. He came back to the apartment, and he said to my mother, 'Come on, we're leaving.' He had wanted to take other relatives, too, but they were afraid to risk escape to the unknown. My father took off his yellow star and very calmly walked out with my mother and me following. The assumption on the part of the guards was that nobody would have the balls just to walk out unauthorized, so they assumed it was okay and didn't try to stop us.

"This was an amazing thing for my father to have done. I've read that one person out of something like three thousand had the courage to walk away from the ghetto or break away en route to a concentration camp. I've tried to understand what it was about my father that led him to take that risk."

SALKA: "He was a nice guy, a good person. I loved him! It must also have helped that he didn't look Jewish. He was tall, blond, and very handsome."

STAN: "I know that he had business connections in Vilna with a Polish Christian family that hid us for a short time. Do you know anything at all about that family, Salka?"

SALKA: "No, only that they were very, very nice!"

STAN: "Do you know how my father knew them?"

SALKA: "No. I only know that for a long time your father had been busy making contacts. When it was time to go, he was prepared. He was out all the time looking for connections, ways out. He always had his eyes and ears open. His brother was taken right away and finished! But my mother used to say that your father would survive—and he did."

STAN: "He was able to get us false papers that said that we were Polish and Christian. Instead of Turecki, our name was now Fialkofsky. To me that sounds more Jewish than Turecki."

SALKA: "No, Fialkofsky is a real Polish name."

STAN: "The next thing I know is that my father joined the Polish underground. For the rest of the war, whenever he could pass information to the Polish underground, he did. From the day we left the ghetto, I was raised as a Christian child. I was taught Catholic prayers, and I was not allowed to pull my pants down to urinate because I was circumcised."

SALKA: "Right. They didn't use psychology, they scared him! His parents told him, 'They'll kill you, they'll do something to you, they'll take you away forever.' "

STAN: "Well, obviously I must have gotten the message!

They also must have watched me very carefully. Then we settled in a small village that was under German occupation. There my father became the right-hand man of the local Gestapo commander. That man really liked my father a lot. He was always saying in a friendly and admiring way, 'Fialkofsky, it's a pity you're a Pole. You really ought to be a German.'

"Apparently I was a happy little boy. I used to take my little bowl of whatever they fed me, cereal or fruit, and I would sit outside on the porch of the house where we lived and sing to myself. That I know. I also learned a lot of Catholic prayers."

SALKA: "He knew everything by heart. The priest was so proud of him."

STAN: "I seem to recall that the village was surrounded by a forest."

SALKA: "Yes! That forest was the place where the Nazis would bring Jews from the Vilna ghetto and shoot them. Stan's house faced the forest, and Stan's mother used to see the shooting in the daytime and hear it in the middle of the night. The Germans would make the Jews dig their own graves. Then they shot the Jews and put them in the graves: cover it up, and that's all! His mother was haunted by those sights and sounds. For the rest of her life she would see it and hear it all happening again and again in her sleep."

STAN: "While we lived there, my father used to pass all the information he could get from this Gestapo officer he worked for on to the Polish underground, who used it to blow up trains. Then at some point rumors began to circulate in this little village that Fialkofsky, of all people, had a Jewish wife."

SALKA: "Your mother did look Jewish. She was dark with green eyes, a real Jewish type, a beautiful woman."

STAN: "That's true. She had dyed her hair red, and she stayed home a lot to avoid close scrutiny. Still, the rumors grew more intense. Finally my father made an incredible decision. Based on nothing but his own intuition and trust, he went to the Gestapo commander he'd been working for now for six months, and he told him the truth. He said, 'My wife *is* Jewish. We are all Jewish.' "

SALKA: "Oh, my God! I didn't know *that*."

STAN: "You didn't? He told him we were Jewish and asked for his help. The man apparently blanched, but because he liked my father so much, he gave us twenty-four hours to leave before he blew the whistle. We packed up and left as quickly as we could. I am not sure exactly where we went. Eventually we found ourselves deep in the same forest, living with a hermit. His name was Franckiewicz. He had dark hair and a beard, but he was gentle, not frightening to me at all. He took us into his little hut in the middle of nowhere. That was where we stayed for the rest of the war. So we were hidden, first by my father's associates when we escaped the ghetto; second, in a funny sort of way by this Gestapo even though we didn't live with him; and then by Franckiewicz.

"In 1945, when the war was finally over, we left Poland and went to live in Stockholm. That was when I saw Salka for the first time since I was a baby."

SALKA: "Yes, you were seven. You stood there in the doorway, and you looked at us. You said, 'You are Jews, and I hate you.' I will never forget this as long as I live! You also had the picture of Jesus Christ or the Mother, whatever it is, hanging over your bed. We couldn't talk you out of it. You used to say the prayer every day, every night. I don't know how you knew we were the Jews. But you said, 'You're *Jews*, and I *hate* you.' "

STAN: "I must have been taught to hate Jews during all

those years when I was brought up as a good little Catholic Polish boy. But there may have been another reason too. I'd just as soon not get too analytical, but I'll concede that it must have taken a lot for me to maintain that pleasant, confident facade all the time we were in hiding. Perhaps this apparently random anger came from that."

SALKA: "He was very wild. He didn't listen to anybody. He was running in the streets. He was a wild animal. But he was wonderful!"

STAN: "Come on, Salka. You can't be like an animal and wonderful at the same time."

SALKA: "You can, and you were! You were very smart. You were talking Swedish, it was unbelievable! And you were athletic."

STAN: "I was a bobsledder. I won the Junior Swedish or Junior Stockholm title. I'd go down that U-shaped bobsled run. The people would link arms over the U-shape as I came down the tunnel."

SALKA: "You said you don't remember, but you do!"

STAN: "We had a good life, and my father made a lot of money. Then the Cold War began. That was frightening for Jews, so we went to South Africa."

SALKA: "Yes, you wanted to go to the United States, but the waiting list was too long."

STAN: "I had a bar mitzvah in South Africa."

SALKA: "Why not? His mother came from an orthodox family."

STAN: "I did go to a Catholic school in Capetown. That was only because it was academically better than the public school; we weren't hiding our Jewishness. When I was fifteen, the great happiness that my parents had enjoyed in Sweden disappeared. My father lost his money, and their marriage really deteriorated. I think for many couples the war was a unifier, a focuser on things that were of such paramount importance that everything else faded into insignificance.

"During the war and hiding, the fact that my parents hadn't been happily married became irrelevant. But later on apparently the chickens came home to roost. I was unhappy because they were unhappy together. There was the gradual dissolution of my parents' marriage, and yet it never fully dissolved. My father would travel between Capetown and Johannesburg, spending many months away from the family.

"I graduated from high school at sixteen, and my parents sent me to medical school. They felt that if I was a doctor, I could never be trapped anywhere, because doctors are needed all over the world. It was in my third year of medical school that I discovered bridge. Very quickly I became a real expert bridge player. That was what I did for most of my latter years in medical school. When I came to New York, it was as much to pursue a bridge career in the mecca of bridge as it was to pursue a psychiatric career.

"There were a number of factors involved in my leaving South Africa. The political situation was a minor factor then. But when I look back, I think it was more important than I realized—not so much that I was making a political statement, but basically because I believe very much in the American system in which you have the freedom to be whoever you are. In South Africa you didn't. That was as much a social issue as a racial issue. Even within white South Africa the prescribed rules of behavior were very much fundamentalist, like Southern Baptist. I couldn't stand that restriction.

"Another attraction was simply going to a city like New York and cutting my teeth there with the big boys, I liked that! In fact it was a very famous professor of psychiatry in New York, named Harry Weinstock, who was also a bridge player, who arranged for my immigration. For the first two years that

I was here, I achieved a level of success in bridge that no foreigner had ever had up to that point. Then, in 1971, I completely stopped playing. This is where my background begins to tie in: the concept of abrupt endings. I learned early that when you're finished with something, you're finished, and that's the end of it: the ghetto, the Gestapo, Sweden, all of it.

"I think all those moves in some way made it easy for me to adapt to new situations. However, it gave me a style of saying good-bye which hasn't always worked well. Of course the positive side of making clean breaks is you're able to move on to new situations in life. I've always been able to do that. It's just the times you really need to mourn and to feel the sadness, that gets a little stunted. When you say, 'That's a closed chapter,' and wash your hands of something, you never give yourself the opportunity to say good-bye from the heart or have the kind of transition that really allows you to feel the good-bye.

"This is a recent emotional insight for me. Both my parents died after I moved to New York. While I returned to South Africa for the funerals and did all that needed to be done, I never really mourned them. A few years ago, after my marriage ended, I met and fell in love with a woman named Roberta, who died a year ago. Today is actually the anniversary of her death. Earlier I'd learned to deal with powerful and difficult situations by distancing, just removing myself. But with Roberta I stayed to the end. It was very painful, but also liberating.

"Another way that my childhood affected me deeply was the fact that we lived in so many different countries. That made me appreciate diversity and respect people for their differences. This ties in directly with my professional work with difficult children. I have a very broad view of normality. I believe that you can be different without being abnormal. This is really what *The Difficult Child* and my new book, *Emotional Problems of Normal Children,* are all about.

"I admit that my normally nonjudgmental approach has a limit, especially when it comes to Germans. I can't accept them! Even the younger ones make my skin crawl. Not that I am afraid of anti-Semitism. I'm not! Nor do I worry about plane crashes or earthquakes. I am not bothered by going down to the Deep South in case the Ku Klux Klan is on the lookout for Jews—though I know many people from my background are. I have an almost instinctive appreciation of the concept of fate and destiny, that certain things happen in life that are beyond our control. Instead of making me scared, that's given me a clearer understanding of what I *can* do something about—and what I can't.

"Finally, I don't know if it's my father's genetic heritage or the result of what I lived through, but I've always been able to go into the unknown and not be scared. When I was younger, I expressed it in silly, stupid risk taking, but as I've matured, it's become a refusal to be intimidated by something simply because it is unknown. I do believe that I would have been a rescuer if the situation had been reversed.

"Certainly, hiding, escaping, and my father's daring were shaping experiences in my life. But here's the important thing: I don't look at it as, 'Oh, my God, this happened to me.' I think that this experience contributed to who I am in many positive ways. I don't like self-pity, and the kind of literature that used to come out about the Holocaust seemed filled with a victimlike attitude. It's only recently that I see the atmosphere shifting toward a recognition of the courage and the nobility of the people that survived. *That* speaks more to me."

AVA LANDY

Ava Landy is pale and poetic-looking with flyaway hair, no makeup, and a black sweater and skirt. Ava works in a cancer-diagnosis lab, and lives in an older New York City apartment surrounded by her own paintings (mostly nudes), Matisse prints, and an enormous amount of blue and white pottery she picked up in Israel, Holland, Spain, Portugal, France, Belgium, and Greece. The three large white bookcases in her living room are filled with books and favorite music recordings, mostly baroque. There are many plants—some six or seven feet tall in tubs, others hanging in front of her two bay windows. But all the apparent serenity is shattered by the sound of the doorbell. Ava's hands shake. "It's terribly upsetting, even when I'm expecting somebody," she admits.

"I was four years old on Yom Kippur in 1942, when the Gestapo burst into our home in Antwerp, Belgium. My mother had put the three of us: my younger sister, Alice; my elder sister, Celine; and me in bed. She had a certificate from a doctor saying that we were all sick. This was important because the Nazis weren't picking up sick children at that time.

"We all froze when the six or seven SS officers came in. There were so many men, all demanding to see my father. I lay trembling under the covers as my mother lied and said that she didn't know where my father was. Actually he was on top of the roof. The SS men searched inside the house, and then they left. Thank goodness! We were safe, at least until the next morning. The SS never came twice in a day. However, this time they did come back! Just a few hours later we heard the dreaded knock. My father turned pale. He had no time to hide on the roof. Quickly he jumped into the armoire and closed it tight. The knocking grew louder, angrier. My mother opened the door. Again she told the officers, 'I don't know where he is.'

"I was too scared even to move as the officers milled around. I don't know if I understood what was about to happen, but I knew it was very serious. I huddled against my sisters for comfort. Suddenly one of the men caught sight of my father's jacket on a chair in the living room. 'Okay,' the officer said to my mother. 'If you really don't know where he is, we'll take the children instead.'

" 'Oh, no, you won't!' my mother cried. 'You'll have to shoot me before you take my children away.' Hearing that, my father came out of the armoire and agreed to go. The rest happened in a flash. My mother gave him some money—or maybe he gave her some. A moment later he was out the door. Just before they took my father away, one of the soldiers who was younger than the others and still had a little decency made a warning sign to my mother to get out or they'd pick us up too. My mother wasted no time. She gathered up our valuables and we fled.

"I wish I could remember where we went. I know we took our most prized possessions to a Gentile friend of my mother's named Maria for safekeeping. Then we went into hiding: a whole succession of different places, first in Antwerp, then in Brussels. We had to stay one jump ahead of the Nazi sympathizers, who were eager to denounce us. I don't recall any of our rescuers' names or faces. I only remember how cold it was hiding in one attic with a broken window and no blankets.

"One night I was walking quickly and silently, holding a strange woman's hand. I whispered, 'I have to do pee-pee.' She whispered, 'Do it right here. Do it on the street.' I said, 'On the street? In front of everybody?' A moment later it was dripping down my leg, making my socks wet, and I was so embarrassed that I'd had to do it in the street. But there was no place to go!

"There were very few hiding places where we could all stay together. Poor Alice, the youngest of us, had the worst of it. When she was only one and a half, my mother left her with a couple who abused her terribly. They got her drunk on beer and wine, just to amuse themselves. They would lock her in the bathroom and leave her there crying for hours. She even had to steal food from the dogs because they didn't feed her. My mother was heartbroken, but she had no other option. She needed a hiding place for Alice. It just shows how desperate the situation was: My mother knew what was going on, but she still had to leave Alice there. As cruel as those people were, my mother felt that they wouldn't hand Alice over to the Nazis.

"Six months after we left home, we found a woman named Madame Louise, who was willing to hide my mother in her attic. Madame Louise also made arrangements for my sister, Celine, and me to go to a convent called Institut Notre Dame des Sept Douleurs, in Weezenbeek outside Brussels. Only the Mother Superior knew we were Jewish. The nuns didn't know, and we had to use false names. Mine was complicated, and I kept forgetting it. Still, I kept up the pose. I knew it would be the end if I didn't. Sometimes Madame Louise would visit us and she'd bring my mother. Because my mother looked very Jewish, we were instructed to run and kiss Madame Louise and call her Mama while our mother sat on a bench in the shadows watching.

"We stayed at the convent for about a year. In 1944 my mother made arrangements with the Belgian underground to get us into Switzerland. A truck came for us in the middle of the night, and I sat on a strange man's lap. This was how we got to another hiding place in France en route to Switzerland. When we arrived at the Swiss border, there was some problem. The adults pretending to be our parents were turned back. I just stood there not knowing what to do. Then somebody shouted to my sister and me to run under the barbed wire; the police would pick us up on the other side and take us to safety.

"I ran—and got caught on the wire. My coat ripped, and I was terrified. It was a coat with a velvet collar that my mother had made for me, and I was afraid she'd be angry. At least we made it across the border. The police took us to a refugee camp. A series of different families took care of us until after the war, when my mother came and took us back to Belgium.

"We did not receive a warm welcome home. Madame Louise, who had helped us so much during the war, was bitter over having lost a daughter. Jealous of my mother for having three children, Madame Louise was now deeply anti-Semitic. Nor was she the only one to betray my mother. Maria, that 'friend' who had been holding our possessions in Antwerp (and who had actually denounced my mother to the Germans earlier) was shocked to see my mother return. Maria muttered, 'What! You survived?' and then she pretended not to even know my mother!

"Shaken, my mother said, 'Just give me the pictures, you can keep the silver and all the rest.' But Maria wouldn't budge. As we were leaving, we saw my father's prayer shawl being used as a tablecloth.

"We were left with nothing. My mother, who had yet to get her life together, placed us in an orphanage in Brussels for almost three years. I didn't mind that, nor did I feel sorry for myself to be there. Lots of children were! I thought how lucky I was because I had a mother, while many of the children there had nobody. We slept in big dormitories, and though we weren't supposed to keep food, my mother sent packages of cake and salami, which we'd hide in the closet and then share with all the other children late at night.

"When I was nine years old, my mother sent for me. I was put on a train to Antwerp. Was it happily ever after? On the surface life was normal again. I was a good student and an athlete. My mother remarried, and we had enough money. When we came to the United States, we traveled with a maid! But the war was far from over for me in a deeper sense. My father died in the camps. We were told he died of typhoid. After the war a man who had known him came and wanted to marry my mother, but she wouldn't marry him because he wasn't religious. She did marry a religious man, but I could never look in his eyes. It's impossible to describe the pain I saw there. During the war he had lost his whole family, his children, everybody. Now he's dead too.

"I was left with many fears. They don't show; there's no way my friends or my colleagues would guess that I had all these problems. But they're there! For years every time I came home to my apartment, I would search for intruders. And until a few years ago I slept with a knife under my pillow. I've put the knife away, but I still get very frightened when I hear a doorbell or the sound of someone knocking, even when I expect friends. For example, my boyfriend has been coming over here for twelve years. He always rings three times on the downstairs buzzer to let me know he's coming up. I still jump out of my skin when I hear him ring. (I know I could give him a key, but frankly I'm embarrassed to let him know how much the ringing and the knocking bother me!)

"I can't hear a plane overhead without feeling panic. Hearing someone walking behind me in boots makes me shake. I'm scared of anyone in uniform. I haven't gotten over that. I find, too, that I'm still afraid of being hungry. I don't remember being scared at the convent, or hungry either. But I never leave my house without some food. Even if I just go down to Bloomingdale's, where there's a good store at every corner, I must be prepared, with a chocolate bar, a banana, or even a piece of bread. I have to take something just in case. Again, I don't *remember* being hungry. I asked my sister, and she said that we were hungry. So I must have been! I just don't remember.

"So much of my childhood between the ages of four and nine is blank. I have *so* many questions without answers! I feel like an unfinished puzzle. It's almost as if my life was smashed into little pieces on that Yom Kippur that my father was taken, and I've been spending my life ever since then trying to put the pieces together in a way that makes sense. The trouble is, when I try to remember, I come up with so little. This ability to forget was probably my way of surviving emotionally as a child. Even now, whenever anything unpleasant happens to me, I have a mental garbage can in which I put all the bad stuff and forget it.

"It's a good defense, but the downside is the fact that forgetting has left me with all those unknowns about myself and what I experienced as a child. Sometimes it really drives me crazy! I wish I could do something to bring it back. When my mother was alive, I didn't ask her, I just didn't think of asking—or maybe I wasn't sure that I was strong enough to cope with knowing. It wasn't supposed to matter, so I didn't ask questions. In any case we didn't talk about it, but after she died, I was sorry that I hadn't asked.

"I lost so many relatives and friends, and all I have of my father is his passport picture. I still have trouble realizing he's gone. Whenever I travel to a new city, I automatically look for his name in the phone book. Once, in Israel, I got off an elevator on the wrong floor, and there was my father's name on a dentist's nameplate. But I knew it wasn't him, so I just got back on the elevator.

"Three years ago I was on vacation at a hotel in New York State. I met a woman named Gilberte who was also born in Belgium and also lived in New York. She introduced me to another Belgian staying there, a man named Willy, who was only a few years younger than I was. As we talked, it turned out that Willy, who had lost his father in the war, had been in the same orphanage as I. Willy remembered nothing, but he offered to show me his photo album back in New York. He said, 'Maybe you'll know some of the people in the pictures.'

"When I saw his book, I couldn't believe my eyes. There was a picture of Willy and his mother with another woman. I screamed, 'That's my mother!' Willy said, 'Oh, my God! Then *your* mother was *my* mother's best friend.' It was true: Willy's mother sold linens, and I actually use some of the beautiful sheets and pillowcases that she sold to my mother in the 1940s!

"That was quite an experience for me. When I told Gilberte, who had introduced me to Willy, she urged me to join her at a weekend workshop sponsored by the child-survivor group that she belonged to. I hesitated, but I went. It was interesting—but also disturbing. If you're not an aggressive person (and I'm not), you're lucky to get to say a few words, because in a group of fifty people an hour and a half is so little time. I found that the few things I said brought no relief, but just opened old wounds. I went home and I was in terrible pain for a week. It was horrible! I couldn't sleep. Everything made me cry. It was the first time I had opened up, and I had no place to go with it! Then Gilberte told me that there was a group of hidden children just forming, and she introduced me to them. That was the first meeting.

"If I'd hoped that this would be a quick fix for my anxiety, I was wrong. In fact, as I got involved in talking with the others, I felt worse. I was actually losing the slim peace or resolution I thought I had. One night, for example, there were four or five of us at a steering-committee meeting. By chance we were all from Belgium. Each one of us had lost our father. We started asking each other, 'So, how did your father die?' 'He died of typhoid.' 'What a coincidence! So did mine.' It turned out that all our fathers had died of typhoid.

"That seemed a little strange. Then I asked the others, 'What's the anniversary of your father's death?' 'The first day of Chanukah!' someone said. Then everybody said, 'Me too.' I thought, Gee, this is *very* strange. Then one of the women explained that in Antwerp the chief rabbi said that all those people who didn't know when their fathers died should light a candle on the first night of Chanukah because that's the easiest to remember. As for the typhoid, she said that even if the men were gassed or killed in some other horrible way, it was easier for the children to hear that it was typhoid.

"Now I felt the old ambivalence. *Did* I really want to get in touch with all the buried pain of the past? At about that time someone on the committee arranged for the *New York Post* to do a feature story on some of us, to publicize the Hidden Child Gathering that we were planning. The reporter interviewed Astrid, Nicole, and me. A photographer came and took our pictures. Then we all panicked! The reporter said he couldn't let us see the story before it was published. I had fantasies of appearing on the front page: HIDDEN CHILDREN REVEALED! Something horrible. None of us wanted it. None of us gave our permission. In the end they were forced to kill that story.

"But we still needed publicity! It was a dilemma. With some trepidation I tried again. This time I wrote a letter to *New York* magazine. I checked the masthead and phoned Edward Kosner, the editor and president because his name looked Jewish. I hoped that he might be sympathetic! What I didn't know was that *New York* magazine is inundated with requests for publicity, and such requests rarely turn into stories. By a stroke of luck Kosner's assistant, Fran Kessler, saw my query letter, liked it, and passed it on to Debbie Harkins, the executive editor, who agreed that it sounded worthwhile. Fran had me send a letter, which she showed to Mr. Kosner. He said that Harkins could assign the story. She did.

"Well, this reporter, Jane Marks, understood how we felt and promised to read us each our quotes before the article appeared. But it was still frightening. There were some delays: An entire issue on the Gulf War, for example, put the article on hold. The last week before it was finally to come out, I was in agony, really petrified: *I felt I was about to be exposed.* Even though I was using my grandmother's maiden name instead of my real name, my picture was there. I'd get home at night and feel terrified.

"I don't know exactly what I expected. The article was dignified. I did receive a lot of feedback, but all of it was wonderful, supportive, and affirming! Even people who had not been hidden children wrote to tell me how they identified with me. Then I got a bonus: a very special letter from the former director of the orphanage where I had been. This woman wrote asking if any of us on the committee knew anyone who had lived at that orphanage during the war. If so, she wanted to contact them. I could hardly wait to respond. Unfortunately that letter was one of the few without a phone number. I wrote to the woman immediately, telling her that I had been at the orphanage. She wrote back and said, 'I remember many of the children.' She sent a picture. In it the faces were small, but I was able to recognize my sister, Celine, and me! I made a photocopy of the picture and drew arrows pointing to us. I wrote, 'This is my sister and me.'

"Was I excited? I was out of my mind! Then she wrote back and said, 'I don't remember you, but I remember your sister.' When I took a closer look, I saw it wasn't my sister, it was someone else, a girl with a crippled arm. I was disappointed! Well, I concluded, at least that picture showed me what I had looked like as an eight-year-old. Until I saw that picture, I'd had no idea that I wore glasses as a child. I wear them now, and I'd always wondered when I started.

"I consoled myself thinking that maybe I would find someone from my past at the gathering, someone who could tell me at least a little more. But as a member of the committee I was so busy! At one point I was trying to help people find the workshops they were looking for, when a woman came up to me. She said, 'I'm looking for people who were hidden in Belgium.' 'Oh,' I said distractedly. 'I was.' She said, 'Actually, I'm looking for people who were hidden at a convent called the Institut Notre Dame des Sept Douleurs in Weezenbeek.' I said, 'How interesting! I was there.' The next thing I knew, she had whipped out a picture. I looked at it. There I was with my sister, and this time there was no mistaking!

"As we talked, it turned out that this woman actually remembered me! She said that I was very weird, that I couldn't say my name and that I seemed to believe that something terrible would happen to me if I did say it! She also told me that

I was baptized, something I don't remember at all. I suddenly thought about the fact that I love sacred music. 'Tell me,' I begged, 'Was there music in the convent?' The woman said no. Oh well, I thought. Even the best detective stories have some false leads. I made several photocopies of the picture. If nothing else, at least I had this as tangible proof that I'd existed in a place at a time that I couldn't remember.

"That was an exhilarating experience for me, but not a cure. I still have nightmares, and I haven't lost even one of my fears. The war is long over for the Germans, but it's still ingrained in every cell of my brain. My life is still very much affected by what happened to me as a child. For example I'm not married. That may not have a lot to do with the war, but it is hard for me to get close to a person. I have a boyfriend named Joe, who is an architect. He is wonderfully understanding. He's told me that whenever I want to get married, we will. All I have to do is say the word. I know I'm so much luckier than the women who are always searching for someone.

"I'm searching in another sense: At night I lie in bed and I try to remember my childhood, but I just can't! I tried hypnosis once. It didn't work at all. Nevertheless I keep hoping and imagining that someday something will bring my memory back. Whenever my sister and I get together, or when I go to Belgium or Israel, we always end up talking about the war. Eventually the reminiscing gets to be competitive. Invariably someone starts to brag, 'If you think *you* know an interesting story, listen to *this* one!' That's been the ritual, year after year. Well, you know what? I'm the one who knows all the best stories! I know a zillion stories. The trouble is, they're all other people's stories. None of them are mine."

THE
HEALING

ANNETTE BASLAW-FINGER, PH.D.

A vibrant and attractive woman, Annette Baslaw-Finger, Ph.D., has short blond hair, hazel eyes, and seemingly inexhaustible energy. A recently retired professor of foreign-language education, she is often away from home: accompanying her husband on a lecture tour, giving her own lectures, or baby-sitting her grandchildren. But even when Annette and Max are at home in their Greenwich Village apartment in New York City, they have something doing every night. Annette admits, "We never just sit home. When I hear people talk about their TV shows, I feel like someone from another planet."

"I was ten years old when the war broke out for us in France. It was early September 1939, and we were on vacation at Touquet Paris Plage, a lovely seaside resort, almost two hours outside of Paris. I remember seeing my mother crying. She said, 'We're at war.'

"I asked her what that meant. My mother, who had gone through World War I and wanted to shield me, said, 'It means you can't get butter and eggs.' That was probably the greatest understatement of my life! But at the time I thought, Well, fine. I can live without butter and eggs, if that's all it means. But of course it came to mean a lot more than that.

"What it meant initially, for me as a ten-year-old, was the end of a predictable, secure, and safe life. I had had a very privileged childhood: We had a lovely home and my parents were extremely devoted to each other. As an only child I was spoiled.

"I did have a first cousin, Frances. My father's sister lived nearby, and her husband was my father's business partner. The four adults made a very close foursome, so that Frances and I were like sisters except that we each had our own parents and our own toys, so there was little rivalry. It was the kind of life that many people dream of. But it came to a screeching halt in 1940, when Paris was bombed, shattering the windows in the family business.

"It was decided that my mother, my aunt, my cousin, and I would go to the country, for safety. The men would take us to stay at a farm; then they would return to Paris to make a living. At that time there were lines of refugees stretching for miles and miles, all trying to leave Paris. Vehicles were packed with mattresses, children, and dogs. Though these were obviously families seeking safety, they became the target of German planes, which would swoop down and machine-gun the lines of refugees.

"One plane came down so low, I could see the pilot's face and helmet. I realized that if I could see him, he could see us. My aunt was pregnant at the time, so my uncle would throw himself on top of her to protect her. We all had to lie low on the ground. My first experience with genuine terror was realizing that one of my parents might get killed. Many people were wounded that day, and it was a dramatic rite of passage from peace into war. This was war, *not* just a lack of butter and eggs!

"I don't know how we made arrangements to stay on that farm, but we arrived there and settled in, and then the fathers went back to Paris. After a few months the mothers decided to go back to be with their husbands. I experienced it as total abandonment, and I asked why we couldn't all go back. My mother said, 'Because it's dangerous.' 'Well, if it's dangerous, why are you going back?' 'Because I have to be with Daddy.' 'What if something happens to you?' 'Nothing will happen.'

"I really didn't buy that. It was safe where we were, but Paris was being bombed. I was scared for the grown-ups, and I missed them terribly.

"The farmers were good people, but it was a very different lifestyle for us on the farm. Frances and I dressed like the farm children, and we wore wooden shoes because of the mud. We attended a one-room schoolhouse. Once, when I handed in my homework, the teacher accused me of having had an adult do it for me. I protested that I had done it myself, but she said, 'No, a child couldn't do that.' I didn't even know what she was talking about. I would never have cheated! I was used to shining in school; my parents expected me to do well. Getting one hundred on a test was normal, expected.

"But here in the one-room schoolhouse I saw that it wasn't wise to achieve. I felt very lonely—even though my parents and my aunt and uncle came from Paris to visit every weekend. Even though the farmers treated us well, they didn't love us. I was used to being surrounded by love, which was something I missed. Weekend love is not everyday love. If you fall and scrape your knee now, you can't wait until Friday to get the hug and kiss. You need it right now. I felt that very deeply.

"Every Sunday morning the farmers would ask if we wanted to go to church with them, and routinely we said, 'No, thank you.' But one Sunday in about the ninth month there, I had a need to pray for my parents' safety. My father had always made it very clear that there is one God. But I figured, Well, all right: God is in the synagogue, but he's probably big enough to come to church also. This would be one way I could reach him. So that day I said, 'Okay.'

"As I was entering the church, I thought, I'm going to be struck by lightning. I was positive that at that moment, as a Jewish child crossing the threshold into a church, something horrendous was going to happen. I was actually surprised it didn't.

"Then when I got inside the church, I had another problem: As Jews we don't kneel. But everybody else was kneeling! I didn't know how to handle that. So I sat there, feeling horribly conspicuous, but knowing I couldn't kneel nor make the sign of the cross. I could be there and pray to our God, but I couldn't do the other things. I prayed with my whole heart and soul.

"When I'd finished, I had to go to the bathroom, but in the worst way! I did not know if it was okay to stand up and walk out. I didn't see anybody else walking out. Everybody else was still kneeling. Finally I couldn't hold it in. The absolute quiet was broken by this awful torrential noise of my bladder finding relief, and I died, I just died!

"Everybody turned because it made so much noise. The sound echoed through the church. It was one of the most embarrassing moments in my entire life. I felt so humiliated. The whole village was there. I said to myself, That was my punishment instead of lightning. I never went to church again.

"While on the farm I would seek refuge from loneliness by standing on a hill and watching the railroad trains go by. One time a train loaded with German prisoners passed. I noticed how young they looked. One was looking out the window, and I could see his face clearly. He looked like a very sad and lonely kid. I felt so sorry that he had been taken prisoner and separated from his parents and that he didn't know where he was going or what would happen to him. But then I remembered that he was German and that I was here on the farm because of what the Germans were doing!

"I didn't want to talk to Frances about being lonely, for fear of making her feel worse. Nor did I want to talk to the farmers about it, because they were being very kind. Nor did I talk to my parents, because I knew nothing could be done about it. But there was someone—a rooster. His name was Cocorico. I used to talk to him. I'd go out early in the morning and tell him how lonely and worried I was, and how I wanted to be with my parents. This rooster used to listen to me, and I guess you could say we became best friends.

"But the end of the rooster story is a sad one. By the time our parents came to pick us up, there was virtually no food anywhere. But to celebrate our reunion with our parents, the farmers prepared a wonderful chicken dinner. I was licking my fingers. It was the best dinner I could remember. I was enjoying myself so much . . . until suddenly, with the fork midway to my mouth, I realized there were no chickens around. There just weren't. The only one was my rooster. Suddenly I felt like a cannibal!

"Of course at the same time I understood the magnitude of the sacrifice the family had made for us: actually killing the only rooster on the farm as a celebratory dinner present for us. But it was years before I could even think about a chicken dinner.

"After leaving the farm, the whole family had to go into hiding. I was allowed to bring only one thing from home, and I chose a doll, Rebecca. That was when we began a year's journey to no fewer than forty different hiding places. We kept moving and moving. We knew there were people who were trying to survive by passing themselves off as Christians. But my parents said we had been born Jews, and we would do our best to survive as Jews. If need be, we would die as Jews, but Jews we were, and Jews we would remain.

"At some point we arrived in Toulouse, which wasn't occupied, but was dangerous, and we children weren't supposed to go out of the house. Our attic apartment was infested with vermin. There were fleas in the mattress, and so many cockroaches that they actually covered the walls and formed black carpets on the ground. We killed as many as we could, but there were plenty left.

"We needed money for visas to Shanghai, one of the escape routes still open to Jews. So my mother and uncle went back to Paris, where we had left our belongings, to try to sell something, while my aunt and my father stayed with us. Paris was occupied and *very* dangerous. It was a real risk to go back there.

"Meanwhile Frances and I couldn't go to school, so we were very restless from being cooped up with nothing to do. One day we did a very stupid thing. We went out to the marketplace, to a stall with cards of buttons, piled high. There on the ground were some that had fallen off the table. We decided that since they were on the ground, it was all right for us to take them. We were on all fours, gleefully picking up those cards of buttons, knowing that they didn't belong to us. We knew, but we were playing games with our consciences. Picking up all those buttons, we had wonderful visions of how we were going to paste them on cards and sew them and do all kinds of things.

"Then the owner saw us and started screaming, 'Thief, thief.' I was terrified, because we weren't legal; as Jews we were living outside the law. I grabbed Frances's hand, and we started running like crazy, dropping buttons all along the way. I was the older one, so I felt responsible. We ran and ran, and people were chasing us—right into a dead end, where they finally caught us. I was sure I had just brought about the destruction of my entire family!

"The stall owners demanded to know where we lived. I was terrified. I left Frances there while I ran up the stairs to our attic hiding place to get my piggy bank. I brought it down, smashed it, and gave them everything I had. Fortunately that was the end of the incident. It could have been so much worse. I could have been the cause of a terrible tragedy.

"Finally my mother and my uncle came back with some money and jewelry, which was incredible timing, as a policeman friend had just come to say that my parents were on the next deportation list.

"We left for Nice. I was able to go to school there, but the teacher was anti-Semitic. I wrote a composition, and I knew it was good. I had put my genuine feelings into it, and I could tell it came out right. Then I saw my grade, which was terrible. In France you're graded on the basis of twenty. I was used to getting eighteen or nineteen, but this time I received just one quarter of a point! Apparently I'd written something that revealed my Jewishness. The teacher's comments conveyed the idea that anyone who was not pure French—like the German pure-race kind of thing—wasn't capable of much.

"I ran away from school that day, crying all the way. There was nobody home, so I spent the rest of the day wandering the streets and crying with homesickness for our old way of life before the war. When I finally got home, my parents were there—and frantic. This was not the time for wandering alone. I remember their anger: They were so upset with me that they didn't hear what I was trying to say about my own disaster at school. Survival was at stake, and it was time to grow up.

"In due time Nice became dangerous for Jews. We managed to get legal visas for Shanghai, but just when we were scheduled to go, they closed that route. So then we had to try to escape illegally by walking across the Pyrenees. This journey was to include my aunt, my uncle, Frances, and her two-year-old brother, Eugene, who'd been born in one of our many hiding places.

"We set out on a chilly November day, a few weeks after my thirteenth birthday. My father had hired Spanish guides to lead us, who explained that we could not take the easy path because that was dangerous. Also, we could not look as if we were off to climb mountains with ropes, shoes with nails in them, or even a lot of warm clothes. We had to look as if we were out for a stroll.

"It was freezing, horribly cold! My mother gave me her fur piece. This had been her elegant fur in the good old days, but suddenly it was the scarf I wound around my neck three times and tied into a very tight knot. It made me feel very loved that she was trusting me with it—especially since it had been slit open to hide my mother's diamond engagement ring and the few gold coins we had left. In my arms, I still had my doll, Rebecca.

"The crossing was supposed to take a day and night. Eugene had whooping cough and was prone to loud hacking attacks. Our guides were worried and said we ought to stuff a handkerchief in his mouth to make him be quiet. But we couldn't do that. Taking the risk that Eugene would choke and die to save the rest of us was not an option the family considered. So we took our chances.

"And chances they were! We knew that some Jews had been robbed and killed by their Spanish guides. Well, ours didn't kill us. But one evening they took us to a mountaintop and announced, 'We'll be back. We're going to check which path to take.' They never came back. Of course we had paid them in advance, with nearly everything we had! There we were, stranded at the top of the mountains with no idea of where to go. But it was vital to know! Getting to Spain could mean freedom. If we ended up in France, we'd be deported and most likely end up in the death camps.

"The crossing should have taken only a day and a night, but we walked for five nights, hiding in caves and indentations during the day—and all this with nothing to eat but one single piece of stale bread. Sometimes there was water retained in the rocks. We tried to lick up the water, while my aunt made the bread softer for Eugene, the only one who got the bread. Frances and I had our tongues hanging out, watching every mouthful he took and thinking, Gee, that must be a feast.

"Down below us we could see the lights of towns and little villages. I could hear dogs barking, which seemed like a very domestic sound. I thought of the children in those houses, tucked into real beds, hugged and kissed by their mothers and fathers after having had a real supper. I thought to myself, Tomorrow they'll wake up in their beds and get dressed and go to school. I wondered if they knew how lucky they were to have the routine of a real life—or whether they were just doing all those things without awareness or appreciation.

"I was hungry to the point of dizziness. The mountains were steep, and sometimes I had to hold my doll, Becky (she was Becky by then) in my teeth. I remember saying to my father, 'I can't climb this mountain, I just can't do it.'

"He said something to me that has been useful all my life. He said, 'You really don't have to. The only thing you have to do is take one step, and I know you can take one step.' He said, 'You don't look down, you don't look up. The only thing you're responsible for is one step. That's all you do: just take one step, and then another. One step at a time.' That concept has seen me through a lot—including the four and a half years when I was getting my doctorate. Many fellow students had a rough time, but I remembered what my father told me on the mountain, and I took one step at a time.

"We finally got down from the mountain and found ourselves in a little village at five o'clock in the morning. Nobody was awake. We had no idea if it was a Spanish or a French town. The first thing we saw was a bakery with cakes in the window. I pressed my nose against that window, mentally devouring those cakes.

"To our great joy and relief the store's sign was in Spanish. We were in Spain! That was such a moment, such a moment! We really thought we had made it, we thought we were safe. We made our way to a big city, which must have been either Barcelona or Madrid.

"My father went to an organization for help, but they refused because he had no papers. They promised not to report us, but they told us we'd better get away, because we were illegal. We had to make our way to Portugal by walking across Spain at night and hiding during the day. Every now and then we'd come upon a small restaurant willing to serve people who didn't have papers, and we'd have a real meal. But usually my father would pull carrots from the fields or apples from trees, whatever was available.

"One time we hadn't had any food for a while, and all we had left was a limp carrot. A single carrot. It must have been a couple of days old. It was flopping over. It was Chanukah time, and I felt enormous sadness because this was all we had. Had I known what was going on with other Jewish children and families then, I would have considered myself very lucky. All I knew at the time was that we had become gypsies, constantly on the move with no place that was safe for us. Our clothes were filthy; we couldn't take hot baths or sit down at a table and talk or have any normalcy at all.

"That particular night we were hiding in a barn, sleeping on hay. I was feeling sorry for myself. I said to my father, 'It's Chanukah. We don't even have a menorah to light.'

"My father said, 'What do you mean, we don't have a Chanukah menorah? We have the most beautiful menorah possible!' With that he opened the door a crack, pointed upward, and said, 'Look up at the sky.' We were someplace in the country. It was a pitch-black night, so the stars were brilliant. He said, 'Pick out the shammash.' (The shammash is the head candle on a menorah.) I picked out the most brilliant star. My father said, 'Good. Now, let's pick out the other eight candles.' So we picked out the other eight candles, and we lit a menorah in the sky.

"It was beautiful! So close to heaven and close to God. Then we went back into the barn, and we played with an imaginary dreidel. We were spinning it, and then we'd call out what we got. Not unexpectedly I won! The prize was the carrot—that carrot, which just a few moments before had been a symbol of deprivation and sadness and loss, suddenly became a treasured prize.

"Magnanimously I shared that carrot with the whole family. In whispers we sang Chanukah songs, and it felt wonderful to be Jewish. That turned out to be probably the most memorable Chanukah I've ever had, and the most joyous one.

"Meanwhile we had to keep moving, hiding all the time. We had to keep rehearsing our assumed Spanish names in case anybody questioned us. I had this enormous name because in Spain you are the daughter of so-and-so and it goes on and on. Eugene was still coughing his head off, as medical treatment was out of the question.

"Finally after many weeks we reached Portugal, where a village had been set up to receive refugees. It was just a couple of hours outside of Lisbon. Within that village we were free! The residents were wonderful, and there the American Joint Distribution Committee was extremely helpful, giving us food and clothing and placing refugees in various homes.

"During our ten months in Portugal the parents pooled their skills and tutored the dozen or so children in the refugee community. Frances and I hadn't been to school for two and a half years. Many times in hiding, my parents would have intellectual conversations that were really intended as lessons for me, and I was always encouraged to ask questions. My parents left me with a great appreciation for learning. I could easily have lost that appreciation in the circumstances we were in, but they made learning something you wanted, something you were really glad to get. By the time we got to Portugal, I was really hungering for school life: to have teachers, books, friends. Just to have my own pen and pencil seemed so great.

"Eventually our immigration papers came through, and we left for the United States on a very old, very rickety Portuguese ship. It was August 1943, so the waters were still not safe. There were German submarines on the seas, and ships were being sunk. I was horrendously sick during that crossing, which took two and a half weeks, because we had to take a circuitous route to ensure safety. What's more, I was frightened. All I knew of the United States was from American movies that had been exported to France—all cowboy movies or gangster movies where people were shooting each other. I was leery, but my father kept assuring me that those were just movies and that I'd learn to love America. But I was skeptical. We sailed into Philadelphia on a Sunday. In those years it was a dormant city on Sundays. A man was there to receive us, but he wasn't very friendly. Since we spoke no English, what I heard seemed like gibberish.

"Even when we were settled in New York, I felt that we were in a backward country. I saw people standing at a Nedicks stand getting hot dogs and drinking orange juice, standing up. This was lunch? In prewar France lunch was an important ritual. The father took two hours off and came home. In our house it included a tablecloth and flowers and wine, and there was conversation. It seemed very civilized. But here people were standing up, and in just two minutes lunch was over.

"I couldn't understand the mentality that didn't provide time for relating as a family and for treasuring some of what I considered great pleasures of life. I saw adults chewing gum and thought they looked like cows on the farm, ruminating. And the music! The then-popular 'Mairzy Doats' made no sense, when I was used to French ballads that tell a story. Nor could I understand the 'animallike' behavior of rush-hour subway riders, shoving each other aside.

"I went to school, but in those days there were no bilingual programs, English-as-a-second-language courses, or any special services for non-English speakers. They simply put me in a class of retarded children, which was their way of dealing with me, but it made any social life difficult, if not impossible.

"I didn't think of myself as retarded. My parents raised me to respect who I was at all times. Even when we were subjected to anti-Semitism, when people would spit at us and call us pigs, my father used to say, 'That judgment is not reality.'

"Still, I felt alienated, and I had nobody to talk to. My mother, believed to be sick but unknowingly pregnant, spent days in bed. My father, handicapped by lack of English, was putting in fourteen-hour work days on a factory assembly line, coming home really wiped out.

"At school my teacher would ask questions I didn't understand, so I developed a system, which was to alternate between yes and no. But one time, after a yes response, the teacher grabbed me by the back of the neck and threw me out of the class. I had no idea what I had done, but she was furious. She took me to the principal; I was in tears. I was embarrassed because I was fourteen and I was crying. They finally called in a French teacher, who became an interpreter. I learned later that the question I had answered yes to had been, 'What do you take me for, an idiot?' And that was why my teacher had been so mad.

"Then and there I decided to learn English as quickly as possible and get into a normal class. And in less than five months I'd accomplished that. In fact I finished high school in three and a half years, made honor roll, and ended up being class valedictorian—a very satisfying triumph over my earlier difficulties.

"People talk a lot about the guilt of a survivor. I know what that is, and it is a haunting feeling. But it has a positive side to it: If you have been saved, as I have, then you have to give meaning to your life. It means you have to really reach out. You have to try to live in the name of those who did not survive: do a few good things and be there for people or try to achieve—not for titles or for success but to give meaning to your survival.

"I think I chose to become a teacher, at least in part because my grandfather was a teacher and my aunts had Ph.D.s sixty years ago when very few women did. I came from a family of highly educated people who were all annihilated, so I thought I'd carry on the profession in their name.

"I got the Ph.D. not for the prestige of a degree but because I felt a real hunger to go on learning—and also because of the encouragement of my first husband, who was such a good person in so many ways.

"I loved being a mother, but I was restless to do more. So my first husband offered to baby-sit twice a week while I took courses. I got my master's that way.

"When I finished my master's, I said, 'Gee, I'm going to miss school.' My husband said, 'Why do you have to stop? Why don't you go on?' I said, 'What are you talking about? I'm thirty-six.' He said, 'So what?' I said, 'Well, I'll be forty before I get a doctorate.' He said, 'You'll be forty anyway.' Thanks to him I went on and got my doctorate in foreign-language education. He was very supportive and very proud. The kids said he cried at my graduation.

"I know that I'm very much affected by what happened to me during the war. I still treasure the luxury of getting into bed at night and having a roof over my head. For years I wouldn't consider moving. I was determined that our children would have a steady, secure, consistent, and predictable space in which to live. I had made my husband promise we would never move, even if we could afford a better or bigger house.

"Also, I think I went overboard in telling my children how lucky they were to have a school to go to and enough food to eat. I know they resented the fact that *I* was in school, which meant I wasn't waiting with milk and cookies when *they* came home from school. They've never gotten over that. All three of them speak of my not being there enough, so obviously it was important to them. It wasn't that I didn't care. I loved being a mother, and I wish it could have been enough, but it wasn't enough. I had this tremendous restlessness. I couldn't be home all the time. Maybe that had to do with being in hiding so long or being in certain spaces where I couldn't move. But I had to have the stimulation!

"I think my children saw me as self-centered and needy. I know I was intense, and that's hard on children too. My children have accused me of role reversal. They point to the way my feelings get hurt easily and my need for protection. Sometimes they feel called upon to protect me, and they don't enjoy that role. They resent it now in retrospect.

"I realize that I have an inordinate need for love and reassurance. Curiously my anxiety dreams are not about me or even my children, but about my grandchildren. I keep seeing them wandering alone in the streets of Paris, with no food or water, no place to go. They're crying. The French are hiding behind their windows and closing the shutters—just as during the war, when many Jewish children died because the French reported them to the Germans.

"When my own children were young, I used to have to get out of bed many times to reassure myself that they were actually tucked into a real bed in a real room. I just had to make sure. That had been something that I really missed for so many months: just the luxury of being safe in a bed with a blanket and a pillow.

"There is also the issue of food. My love for food plays havoc with dress sizes. I'm always on the way up or the way down, to the chagrin of my daughter, who is a dietitian. Food is very, very important to me, and I really love eating. When I wake up in the morning and I can sit down to a cup of coffee and bread and anything I want, I feel such a sense of luxury, such joy, and such thankfulness. To this day I get an infinitely more secure feeling from opening a full refrigerator than from trying to save money in a bank account.

"A bank account doesn't mean anything to me. Money can be taken away from you; things can be confiscated. Those things happened to my family during the war, and we were literally penniless when we came to the United States, even though we had been very comfortable before the war.

"Another thing is that I have very, very intense, close relationships. I don't have time for anything superficial, because I feel time is limited, and I don't want to waste it. I don't have any acquaintances. None! My time is spent exclusively with the people I love with all my heart.

"I admit that some of this goes back to my intense fear of abandonment. I think the psychological reason that I have so many really close, intimate friendships and relationships is to make sure there will always be someone there.

"As for my moods, those are also intense: When I'm happy, I'm very, very happy—the way a child is happy. Of course when I'm unhappy, I'm beyond consolation. That's the other side of the coin. My first marriage ended tragically: My husband suffered a massive coronary two days after our daughter's wedding. The very last thing he ever heard was, 'I love you,' because we were talking about our daughter's wedding and the fact that *we* felt so in love. I said, 'I love you.' That was the last thing he ever heard.

"What followed was a terrible period of grief. I felt abandoned and frightened. Sometimes I would drive home and see the house in darkness, and my heart would pound with fear. I had visions of people hiding in the bushes, and I was terrified. As a result two dear friends gave me keys to their homes, where each had a room set aside for me if I needed it. Nevertheless I admit I came very close to dying, I really did. It was very hard.

"I remained alone for the next ten years. It took that long to feel single again. I still felt married for a long time after Al's death. Then Max came into my life, and we love each other like eighteen-year-olds. It's really miraculous!

"In a way I think my first husband had something to do with it. I see him in heaven, close to God, pulling strings. I think he knew when I was ready. It was ten years precisely. He must have felt, Okay, this is the right person, and somehow helped to bring our meeting about.

"Now I'm very happy with Max, but we don't just sit around. I took early retirement to travel with Max, who is a retired ambassador and professor. He gets invited to lecture in wonderful settings, including on luxury cruise ships. So we're off! It's really heaven. We also have a place in Florida where the kids join us for holidays and so forth. I thank God a million times.

"I'd feared that I might feel guilty about retiring and not doing anything 'useful.' But it hasn't worked out that way. I'm ashamed to say that so far I feel wonderful and not guilty at all! There is time to see all the people we want to see, to do all the things we want to do. Max just turned seventy-six, a very, very young seventy-six. But the calendar says he's seventy-six. I don't know how much time we have left, but we're going to really make the most of it.

"I'm constantly busy. But I mean constantly! I need an enormous amount of stimulation, which I'm sure is related to those months and months of total suppression: don't make noise, don't talk, don't move, don't go out. Now I've got to get out. I'm incapable of staying home. I can't even sit during the day and read a book, even though that would be a pleasure. I fill my days with activities, people: Max, children, grandchildren, friends! Thank God both husbands understood that. Max and I may be retired, but our way of life would kill a twenty-year-old, I'm sure! It's very exciting and interesting and fun. I can't bear to be closed in or bound to a predictable schedule.

"Life is dear and precious, but I never have a sense of the

future. Never! I'm so surprised that I've lived to age sixty-two. I never expected it, and I'm surprised to be here. I feel like I'm on borrowed time. I was always convinced that I would die very young. Now, every time I have a birthday, I'm surprised. So I celebrate each one as though it's the last.

"I met another former hidden child who asked, 'Was there anything good left from all this?' For me, yes! It is this deep appreciation for every good moment because I always feel that this moment may be my last one. I know that the roof can cave in at any second, but for this one moment I'm alive, and I have food and I have people I love. Even if it's only for this one moment I am safe!"

ASTRID JAKUBOWICZ

Married and the parents of a son and two daughters, Astrid Jakubowicz and her husband, Wolf, live in a spacious and sunny apartment in Forest Hills, Queens, New York. The traditional prewar building is set back from the street, with a lovely rock garden in front. Astrid is in the custom linen business, catering to celebrity clients. Dressed to meet a client in a tweed suit and a very expensive and beautiful silk blouse, Astrid reflects on her looks: fair skin, blond hair, and blue eyes. "My looks were a gift from God!" she says. "I'm referring back to the Holocaust. Not looking Jewish made a child better merchandise, easier to place—and a lot more likely to survive."

"I was born in Belgium in 1937, and I was named for the queen. That wasn't just a sentimental, patriotic whim on my parents' part. There was a reason! My parents had recently come from Poland, my father illegally. Shortly after they arrived, my father was arrested as an illegal alien and sent to jail. I don't know what possessed my mother, a poor immigrant diamond cutter married to a jailed waiter. But she wrote to the king of Belgium and asked for clemency. My mother told the king that she was pregnant. She promised that if she had a daughter, she would name her after the queen, who had just died in a car accident. The upshot? My father *was* released, and I was named Astrid.

"I was the only girl in the whole extended family of cousins. Everybody kind of spoiled me, saying I was the prettiest, the smartest, the best; everybody made me clothes. I was feisty! I fought with my cousins, even though they were boys. My aunt would come over to complain to my mother about me. One time when I heard my aunt coming, I knew I'd be in trouble. I hid under the table and distracted everyone by peeing on the floor. It seemed like a good diversionary tactic.

"I loved my mother and my little brother, Paul, but I was closest of all with my father. He was a slim and very handsome man with black hair and dark eyes. I spent as much time with him as I could. I have very warm, fond memories of our going for walks together. We also used to stand at the window together watching trains go by. Sometimes he would take me to the chicken coops in the backyard. There he'd take warm eggs and cover my eyes, which, according to superstition, was supposed to make them beautiful. My mother always said to me that I was my father's little girl, and he really adored me. It was a happy time.

"But those innocent prewar days were numbered. In 1942 my father received a document saying that he must report to Maline, Belgium. The document said that he'd be assigned to a work camp. That sounded innocent enough, but my mother had heard sinister rumors about what really happened. She pleaded with my father to take the money she had earned selling food on the black market. With the money perhaps he could escape to Switzerland. My father refused. He was afraid that *we* would get into trouble if he didn't report to Maline.

"The day he left, I sat and watched him pack. Then I

walked him to the corner. I kissed him good-bye and I gave him a chocolate that I had saved from nursery school. Walking back home by myself, I felt a terrible emptiness. He had only been gone for a minute, but I already missed him terribly. Some weeks later my uncle went the same way. At that point the remaining grown-ups in the family decided that it wasn't safe to stay where we were anymore. I thought of the Nazis as some kind of menacing, predatory birds. I was scared. Where would we go to get away from them?

"As a family we were lucky! My uncle had a friend named Franz Rosseels. Franz was outraged at the Nazis, and during the course of the war he became one of the big Belgian hero rescuers. He saved countless Jews, and even later on when he was caught, he knew where we all were, but he never told. It cost him his life. That very rugged-looking man with his strong, tattooed arms and a leather jacket, became our family's protector. Franz found an apartment somewhere for my grandmother and two aunts. My mother, brother, and I went to live there, too, for a while. Then we had to split up, which was the last time the family was together.

"It all happened quickly. My brother, Paul, and I were sent to stay with an Antwerp woman and her husband. I was miserable there. The man sneered at me when I asked if I could have a piece of bread with onion on top. 'We're not Jews here!' he snapped. I didn't know what he meant, and I still don't! But it was traumatic for me, as it was my first personal experience with anti-Semitism. One day when I was alone with him, he took his penis out and made me hold it. I was disgusted, but as a child I didn't dare refuse or think of telling anyone. Finally the couple decided that it was too dangerous for them to keep us anymore.

"Paul and I were packed up and taken to another hiding place, this time with a woman who often had lovers. Whenever one of them came for a tryst, Paul and I would be stashed in the attic. Once, she left us up there for such a long time, and we didn't know what to do. Just to entertain ourselves, we rubbed saliva on our bodies. Then we picked up the dust from the floor and made ourselves completely black. When she finally came up to get us, she was very upset. However, she was not so fastidious herself! She used to pee in the coals and wipe herself with a dishtowel. I was a child, but I knew this was wrong. Her strange, dirty habits just emphasized to me how very far we were from home and family. Still, she must have been a good person to have kept us in spite of the danger.

"After a time even this woman got cold feet and made us leave. I can't blame her. It was pretty close living, and it was too hard for her to keep us out of sight all the time.

"Our next rescuer was a woman named Netje, who lived in a walk-up near the port of Antwerp. That was a brief stay. The moment neighbors caught on or suspected that there were Jews in the house, we had to go—and quickly! Franz showed up again to take us away. This time Paul and I had to be separated. I felt badly about that. I adored Paul, and I knew how much I'd miss the way he sat in his crib in the morning making up stories.

"Franz whisked me away. He held me against him, and we jumped off a moving tram. He was a very strong man. I stayed with Franz and his wife for a brief time, but that was especially dangerous because Franz was a known member of the underground. I didn't know where Paul was.

"Then Franz took me to Nora, with whom I stayed for the next two years. Nora was a very pretty woman with dark hair, brown eyes, high cheekbones, and a lovely figure. She was very soft to me, very nurturing. I considered her my second mother. Her home was a little house on the grounds of a château in the outskirts of Brussels. The house itself was tiny, but we had a vegetable garden, gooseberries, currants, goats, and rabbits, which made delightful pets. I even had someone to play with: Louise, another Jewish girl Nora and her husband were hiding.

"Still, it took some adjusting. I was six years old when I arrived there. I spoke both Flemish and Yiddish, but now I had to learn French. According to Nora, I was a very, very difficult, spoiled child. I was terrible at sharing, and I gave Louise a tough time. But Nora took beautiful care of me. She indulged me, not so much with material things but with love and attention. When she bathed me, she always sang a pretty little song about closing the door so that little Astrid in her undershirt wouldn't catch a cold.

"I also had to learn to get along with Nora's husband, a much older man with a very violent temper. One day he grabbed my favorite little bunny by the ear and started hitting it. He beat it to death. Then he skinned it, took the entrails out, and hung it in the basement. Later Nora cooked it. I was really upset and I wouldn't eat it. Unwilling to take my rebellion sitting down, he carried me down to the basement, lifted me up by my hair, and he hit me. I'm sure he felt frustrated by this dumb child refusing to eat good food, but what could I do?

"He probably loved me in his own way. He made me lots of toys, including beautiful jointed wooden animals on wheels. But he had an uncontrollable temper. Nor was he the only one with a temper! His daughter from an earlier marriage was also around there some of the time. One day this girl, who was just as irascible as her father, got mad and she threw a fork at me. It landed next to my teeth and it stuck in my face!

"Poor Nora put up with a lot of physical abuse at her husband's hand. She could have left him, but she chose to stay with him until the liberation—just because of us: the children! That was an incredible sacrifice. When the war was over, Nora did leave him. She got a job as a live-in maid in someone's house. But that was only after Louise had been reunited with her parents and another home had been found for me. I still needed a foster home because my mother had not yet appeared. Nora arranged for me to stay with a lady I was taught to call Marraine, which means 'godmother.' She seemed nice enough, but I didn't want to go to her. I was still very, very attached to Nora. I hated leaving. I had such a heavy heart as Nora, who was carrying my little suitcase, walked with me up the three flights of stairs to Marraine's apartment. I didn't want Nora to leave me there. I couldn't bear it. But I had no choice.

"Marraine was delighted to have me. She had a grown son, but she said she really wanted a little girl. She even made a point of telling me that she hoped my mother wouldn't come back so she could keep me. Marraine was very Catholic. She'd take me to church very regularly. On days when the weather was bad, we would sit next to the coal stove because it was the only warm place in the apartment. There, among all her gleaming copper pots, we would pray together. Marraine taught me to use the rosary beads.

"Thanks to Marraine I was a devout believer. I would even stop off at church to pray on the way home. But part of me was also afraid of church. It was so big on the outside and so imposing on the inside. It was as if most of me had become Catholic, while another part deep down inside was still distantly but unmistakably a Jew.

"One day when I was eight years old, I was on my way home from school with my friend, Elaine, when the maid from the pharmacy downstairs came running to tell me that my mother had arrived! I turned the corner, and there she was in a huge brown coat with a stick in her hand and a turban on her head. She was so thin! She was recovering from typhus, she had no hair, and she was using the stick as a cane. I don't know if I was happy to see her or not. At least she didn't take me home. She was living in a crowded rooming house, where there was no place for me.

"I stayed at Marraine's for that whole first year after liberation. I had a crucifix over my bed, but as I was also seeing my mother and beginning to remember my Jewishness more consciously, I asked Marraine to take the little Jesus down from the wall. She did what I asked. That night I didn't sleep. Marraine smiled knowingly. 'Of course you couldn't sleep,' she said the next morning. 'Jesus wasn't there to protect you.' Back went the little crucifix, right above my bed.

"My mother had not found my brother, Paul, yet, but she hadn't given up. She went from one children's home to another, pulling out every six-and-a-half-year-old boy. Finally she found him in an orphanage in Weesenbeek. The way she identified him was by looking for certain marks. He had fallen off his high chair as a baby and had stitches in his tongue. He also had a birthmark on his ear, which was shaped like a mouse, presumably because my mother had been frightened by a mouse and had grabbed hold of her own ear when she was pregnant with Paul. I was happy when I saw him. He stood there with snot running down his nose. He was kind of dirty. I had missed my little brother very much.

"Finally, when I was nine, I went to live with family again: my mother, Paul, and my new stepfather, Herman Goldberg, who had lost his wife and children in the war. I hated him! He was short, skinny, and bald, with a mustache and a Napoleonic complex—always putting others down to make himself bigger. I called him Hitler. I called them both dirty Jews. I had such mixed-up feelings! I was Jewish, yet I was Catholic. I was learning Hebrew, but I wanted a Communion.

"Night after night I would think about my real father and wonder if he'd really died in the concentration camp. There was no proof. There were no witnesses. I imagined that one day the doorbell would ring and my father would be standing there alive! In my mind he *was* alive. He was suffering from amnesia, or perhaps he was lost somewhere. In any case he was going to come home. Then what would Mama do? Of course she would throw this other man out, this intruder named Herman who was not my father at all.

"My father became even more special because he was dead. Idealized. Untouchable. I never had a fight with *this* father, he was great! I was never angry at him. When Herman would say, 'You have to come home at eleven,' or 'You can't go camping,' I felt certain that my real father would have let me do what I wanted. Eventually I made peace with Herman and shared his love of Yiddish music and theater. Still I continued to miss my father in the worst way.

"That was a long time ago. For many, many years I refused to allow myself to dig into old memories. Then six years ago I began losing people. First my brother, Paul, died, which broke my heart. Three years after that my mother passed away. Suddenly hearing anything about the Holocaust made me cry. Everyone but Nora was gone, and here I was, the matriarch of the family. People who knew my story would praise me, telling me how well adjusted I was in spite of everything. Yes, I agreed. Secretly I said to myself, They don't know how screwed up I really am.

"I was walking around that way for a couple of years, feeling aggrieved and reluctant to be the grown-up. Then, one day just this past month, my husband, Wolf, and I were burglarized. This was devastating. Wolf had spent thirty years in the jewelry business, and I had many, many, many pairs of beautiful earrings. Now they were all gone. God, I felt so sorry for myself!

"Then one morning a few days after the robbery I had a revelation. I said to my husband, 'Look at me, how bad I feel, losing the jewelry!' But you know what? The jewelry was nothing but metal and stones. They were *things* that couldn't hug me or kiss me. For the first time I tried to think of how my parents must have felt, *losing everything*! For the first time I thought about how it must have been to lose all their possessions, their home, *each other*, and maybe worst of all their children. Up to that moment I had never thought of what went on in my father's heart when he said good-bye. Nor had I thought about my mother's losses. I had focused only on the feelings of the child.

"I'm fifty-five years old now. Is it possible that maybe I am finally growing up?"

THE LESSINGS

Ed and Carla Lessing live and work in a sunny carriage house in Westchester, not more than forty minutes from Manhattan. Carla, a psychotherapist, sees patients in a downstairs office that was once her mother's room, while Ed, a graphics designer, works in his studio on the floor above. The Lessings' son and daughter, both married with children, live nearby, but until recently they knew only bits and pieces of their parents' war experiences. "Of course we didn't talk about it," Carla admits. "Ed and I didn't even share the stories with each other. Neither of us wanted to know how much the other one had suffered."

CARLA *is five feet one and a half, with short dark hair and glasses. Her black skirt and white blouse are feminine but plain, subdued, toned down, just like her makeup and jewelry. "If I wore red, I might be noticed," she explains. "It's a habit of thinking that is still hard to change."*

"We didn't go into hiding until 1942, when I was twelve. But I was trained not to be seen and not to be heard a long time before the war began. When I was five, my grandfather in Gelsenkirchen, Germany, always told me, 'Don't make noise, don't skip. When you're in the street, just make yourself very quiet.' I got the message: We were Jews, and it was bad for Jews to call attention to themselves. Looking out the window of their apartment, I could see anti-Jewish graffiti scrawled on the big department store across the street. I also knew that Jews were banned from the neighborhood swimming pool.

"Putting it all together, I realized that if I was noisy or called attention to myself in public, I would embarrass the family and possibly get us all into some kind of trouble. Clearly, to act like a child was a luxury I could not afford. Later, back home in Holland, I felt increasingly conspicuous. I was after all a dark little girl with a Jewish face in a country of blond-haired, blue-eyed people. I tried in vain to blend in, not realizing that it wouldn't be many years before I would have to disappear in a much more radical way.

"In 1940 the Germans occupied Holland. Our lives changed dramatically. Jews were ordered to turn their valuable jewelry in, and I had to give up the possessions I valued most in the world: my bicycle and two small golden rings my mother had given me for my birthday. Jews were no longer allowed to attend public school. My brother, Herman, and I were sent to a special Jewish school, which we actually enjoyed, thanks to our wonderful teacher, Mr. Engelander, who loved music and helped us stage our own operetta.

"But something very sinister was happening: One by one my fellow students stopped coming to school. Even Mr. Engelander didn't seem to know where they were or if they were coming back. The worst shock of all was the day I went to play with my best friend, Fanny, who lived around the corner. I stood at the door knocking, ringing the bell, and calling her name over and over, but nobody came. I waited and waited: still nothing. The family had vanished. My very best friend had not told me she was leaving.

"My mother, a widow raising Herman and me alone, didn't seem too surprised. She explained that many Jews were fleeing over the border or going into hiding. I asked if we would go too. She did not know her plans yet or was not ready to share them with me. At night I would lie in bed straining to hear as she talked on the phone. Everything was secret. This was a time when adults believed that the less you tell children about the bad things going on, the less upset they will be. For me that secrecy only deepened the mystery—and my growing sense of dread.

"Suddenly it *was* our turn! My mother learned that we were going to be called to the camps, so she arranged for the three of us to go into hiding. A Jesuit priest found us a place in the Hague with an elderly lady named Mrs. Van Nooyen. One night in August we left our home to go into hiding at her place. I was twelve. I had been wearing a Jewish star for months. That evening, just before we left, I was told to take off my vest with the star sewn on it. When we went outside, I was to throw it in the gutter. That was very, very hard for me! It seemed so dangerous. What if I was caught without it and they knew I was Jewish?

"It wasn't just the risk that bothered me. My reluctance to part with the Jewish star went beyond that. My star had come to feel like an essential part of my identity: something I put on every day, like eyeglasses. How could I be me without my star? Taking it off made me feel like I was throwing away a part of myself.

"Our room in Mrs. Van Nooyen's apartment was dark and small, and extremely stuffy. Bored and restless, Herman and I bickered constantly, but only in whispers of course. We certainly didn't dare raise our voices. We couldn't even go to the bathroom without permission. Herman, who was having frequent asthma attacks from the anxiety, was not even allowed to cough, except under all the blankets, because we were surrounded by neighbors. There was a dictionary in the room, which kept us from extreme boredom. We spent many, many hours looking up words. Still, most of the time we felt like caged lions.

"Mrs. Van Nooyen welcomed us. She believed that God would forgive her sins if she rescued Jews. She was a very obese old lady and a good cook. She made us kidney bean soup, which was delicious. The problem was she was extremely nervous about having us there. In fact she was so fearful that she couldn't sleep at night. After three months her son told us that we had to leave. This was devastating news for us. However, it turned out to be incredibly lucky! Just one month after we left the Van Nooyen apartment, a neighbor in the same stairwell was picked up by the Germans, and that was just for storing Jewish property, not even hiding people! If we had been there, they would surely have found us too.

"Arrangements for our next hiding place were made through the Catholic underground. Late one night we set out for the train station. This time just stepping outdoors in the air felt so dangerous! We hadn't been outside the apartment in three months. Even as we tiptoed, our footsteps sounded so loud to my ears. Each time we turned a corner, I held my breath. You didn't know who might be out looking for Jews on the run. It seemed strange to see lights and trolley cars. Until now I had almost forgotten that life was still going on for most people! That awareness made me feel even more that I didn't belong out in the world where people might see me.

"All the way to Delft I was terrified that we'd be caught and arrested. Somehow we made it to our new hiding place in the home of a barber named van Geenen and his wife, a beautician. They had seven children, ranging from two to eighteen. My mother and Herman and I were to join this family of nine in their small family quarters above the shop. It was pretty tight living. There was a kitchen and dining room downstairs and then a little staircase with two small rooms and a hallway. Mr. and Mrs. van Geenen slept on Murphy beds in the dining room. Our family and the eldest daughter slept in the front room upstairs. The other children all slept together in the back room and the little hallway. Certainly there was no privacy! Their street was a market place and very narrow, so we could not go near the windows. During the day we couldn't walk around or use the bathroom for fear that the customers downstairs would hear us.

"At least my mother and I were able to do some helpful things like peel the potatoes and cook. We could even do the dishes, letting the water run very, very slowly so it didn't make any noise. We would also darn socks. We read, but the van Geenens were not really readers, and a lot of the books were like today's Harlequin romances. We read whatever we could get our hands on, and we were grateful for that. The other big activity was sleeping. Going to bed was a refuge from the boredom, fear, and sadness, a way of passing the time. By then I was very well conditioned not to even think of wanting to shout or jump around.

"Fear was the dominant emotion. I lived in constant terror that we would be discovered and hauled away. The most frightening thing for me was the sound of a truck. If it stopped, that meant they were going to search the house or that they knew someone was hiding there. Every time I heard a truck, I'd hold my breath and hope it wasn't stopping. Especially at night, when it was quiet and dark. Even now I panic if I hear a truck at night. It still sounds ominous!

"Sometimes German soldiers who had come for a haircut would want to use the bathroom upstairs where we were. I don't know how we managed to hide from them, but we did.

One time some German soldiers came to search the house for blankets, other times for young men over sixteen to send to the ammunition factories in Germany. My mother and my brother and I were sneaked out to the Catholic church around the corner. Thanks to the very compassionate priest, we stayed there for three days while the police made thorough searches of all the houses in the neighborhood.

"Our stay with the van Geenens was meant to be short. But with no place else to go, we ended up staying there for thirty months. Understandably the hiding mother was very nervous. It wasn't her idea to have us there, it was her husband's. He was a great man, extraordinary! He was in his glory helping people and fighting authority. These terrific people never demanded that we join them in saying grace, for example. But I always felt awkward and apologetic when they were praying.

"There was also the food issue. There were quite a few teenagers there! One of the boys was my age, so there were already two thirteen-year-olds. One was a year younger than my brother, who was seventeen, and one was older. So you can imagine how much food was actually needed! Of course there wasn't nearly enough. I can only imagine how hard it must have been for the hiding mother to give away the food her children would have gladly eaten. She never said anything, but she always seemed to be trembling.

"I knew that we were causing trouble by just being there. I felt responsible for seeing that I didn't cause any additional trouble or do something wrong. For example, if I went too close to the window, then someone might see me and inform the Germans. Then we'd be put in camps and possibly killed—not just our family but the hiding family too. I felt very, very guilty when the van Geenens' eldest son, Walter, got a letter demanding that he go to a work camp in Germany. I knew that if we hadn't been there, maybe he would have opted to go into hiding or run away. During that time they speculated that he suffered a lot, and after the war it was frequently mentioned. All through the years I felt guilty that he suffered because of us.

"Herman sometimes picked arguments with the van Geenens. It made me uncomfortable. Most of it was about politics, based on items Herman read in the newspaper. It upset me. Hadn't we been taught that children aren't supposed to express their feelings or their thoughts? Even before the war we had been told repeatedly by the adults, 'You are just a child, you don't know.' Herman seemed outrageous—which made me even more committed to being good. I was careful to say as little as possible, for fear that I would say the wrong thing and end up out on the street.

"Needless to say, under those pressures you lose spontaneity and become inhibited. That was what happened to me. I became a mouse: timid, silent, invisible. Even when we heard that the war was over and we could go outside, I didn't dare. I cried. I was so afraid it wasn't true. I said, 'I'm not going out there.' They finally convinced me to go out in the street, and there was a lot of joy, but I still couldn't believe it was over. After several months my brother was drafted and decided he was not going to fight in Indonesia to lose more years, so he went to Israel. My mother and I stayed behind. I went to school both day and night. Then I met my husband, Ed, and we immigrated to the United States. By then I was just nineteen.

"For many years my mother never talked about the hiding experience. It was over and done with: time to start our lives anew. But it was hard.

"This past year I went to Holland. My hiding mother was ninety years old, and I felt that I needed to go. Of the seven children five were there, and we did a lot of talking about the war years, which we had never done before. They told me how much our being there upset the family, how the oldest daughter married much earlier than she had planned because the house was too full . . . and, again, how the oldest son went to Germany when he was drafted to a work camp, even though he didn't want to, because refusing or hiding would have put us in too much danger.

"One of the children who was twelve when we were in hiding expressed a lot of anger. He felt that my mother, who was a very poor widow, should have given his father more money. When I heard that, I ignored it like I used to back then. It was only when I got home that I could even think about it. The eldest daughter, Corrie Duppen, is the one I've really kept in touch with. She's now almost seventy. She was able to say, 'My mother wasn't always so nice to you.'

"I know that the hiding experience took a toll on me in all kinds of ways. For example, I never lost the old feeling of anxiety. When my children were growing up, if they didn't come home on time, I would always think of the worst thing, imagining they'd been hit by a car. Even now I suffer from sleep disturbance. I wake up startled, with palpitations. It all has to do with a sense that the world isn't safe, which is something I probably conveyed to my children. I lost much of my capacity to enjoy life. This comes from years and years of holding myself in so tightly. When you live a life of secrecy in your formative years, it becomes a part of your personality. I did all the normal things—I went to school and college and graduate school, I went shopping. But underneath there was always fear, feeling out of place and in hiding.

"Therapy has helped me a lot. But the dramatic break-through for me came directly from my work in planning the Hidden Child Gathering. I'd never felt any strong ties to any kind of organization: not any professional organization, not Hadassah—nothing! However, when I got in contact with the people who were planning a gathering for the hidden children, I realized that this was different.

"Almost at once I was deeply involved. For the first time in my life I had a real sense that I belonged with these people who had also been hidden during the Holocaust. I worked on the project from June 1990 to May 1991—and I mean I really worked. I devoted virtually *all* my free time to it. It was so important! For the first time I could relate to that part of my life, a part I hadn't shared comfortably with anyone, not even my family. In the past when I had shared parts of my hiding story with good friends, I found it very painful to watch their faces; they expressed pain and suffering, probably reflecting my own. I even felt guilty, as if I were inflicting the suffering on them.

"As I gradually overcame a lot of my discomfort in opening up, I found I was reaping incredible rewards: As a member of the steering committee I did things I had never done before, such as reaching out to get other people involved, making decisions, and chairing large meetings. As a result I felt my self-confidence grow in ways I'd never dreamed of. It occurred to me then that a part of my personality had been dormant, almost dead, but now it was coming to life! It seemed to me that in working with other hidden children toward the common goal of the gathering, this whole hidden-child part of me that I'd left in the closet, so to speak, came out because I was allowing it to. How wonderful it was to find that I could talk about the past and express my feelings and know that others not only heard me but also accepted what I had to say.

"People say my whole demeanor is different now, that I'm jollier, more outgoing, more relaxed. I'm sure it's true. I worked very hard, but I wasn't *just* helping others; I was also freeing myself.

"There has been another force at work in my healing, and that has been my continuing joy in seeing our children and our grandchildren living happy lives. For so many years I carried tension and the fear of death. Now I can actually see the family expanding with new life. What a difference that's made! Recently my husband, Ed, threw a big surprise party for my birthday. I was surrounded by friends and family, with babies all over the place. It made me think of life instead of death. It felt like a new and very hopeful beginning."

ED, *a graphics designer, is whimsical, expansive, and friendly. His hair and beard are reddish, with hints of gray. His studio is spacious and sunny, with fancy computer equipment, neatly organized drawers filled with art supplies, and several bright Mexican serapes hanging from the ceiling. Ed works virtually undisturbed, except by Sam, the Lessings' tabby cat, who frequently meows to be let out or to be let back in.*

"I was born in 1926, into a Dutch Jewish family that wasn't very much aware that they were Jews and never went to synagogue. My father, a musician, was actually sort of an atheist. As fairly poor people who were struggling, they didn't pay much attention to what was going on in the world. We weren't a politically aware family, just a happy family struggling along.

"In 1940 we were living in Delft, right on a canal. It was two days after my fourteenth birthday when we awoke at five A.M. to gunfire. I looked out, and in the distance paratroopers were dropping to the ground in big white parachutes. I thought it was some kind of exercise—great fun, all this shooting and noise. I went up on the roof to watch. My father pulled me back. He'd just heard on the radio that Germany had invaded. The disaster came over us literally out of a blue sky. In five days it was over: the Germans had bombed the Dutch into submission.

"After that, life went on as usual, except there were men in uniforms marching through the streets. They were hated, but nobody stood in the streets shouting to them, 'Get out, you bastards.' Once the official anti-Semitism started, there was a new decree every week, and we, as good little Dutch people, believed that you don't break the law; that was unheard of. Nobody in Holland broke the law. Within two years we were not allowed to go into parks, not allowed to own a bicycle or a radio, not allowed to go to school or have a job.

"Pretty soon they issued the decree about wearing stars, but even at that point it didn't feel dangerous. Maybe that was because many Dutch Christian friends were saying to me, 'You should be proud of that star! Do feel that we think you're wonderful people.' That sort of thing. The first real major insult to me was when I was walking in town with my cousin. We looked almost like twins, but I had a star on my coat, and he didn't, because his father was a Gentile. We met up with a German officer, who stopped us and asked for our papers. Mine had a big *J* stamped on it, and my cousin's didn't. The officer told me I had no right to walk with someone without a star. He hit me in the face so hard, I fell on the cobblestone street. He said to my cousin, 'If I ever catch you walking with a Jew again, *you're* going to jail.'

"Shortly after that incident my family was summoned to a work camp in Poland. My parents were ready to go, but my grandfather from Amsterdam, said, 'You really think you're going to survive if you go? You're crazy!' My parents were shocked. First you didn't break the law, nobody did. Also the idea that they could get killed was absurd. Yet here the grandfather was telling them that they would never come back.

"Finally my parents decided that my grandfather might be right, that the only hope for us was to go into hiding. That was the day we walked out of the house. We just walked out with nothing. By nightfall my two brothers had been taken to hide in Amsterdam. My parents were with friends, and I had been left with two old people named Nieuwenhuizen and their surprisingly young daughter, Iens. There I was, suddenly, with no mother, no father, no brothers, and no home. Only God knew what was to come.

"I spent much of my time there looking at Iens because she was very pretty. She didn't pay much attention to me. In the daytime I stayed in my little room on the second floor and read. At night I could walk around their very quiet neighborhood because it was completely dark. The only lights were little blue slits of light on German trucks.

"Like many rescuers the Nieuwenhuizens were not prepared to keep me long-term. Before long I was sent to Utrecht, to the home of two elderly ladies named Troost. They were kind, but they, too, had a limit on how long they were willing to keep me. It was very much in the spirit of: 'Listen, yes, I can take your son, but only for a few weeks or months, and that's it. I'm afraid to do it any longer.' Many people were willing, but just dead scared!

"After that I spent brief periods hiding with different relatives. However, life was becoming more dangerous. My parents knew they had to find a steady place for me, and the likely choice was a farm. My mother took me to a small farm in Hollandse Rading, a tiny town near Utrecht, and presented me as an underfed kid from the city who was hungry and could help on the farm in exchange for room and board. That was the first time I went as a non-Jew and even dyed my hair blond.

"As a city kid I'd never done physical work, but now I had to get up at four A.M. to milk the cows, even though my feet were bleeding from wooden shoes with no socks. It was hell! There were ten cows to milk, and then the full twenty-gallon milk cans had to be dragged over to the canal, where there was a little rowboat. I'd haul them into the rowboat and row them to the end of the canal, lift them out, and drag them up to the road, where the truck picked them up. Then I had to take the empty cans from the day before and put them back, care for the horses, clean the pigsties, cut greenery, and dig sugar beets for the cows. I knew nothing when I started, but I learned fast! Everything ached.

"I felt very, very sad—abandoned and abused, like someone out of a Dickens novel. The farmer was just like his farm: thin, emaciated, dirt poor. He never spoke except to tell me what to do. I was so depressed, I really considered turning myself in to the Germans. At least then the tension would be over! But my mother wouldn't let me give up. She insisted that the war would be over before long. But would it? When the Germans first invaded Holland, we'd all felt so confident that the English and the French would beat the hell out of the Germans and the war would be over in three months. But it lasted and lasted, and the Germans only seemed to get stronger. It seemed rather hopeless to me, but I didn't surrender. I stayed on that farm for about six months.

"Meanwhile my parents were hiding with a childless couple and experiencing a lot of tension. Those people were nice, but no matter how good you are with people, just take two strangers into your household for, say, a month, and see how long it lasts before you start arguing: 'He doesn't hang up the towels right,' or 'She doesn't wash the cups.' Desperate for a breather, my parents decided to spend a weekend in a little hamlet called Lage Vuurse, which was only a twenty-minute walk from where I worked. They thought they would be safe there, but almost as soon as they arrived, there was a knock at the door of their hotel room. It was a policeman.

"My parents were terrified. The policeman said, 'Relax, I know you're Jews, and I want to help you.' To the world he was a Dutch Nazi; secretly he was one of the people who had helped organize the Resistance. He told my parents, 'You can't stay here, they'll spot you.' Instead he took them to a group hostel for nature lovers. There they would be safe to spend a couple of weeks before returning to their rescuers. I spent a few days there with my parents. I dreaded going back to the farm so much that the policeman arranged for me to go into a nearby Resistance camp, hidden deep in the woods. There was a very complicated zigzag path in, which went around and around. Somewhere in the middle was a large hut, and that's where I stayed for several months.

"It was very exciting there. This wasn't working your butt off on a little stinky farm! We lived in a hut that had all the trappings of my boys' adventure books: half underground and camouflaged with little trees. As the youngest person there and the only Jew, I wasn't welcomed with open arms, but I was tolerated, and now at least I had people to talk to. There was a young shoemaker, an older fat man, a bookkeeper, a red-headed man with freckles, and a Communist. There were some Catholics. All of them had one goal: to defeat the Germans. They would go out on nightly raids to break into town halls and steal the materials needed to make fake identity cards.

"I was still only sixteen, but I was given a pistol to carry. They didn't take me on raids, but my job was to watch the English, Canadian, and American flyers who had been shot down to make sure that none were German spies. Little by little I got to feel like a member of the group. I gradually acquired patience: you just waited, hoping that nobody would discover you and that you stayed alive.

"After I'd been there for six months, my friend, the policeman, came and told us of a rumor that our camp would be raided by the Germans. In response we set up shifts for guard duty: two men, four hours each, which went on for days. One morning I was on the four-to-eight morning shift with the shoemaker. It was still dark when we heard trucks coming up the road. We saw two headlights, then two more and two more. It seemed like dozens of trucks. We heard commands shouted in German. We saw their searchlights, their dogs, and their machine guns.

"Quickly we crept back into the woods. When we reached our hut, we screamed to everyone in our shelter to get out because the Germans were coming. It took a couple of minutes to wake them all. Then we ran! It felt like we ran for hours. It was the most frightening thing that had ever happened in my whole life. Afterward I kept thinking about the others, who had all been in underwear or pajamas. I don't see how they could have gotten out. Following that incident I wound up with my parents again, but I was a total wreck. The sound of a truck just sent me into shakes.

"Our friend the policeman, who knew exactly what had happened, found me a place to stay in a town called Hilversum, with an older man and his sister, who were very old-fashioned patrician Dutch people. To my amazement this place was luxurious! I came from a poor Jewish family, and our friends were all kind of lower middle class, but this was upper middle class. For the first time in my life I had my own room, with nice furniture and carpeting.

"So that I wouldn't be seen downstairs in the daytime,

the maid brought me my breakfast and my lunch on a tray. I remember toast and boiled eggs. At night I had supper with the man and his sister, who were both very upright Dutch people with stiff collars. They were beautiful people, very sweet. I recuperated quite a bit there.

"While I was there, something incredible happened to me. There was a Bible in the house, and though I'd never read a word in it before, I read the story of my people: the story of persecutions. This Bible said, 'You will try to hide, but there will be no hiding place.' I felt like a prospector finding a rich vein of gold! All of a sudden I had something that filled my life. I read the Old Testament from cover to cover. It was like food for me. I got myself a Bible from the Christian Bible society for free. I carried it everywhere. I read it every night before I fell asleep—and I became a Jew! I promised God, 'I will follow these laws as best as I can in my circumstances if you will save my family.' Now for the first time in months I had real hope.

"When I had calmed down some, the policeman found me a farm where I could work. This one—unlike the first place I'd worked—was great, much like those farms you see in Dutch paintings, with fat, jolly farmers dancing at parties. The farmer's wife was fat, his daughters were fat, and they had lots to eat. They were just wonderful people. I stayed there for several weeks. Then inevitably rumors started, and it wasn't safe for me to stay any longer. From there I headed down the road to another farmer . . . and then another. You couldn't stay anywhere for long, it was too dangerous.

"Each time, I presented myself as a Christian. But now, in my heart, I was more of a Jew than I'd ever been in my life! Sometimes the farmer would tell a story about 'an avaricious bastard, you know, like the Jews.' I'd sit there and smile, but it was a dagger in my heart.

"It pained me that I wasn't a worthier Jew. I had made up this religion by myself. *My* Judaism wasn't what you'd find in a synagogue. It was homemade and riddled with compromise. For example, I had to eat bacon because one of the main staples of a farm dinner was potatoes with strips of very fat bacon. I said a silent prayer every time I ate bacon: Please, God, I have to do this. Nor was there any way I could observe the Sabbath when I had to work on Saturdays. Most troubling of all, I felt impure because I spent so much time thinking about sex. I worried constantly that God would think I wasn't keeping up my end of the bargain.

"At least by this time I was pretty convincing in my role as a well-trained farmhand. I could plow fields with two horses, I could cook, put up barbed wire. On the last farm where I worked in the winter of 1943, the Germans used to exercise and train right there. I could even tell which Germans were really dangerous and which ones weren't. For example, a bunch of German soldiers practicing with a gun was like nothing to me. They didn't even look at me, but I looked at them. I got a real kick out of officers stepping on soldiers: If they didn't lie low enough, the officers would press them into the mud with their heels.

"Once, I got frightened out of my wits. I woke up, saw a truck, and heard German voices arguing. I thought: This is it, say good-bye. But they didn't want me—they wanted two cows! They got two cows from the farmer I was living with then and took off. The farmer protested and screamed. I commiserated. I said, 'How scandalous!' It was so hard not to smile with relief.

"That farm was next to a beautiful, really wild wood, and there was a gamekeeper much like the character in *Lady Chatterley's Lover*, with a green suit and a hunting rifle—and a gorgeous daughter. I had never been with a girl, yet here was a girl in love with me! When I told my mother, she said, 'You're crazy. If you want to get killed, this is what you do. If her father has any Nazi sympathies, that's it.' That was the end of my one and only love affair in all those years.

"At that point my mother had a great idea, which was to rent a remote little summer cottage in the woods. There she and my father could get away from their rescuers, with whom they had so much friction. Also they could be with my two little brothers. My mother went ahead and rented a place. However, in traveling to find places for my little brothers, she was caught by some Gestapo, who spotted her false identity card. The next thing we heard, she was sent to Camp Westerbork in the east of Holland. This was a holding pen from which 110,000 Dutch Jews were sent to their deaths.

"My father went to that little house, and my two brothers were delivered there from Amsterdam by an aunt. I was only two hours away on the farm where I was working. Sneaking over to see them, I took one look at my father, who was not too handy, and these two little kids and I said, 'I'll join you.' It was a little wooden house at the end of a dirt road. The owner lived right next door in a large house. He was not a farmer but a refined gentleman named Mr. Hamburger, who loved Mozart and grew apples and pears and other fruit untainted by artificial fertilizer. He had a shack with about ten thousand produce jars.

"Mr. Hamburger asked my father, 'Isn't your wife coming?' My father said, 'Well, she had a terrible accident. She was at the train station in Amsterdam and about to come here, and she fell and she broke her leg.' 'Oh,' Mr. Hamburger said, 'That's terrible.' 'Yes,' my father said, 'She's in the hospital.' After a few weeks Mr. Hamburger asked, 'How's your wife's leg coming?' 'Well,' my father said, 'Complications have set in. She got gangrene, and her leg had to be amputated.'

"Another month went by. Mr. Hamburger said, 'Is your wife coming soon?' My father said, 'It's so terrible! She got so depressed over the leg, she's now in an insane asylum. Now they'll never let her out.' Today we laugh when we think about those stories, but at the time, it wasn't funny at all. We got word that my mother had been shipped to the notorious death camp, Bergen-Belsen. It would be a miracle if she survived.

"Mr. Hamburger seemed to like my father. One day he gave my father a tour of all his trees and produce. As they walked, Mr. Hamburger said, 'The war is a terrible thing, isn't it?' 'Oh, yes!' my father agreed. Mr. Hamburger said, 'These Germans, they're really very bad.' 'Yes,' said my father, encouraged. 'Yes,' Mr. Hamburger nodded, 'The Germans are *terrible* . . . *Almost* as bad as the *Jews*!' We spent the last winter of the war selling all Mr. Hamburger's jars to local farmers in exchange for food. We stole as much as we could from him.

"That winter of 1944 to 1945 was a hell of a winter. Everything was snow and ice. I can't say we didn't have food. We had gathered and begged for potatoes. With my farm skills I had dug a hole underground for storage, lined it with straw, and then covered it up with dirt to keep the potatoes from freezing. We had lots of turnips, and the only place we could put them was in our outhouse toilet.

"We even made salt by stealing cows' salt licks, breaking them into pieces, and boiling them for three hours. My father found a place where they had a supply of cough syrup for children. When nobody showed up, he stole some and we'd pour it over bread. We had a whole survival industry going!

"My father made shoulder bags for my two little brothers. Whenever we heard the peculiar whining sound of a threshing machine off in the distance, my father would say, 'Okay, get the bags.' He'd give the boys a couple of guilders, and they would follow the sound and stand there in their little wooden shoes with their bags, and they'd say, 'Please, Mr. Farmer, could we have a pound of wheat?' Then, I'd grind up what they brought back, mix it with water, tie it up in an old stocking, and hang it in a pan of boiling water for an hour. Once cooled, it was a little bit like a bagel.

"Everyone had a job. The boys carried water. Every night my father and I would cut down a tree and carry it home. We'd roll it under the cottage. In the morning we'd cut it into firewood and use it, wet as it was. We were busy from morning to night just surviving. Finally it was the spring of 1945 and gorgeous weather. Every night we heard V-1 missiles overhead. Sometimes they would stop rumbling, and then your heart stood still because they'd come down in a terrible explosion. One day I heard a hissing sound way up high. I looked through some old binoculars and saw this little plane flying at a speed I'd never seen before. Shhh. It hissed through the sky. It had double jet engines. I thought that it was another secret German weapon. I feared the Allies might yet lose the war and we our lives!

"We also heard gunfire, and within hours it got very loud, with bullets whistling through the trees. We didn't see anybody shooting. It got heavier, and little branches were being shot off the trees and falling down on our little cabin. Pop said, 'I think we have to go into the bomb shelter with Mr. Hamburger.' Just then a farmer showed up with a duck. He said, 'You guys want a duck?' My father asked, 'What's wrong with the duck?' It was dead. It seemed that a shell had exploded in the man's backyard, killing the duck. Now the duck was full of shrapnel. We hadn't had meat in God knows how long, so we took the duck, removed all the steel, and put him in a pot on our stove outside. 'Oh, duck!' we told each other happily. 'Tonight we'll have duck!'

"In the meantime the fighting was coming closer and closer. Huge grenades started to be thrown over, and there were thunderous explosions, and the ground shook. We hustled my brothers into the shelter. However, the duck still had fifteen minutes to cook! By the time we got the duck done, my father and I were on our bellies, crawling to the shelter with the duck. There we stayed for three days, under constant shelling. It was no longer a matter of who was Jewish and who was anti-Semitic. We were all just people under bombardment. We sat there with the Hamburger family of course. At one point the little Hamburger boy started crying, and his sister, who was taking care of him, said, 'You'd better shut up, or I'll put you outside in the bullets.' He shut up right away.

"Then all of a sudden the noise outside stopped, and we could hear voices. Cautiously I looked through a little opening, and I saw three German soldiers with machine guns running by—and those were the last free German soldiers I saw! Then there was more shooting and finally silence. My father said, 'I think it's over, let's go outside.'

"Our legs were so cramped and stiff that we couldn't even stand up at first. Finally we got outside in the gleaming sunshine. I expected to see thousands of mighty Americans come marching in formation, waving American flags. Instead we just heard this grinding engine sound. We walked over to the field where the sound was coming from. There was a whole new road where there had never been a road. On this road there were tanks and personnel carriers, one after another. I looked up at these guys with helmets and Eisenhower jackets. We were all crying and screaming, 'Hello, hello. Welcome.' The guys just said hi. They probably saw ten thousand people waving hello to them. They would never, ever understand what we went through!

"After that life improved rapidly. My father and my

brothers and I went back to Delft. I was standing outside at twilight when an English army truck stopped in front of the house. A woman in a jumpsuit got out. Smiling, she said to me, 'Excuse me, sir, do you know where the Lessings live?' *It was my mother!* She was back! She told us the story of how she had been in the camp, lying in a bunk bed under three or four layers of people. She was very sick, but she had a dream about a newspaper dated January 15. It said something about freedom. The dream gave her hope to go on living.

"Then January 15 arrived, and my mother was exchanged for a German prisoner! Naturally we were all overjoyed to be together once again. I realized then that God had kept his end of the deal, despite my bacon eating and the other sins. God *had* kept our whole family safe, a remarkable gift!

"Shortly after that we got a house that had belonged to a Nazi. People in Delft were very nice and said, 'Lessing, what else do you need?' He said, 'Well, I was a piano teacher.' So they said, 'We'll give you a piano.' My parents also received a set of silver with strange initials on them that had belonged to Dutch Nazis.

"Normal life resumed. I joined a Zionist organization, not because I was political but because I wanted to meet girls. I did—and quickly fell in love. Then I went to the United States. My father and I came first. A year later my mother and two brothers followed. Later Carla and her mother immigrated to the U.S. Carla and I were married. The years went by quickly, as we built a family. We didn't go back to Holland very much. Even at home we didn't speak a lot of Dutch. After all, our children were American, and the past—I felt sure—was firmly behind us.

"Still, the years were racing by. Then it was 1990, and

Carla was very involved in planning the Hidden Child Conference, something I had no special interest in. At some point Carla asked me if I was coming to the conference. At first I said no. ('Really, all that was so long ago!') Then I decided I had better come. After all, she had done so much to organize it. I thought it would look funny if her husband didn't even show up. I had no idea that that weekend in New York City would change my life!

"This was what happened: On the Saturday night, we arrived at the hotel. I saw them all around me: hidden children, pushing to get their tags and meal tickets. Here they were by the hundreds, rising as out of hiding, coming up on the elevators. But they were not the children they once were, fearful in darkness, threatened with death at every street corner. Now they were gray-haired men and women in suits and dresses, reading their programs with glasses. They wanted to register. Their eagerness energized the very air. Excited, I began to feel a stirring in my soul.

"Sunday morning I found myself standing in a sea of hidden children. With a Danish in one hand and orange juice in the other, I watched them as they dashed by and hugged and talked—and oh, how they talked. It was as if they had not had a chance since they came out of hiding in Poland, Belgium, France, Holland. I was astonished. I never knew there were so many like me, saved from hell's fires. I thanked God they were here with me now.

"For two days we listened to the speakers, and we cried—for the dead, for the speakers, for those in the workshops whose suffering was far from over. Many were still alone, still full of fear. In the evening there was dancing. Was it possible for us to dance? It was! On the seventh floor in the back of a room stood a bulletin board. There I read letters thrown out of cattle cars by Jews unaware of their coming death. 'We are going to Poland to work. Do not worry about us,' the letters insisted. I shed more tears.

"On Monday, the last day of the gathering, a group of ordinary-looking men and women gathered on the stage. These people were rescuers: fearless, determined, the righteous of the world. I was deeply moved. That evening the conference ended. I said my last good-byes. It was agony. I was losing all my new brothers and sisters all over again. For the first time in two days we went outside the hotel just as a furious thunderstorm was breaking overhead. Carla and I drove home amid flashes of lightning and crashes of thunder. In our hearts we carried with us all the stories we heard, and the faces we saw of the hidden children who were there.

"As a result of the conference hidden children were suddenly receiving a huge amount of media attention. Shortly after the conference I appeared on a *Good Morning America* broadcast. It was very short, wedged between the weather report and the traffic. One thing I said was that for me the main thing that came out of it was intense gratitude that Carla and I had survived. I thought of our family as a plant that had been cut off at the roots, but sprouted new growth. It's true! We have children, and now *they* have children. Our family is growing. We didn't die, we didn't get destroyed. We didn't get murdered, and look: We're still here!

"That was my conclusion back in May 1991. But wait: There's a postscript. What do I have now that I've lacked for the fifty preceding years? Did the gathering make any real changes in my life? Listen! A few months ago Carla handed me a letter from a hidden child who could not come to the gathering. Carla said that maybe I should contact the man, who lived nearby. And so I met Eddy Strauss.

"One evil night in 1942 Eddy went out to play, promising

his mother to be home before the six o'clock curfew. He came home at seven and was hauled into a neighbor's house just before he reached his front door, where Germans were dragging his mother, his one-year-old baby brother, and his beloved three-year-old sister into their trucks. 'You know,' says Eddy, 'What drives me crazy is that the Red Cross report states that all three were dead the same day that they arrived in Auschwitz.'

"Eddy came to America, received his education, and joined the United States Army. He served in Germany with the adjutant general's staff on denazification cases. He married a lovely girl, and they were happy. However, she couldn't have children; then she died of cancer in 1975. Eddy, in a rage with God, destroyed every picture of her that he could find. It was about the same time that Eddy, through an accident and diabetes, had to have his right leg amputated. Was it any surprise that he tried to kill himself?

"Eddy now spends his days in a wheelchair in a small apartment reading, listening to the radio, and watching the ball games. He is in debt to the pharmacy for hundreds of dollars because he cannot pay for his medications. Surely in that fifty-nine-year-old damaged body of Eddy lives a fourteen-year-old boy. That little boy lost the father he adored, his mother, his little sister, and his baby brother. When he went back to his old home in Antwerp, Belgium, and asked the new occupants if there were any pictures in the house of those who had once surrounded him with love and care, he was told, 'Go away, or we'll call the police.' I wound up with everything while Eddy, my namesake, ended up with nothing. At least I'm here for him now as a brother. I go to see him often, and if nothing else at least I can help him with some of the love that was stolen from him fifty years ago.

"Before the gathering I pushed it all away. I didn't want

to think about the past. It took all these years to begin, but now at sixty-five I'm reading and I'm weeping. I'm beginning to understand how it happened and what they did. What they did to me. What they did to all of us Jews. In a sense I feel like I'm just waking up."

JOSIE MARTIN

Josie Martin, a delicate, youthful-looking mother of a college student, has light gray eyes and shining hair. As she talks, there is no clue to the fact that she didn't speak English until she was nine. Josie is a school psychologist and a writer. She lives with her husband in an old, rather stately part of Los Angeles called Hancock Park. There, in her house, her sunny bedroom is filled with her various collections: baskets, tiny boxes, small sculptures of mother and child. Her dining room is furnished in country French, which she says she didn't do deliberately. "It just happened. Then I realized how much it reminded me of such a room in one of the farmhouses where we hid—talk about déjà vu!"

"I was born in 1938, in a town almost on the border between France and Germany. When the Germans invaded in 1939, we evacuated to a little French village, where we rented part of another family's house. There weren't many Jews in the town, but we were well accepted there. As time went on, I even went to nursery school. However, by 1944 there were Nazi sweeps taking place. That was bad enough, but the greater danger was from the French police: the real super Gestapo, forever trying to show the German Nazis how loyal they were by betraying Frenchmen who were helping Jews.

"My parents were terrified. We left our little two-room home and went into hiding temporarily with a farm family. One farmer and his wife, who were friends of ours, offered—and actually begged—to adopt me. Even though they were worried about me, my parents refused to consider such a radical step. Then another friend told them of a nun who ran a small girls' school in a very small village in L'Esterps, which was fifty kilometers away from where we lived. My parents established the contact, and the nun agreed to take me. The school was a day school. There were no other children living at the convent.

"My parents were so befuddled, so terrified and overwhelmed, survival was the only thing they could focus on. When they dropped me off at the convent, they really didn't explain anything to me beyond the fact that my name would no longer be Josie Levy, it would be Josie L'Or. No doubt there was a fond good-bye, but I cannot remember it.

"The nun was a no-nonsense person and a woman of great importance in the small village. She was very political and very involved in helping the villagers. For example, she was the one who would write to the front and ask about missing sons. In some ways she was almost like a social worker. I developed tremendous admiration for this woman, who was strong, important, and very different from the typical French farm woman of the region. Even I felt a sense of importance in being 'her' child.

"My immediate caretaker was a young woman I did not like at all, who did not like me either. She didn't know that I was Jewish. That was lucky, because she turned out to be a Nazi collaborator—a fact my parents did not know until afterward. So much for their effort to put me in a safe place! Of course the nun didn't know about this woman's Nazi connection either. By the time she realized it, she couldn't do anything because of her own vulnerability.

"During this time the Americans landed in Normandy. The Germans, in retreat, knew they were going to lose. Abandoning all civility, they went about burning crops. One Saturday, in the adjoining village, Oradour sur Glanes, the Germans rounded up all the men, women, and children and systematically set fire to them. Six hundred seventy people were killed; almost none escaped. None of these people were Jews. The attacks had nothing to do with being Jewish. Nevertheless it was terrifying, because we all knew that our village would be next. For several days we had to hide in the woods.

"For the adults it was unmitigated horror, but I felt fantastic excitement from being a little person and getting to do what the big people were doing. Imagine getting up in the middle of the night, getting dressed, and then heading for the woods, where we bedded under the stars! I tried not to think about my parents. I had transferred most of my loyalties to the nun, and it didn't even bother me very much when the lines of communication were down and we stopped hearing from my parents.

"One Sunday morning in August 1944 the doorbell rang. I peeked outside. My parents were standing there. I took one look and I knew I didn't want to go with them. I even pretended that I didn't know who they were. (Actually I knew exactly who they were, but I thought I could get away with it.) As we gradually got reacquainted, my mother was shocked that I had become such a silent child. Apparently I had learned silence well. The nun had enforced the practice of silence. Silence was part of the religious tradition, but I'm sure she also did it to shut me up, because when I first got there, I was such a demanding, talkative child.

"Looking back, the worst abandonment was not when my parents left me at the convent. It was afterward, because in the months and years that followed, the theme of abandonment got played out again and again in endless ways. Years later friends would say to me, 'Well, you were only gone six months.' Only? Much later, when I became a mother myself, I saw how much preparation I would go through just to leave my son with a baby-sitter for a couple of hours!

"That's why I feel that my parents were incredibly naive—not just in having failed to prepare me but more than that, in their lack of attention afterward to what the separation had really meant to me. It wasn't that the subject of the war was taboo, as it was in so many Jewish families. In my family we did talk about the war. But in these discussions the message to me was clearly, 'You were lucky, you have no right to complain.' After all, our branch of the family survived, so whatever happened to us didn't count much.

"One aunt told stories about her experience in a concentration camp. As I listened, one thought always came to me: It seemed more secure to me to be in a concentration camp instead of having to go and hide and wonder if you'd be caught tonight or tomorrow or the next day. When I shared that observation with my parents, they did what any parent of that background would do, which was to say, 'You're a little kid. Who asked you?' Since that was their attitude, I had no opportunity to process my feelings.

"The bleakest time of all for me was when we immigrated to the United States. We were so foreign, so poor, and we spoke no English. My father was forty-eight years old. He had no job or skills, so we were at the mercy of relatives who had already come here. We moved to a part of Los Angeles that had no Jews. There was nobody like me there. A lot of World War II G.I.'s lived there; many transplanted from the Midwest.

To these people World War II was Japan. They didn't know about Europe or Jews or concentration camps.

"Nor were the teachers in the elementary school any help. If anything, a child who spoke three languages was an object of curiosity to them. They would come up to me and tell me to say something in French. It made me want to cry, because I hated being different. My parents, too, were victims, and they were doing their best, but I felt so abandoned: They had no sense of what I had to go through at school without a word of English.

"I was determined to master English as soon as possible, and I did it! In three months I was speaking English. But in addition to liberating me, that new skill just saddled me with still another responsibility. Now I had to be the family translator. That put me in a quasi-adult role, as, quite literally, I had to interpret the outside world to my parents. It all boiled down to coping and survival, but to me it meant that childhood was over.

"Of course I wasn't a real adult, and the discrepancy between how I felt and how I had to behave produced some massive anxiety attacks. I was terrified that my parents would be killed on the Los Angeles freeways. Whenever they went out, which wasn't often, I was frantic if they were two minutes late! I was beside myself. But instead of recognizing the fear and maybe even saying, 'Gosh, it must be hard for you,' my parents chastised me for being such a baby. Finally even I began to doubt that my feelings made any sense at all, but that didn't stop the feelings. At eighteen years old I still sometimes found myself standing by the window immobilized as I waited for them to come home. I had no real understanding of what I was feeling, much less where the pain was coming from.

"In college I wrote term papers about having been hidden in World War II, because it was a very quick sell. The first time that I decided that maybe my early childhood was more than just an interesting anecdote was when I was actually beginning therapy as an adult because I was trying to leave a marriage and I didn't have the courage to do it.

"I said to my psychiatrist, 'Oh, by the way, there is something about my childhood that maybe you should know.' I spoke of being hidden, away from my parents, at the age of six. I was a teacher at the time, and I knew just enough about psychology to think that maybe my experience *had* been more important than anybody realized. He listened to the story. Afterward he looked at me and he said, 'Gee, that's very interesting, but nothing major happened. You weren't abused, and your parents lived.'

"So I decided that he was right, that my childhood did not account for my *mishegas*. The doctor stated that what happened to me was nothing compared with the suffering of children who had lost their parents in camps and/or who had actually been in camps. Once again I managed to bury my feelings. That worked fine—until a few years later. I was then divorced and remarried and I had a son.

"Finding myself in a very protracted postpartum depression, I sought counseling again. Through very hard work I came to realize that the small child that I had never been and had never been allowed to be was now in desperate competition with a real child. I tried not to let it show: I was always careful to be very warm and loving with this little baby, but I felt awful. When he was not particularly responsive, I became outraged with him (and then of course with myself). I was filled with guilt at not being able to cope better.

"That was when I really began to get in touch. My new therapist was a young woman who simply believed that her 'high-achieving' clients were too serious, too contained, and needed to pay attention to the needs of that other, less civilized being that also resided inside (and who, when ignored, caused enormous unrest). This therapist was not especially familiar with Holocaust survivors. However, she had an acute sense of the individual's tendency to abandon the child within. She also knew that this was often the origin of personality maladjustments.

"She helped me to see that I had incorporated into my general behavior the same abandonment that had befallen me as a child. In other words I had abandoned the child's needs and demands the same way my parents had. I speak not only of the abandonment of being left with a stranger when I was six but also of the abandonment throughout my childhood and adolescence: failing to note most any of my needs beyond basic food, shelter, and not much else.

"My therapist encouraged me to do things almost ritualistically for the small child who had really been so deprived and misunderstood. She encouraged me to make amends to my own inner child by urging me to buy myself little trinkets that I wanted and had never had, things I would mention as being 'so cute, but aren't they silly?' She said, 'I want you to buy them!' That was how I began a very slow recovery.

"I didn't lose my fear of abandonment, but I learned to recognize its negative impact on my life and to try at least to reassure the interior child when 'she' becomes exasperating and uncontrolled. Of course, as with most dysfunctional behavior, one tends not to be conscious of it when it is at its worst. Thankfully these episodes became much less frequent. For example, when my son was in high school, he was often late and not very good about calling, which made me anxious! I would also worry if my husband was late—something he didn't understand at all in the beginning, and he felt that I was being controlling. So I had to take him with me to therapy and literally tell him what was happening.

"For a long time I was afraid that I would pass these clinging, clutching, worrying feelings on to my child. Thank goodness, it didn't happen. I'd love to take credit for that, but I think it's just that he has a different temperament. He was born thinking, The world will take care of me. Even as an infant he had no separation anxiety. He is the most secure human being, and I'm grateful for that.

"Sometimes, when I think about what happened to me, I try to figure out what I would have done if I had been a parent during the war instead of a child. I don't think I would ever have let my child go. He would die with me, I'm convinced of that! That was one of the things that came up as soon as I had a baby. I thought, My God, I could be in that same position and what would I do? Of course it's easy to be the salon liberal and say things without having to prove them.

"I also wonder if I could have been a rescuer. When I think of that, I'm always struck by how heroic that nun was—not just for the obvious reason of risking her life by taking in the enemy or a perceived enemy. I also think about the upheaval it must have caused for this woman to take in a child! I know what a disruption it was when my own son was a little boy and would have friends spend the night.

"Maybe a lot of us would rise to the occasion at a time of danger, but I'm extremely aware of how even the young woman who took care of me was hassled. Her job was to teach the girls at the school, and suddenly she was told, 'You're responsible for this little girl.' I can understand why she didn't like me. I was probably this sour-faced, grieving, mournful little person.

"Perhaps the most dramatic healing of all came from the change that took place between my parents and me when I was thirty-three and had recently become a mother myself. I had never rebelled as a teenager. However, real friction developed when I was in my early twenties. I announced that I was leaving Bob, my first husband, after four years of marriage. My parents became terribly disapproving of the dissolute life they imagined I was leading. In 1964 nice Jewish girls didn't leave husbands! It caused them no end of anxiety.

"At that point in my life my parents and I clashed on nearly everything. They were worried sick that I was dating Gentiles—and I was! I lived with one Christian man for a brief time. While my parents weren't supposed to know about it, I was all too conscious of how they would feel about it if they did know. By the time I met Ed, my present husband, my parents were fearing the worst, that I would marry a Christian. When I did that very thing, they began to realize that at age thirty I was on my own. They could no longer do anything about me. In a burst of uncharacteristic wisdom they accepted it!

"Actually it turned out to be much easier than they'd expected. My new husband was a lawyer—and very likable. Our financial security pleased them, and also the prospect of a grandchild delighted them. When my son, Geoffrey, was born, I went through some very rough times, as I mentioned before. That was when so many unresolved feelings about my own childhood—or more specifically the lack of it—came out. It was at this point that both of my parents realized, unconsciously perhaps, that their child was in trouble.

"They offered help and support in every conceivable way—from taking the baby for weekends to encouraging me to hire more help (which I'd felt reluctant to do, for fear that it would be further proof of my unfitness). It was my mother who insisted that I *deserved* to be relieved. I don't remember her ever taking such a generous stance with me before Geoffrey's birth. *But now she truly mothered me, as if for the first time*; and she took wonderful care of Geoffrey whenever she had him.

"She also gave me valuable perspective. I read too much about growth and development, and I was fearful that he wasn't developing in the expected ways. While I was harboring all sorts of misgivings about Geoffrey's possible developmental delays, my mother saw him simply as a wonderful little baby. My mother didn't minimize my concerns, but she simply didn't join me in my totally unwarranted craziness. That fact alone was enormously reassuring! It actually strengthened me at a time when I was extremely vulnerable.

"It surprised and delighted me to see how much joy they were capable of feeling. I'd had no idea that they had it in them! Maybe all grandparents are a bit daft over the first grandchild. I wondered if they had once been joyous over me. Surely this was the first time in all my life that I felt my parents' unconditional love. There was no demand, no disapproval, only a genuine appreciation of this dear grandchild and an instinctive sense that their own child needed them in a way that she had never perhaps shown before.

"I had been so overwhelmed, so unable to control the feelings that were assailing me from all sides, I was having a kind of a breakdown, I think you might say. My parents came to my aid as never before. Finally I had ceased being the daughter of strength. My parents were in good health, had just retired, and were reasonably secure financially for the first time in their lives. In short they were better off than they'd ever been. This allowed them to be the parents and givers that they could not be at those critical times in my childhood when I so badly needed them.

"Before all this I saw my parents only as weak, needy, ineffectual, needing to be spared from any additional burdens, overly critical, and almost never the source of comfort or security. So I, too, had to revise my perceptions, didn't I? Now I realized in a whole new way how cruelly the war had prevented them and me from experiencing each other at our best. How the real and/or imagined threats had so blackened their *Weltanschauung*, that we had lived in a long period of 'endarkenment.'

"The coming of the grandchild was a time of reconciliation and mutual appreciation that I still deeply cherish. I often think how tragic it would have been if one or the other had died early and I would have gone through life thinking of them as faulty, incomplete, morose human beings. Indeed they had been all these things, but they were also capable of more love and caring than that. It took a lot of time for this healing to happen. What great fortune that we were granted it!"

ANN SHORE

Ann Shore is slender and flamboyant-looking, with a mane of blond hair and dramatically made-up eyes. A successful artist, Ann lives on Long Island in a home that's pleasant and inviting, with her vibrant paintings on the wall, many plants, a green parrot perched on top of its cage, and cats all over the house. Ann, a wife and the mother of three creative grown children, is effusive and upbeat . . . until she begins to tell her story and the pain becomes overwhelming. She chokes with emotion, tears come. Self-conscious, she chuckles with embarrassment. "It was so confusing for a child to experience such brutality," she says in a strong Polish accent. "What was it I'd done that was so bad? I couldn't figure it out. People had always said I was a good little girl!"

"I was twelve on the morning in 1942 when the police in Zabno, Poland, where we lived, stuck a gun to me and asked me where my father was. I said I didn't know. The police ran down to the basement where my father was hiding, and they shot him to death. My mother and my sister, Rachel, and I had to flee to a nearby farm.

"After a few weeks the farmer decided that he couldn't keep us any longer. My mother remembered a very poor widow with many children who used to come to my parents' shoe store. My mother thought that if we could find this woman and tempt her with money, she might take us in. That night in a thunderstorm we trudged from village to village, peeping into windows in search of that woman. At last we found her! The woman agreed to let us hide in her barn in exchange for all the money we had. After a few months, however, she tried to make us go.

"My mother refused. She said, 'If we leave here, they will kill us.' She was right! Grudgingly the woman let us stay, but she totally ignored us. We stayed for two and a half years. In all that time she never gave us even a glass of water. We lived in an open hayloft with nothing but a single goosedown cover for the three of us to huddle under. We froze! Our fingers were swollen and stiff from the cold. The farmer woman took away the ladder. She would take away anything, just to make it difficult for us. My mother and sister called me the monkey, because I had to jump and climb. At one point I got jaundice and I almost died, but there was not a cup of warm water, much less medicine. As I was gradually recovering, Rachel got very sick. Then my mother got sick, too, so I had to go out alone to steal food.

"I could go out only when there was no moon. If anyone saw me in the moonlight, I would have been a goner. It was so tense! In a city like New York City you might get an anxiety attack if you believe that someone is following you. But that was how it felt to us for the whole two and a half years we were hiding. I would go to this terrible lake, which had moss in it. I can still taste the dirty water. Sometimes I would milk a cow. I would steal potatoes from the pigs. Anything, because we were starving. There wasn't a moment without hunger pain.

"We had to whisper—for two and a half years we never once spoke above a whisper! Nor could we go out in the daytime. The farmers' children would be playing outside in the field, and I would want so badly to go out and play with them, but I knew that was impossible. We were hanging on to life by a thin thread, always cold, scared of shadows, running, listening. Each day, each night, brought fresh terror. It was a terrible existence in so many ways, but as frightened as I was, I never even thought of giving up. I would look at pictures and see how fortunate and loved I was as a little girl before the war, and that gave me strength.

"Once, about six months before the end of the war, we heard a lot of Germans in the back. We were convinced that they had come for us. We panicked, but what could we do? There was no place to go. We were relieved when we realized that the soldiers were just resting for the night. However, this was the night the young men would be coming! Three young Jewish men who had worked for my father were hiding in the woods not far from the farm. Once a month they would sneak over to where we were with a loaf of bread or an old sweater. They were coming tonight, but how could I let them know that Germans were here?

"I listened carefully. The moment I heard our friends tapping, I swung down silently and made a sign for them to run. Thank God, they took off at once, and the Germans never saw them. The German guard was sitting there with a gun—but he had fallen asleep! What a relief! I often think it's amazing any of us survived. Under those circumstances anyone's survival was purely by chance.

"As soon as the war was finished, I was determined to put the whole experience out of my mind, as if it never existed. When I came out of hiding, I just went for it! I went to school, I took dancing and horseback riding. I felt like I had been given another chance, and I wanted to celebrate life. My mother—until she passed away in 1983—was totally obsessed with the Holocaust. I used to find that embarrassing. I just wanted to be like everybody else. You don't want to be different! I know it's a characteristic of abused children that for some reason the children paint the guilt upon themselves. I can't explain it any other way.

"For years and years I never wanted to talk or think about my experience during the war. Just thinking about it brought up such pain! I'd even managed my life to avoid other Europeans, for fear that they would remind me of the awful reality: Out of several hundred Jews who lived in Zabno, only fifteen survived! Strangely enough I knew one woman from Zabno named Genia, who lived only five miles away from me. I tried my best not to see her. I always felt that the past should be left behind, and I didn't even want to discuss it.

"Over the years I made an occasional effort to tell my children about my childhood. When I did try, I found I had blocks remembering it all. For example, there was one incident shortly after my father died. We were still in our town, and two German soldiers beat me up. I spoke to my sister the other day, and she says that one of the Germans wanted to kill me, but the other said, 'No, let her go.' I had blocked that out because it was so horrifying! My husband, Sidney, comes from Rumania. He was very fortunate because he comes from Bucharest, and at that point they had not done any real harm in the city. Just to show you how little we talked about it, my husband said to me, 'Well, you're not a Holocaust survivor. The only survivors are the ones who were in the camp.'

"Shortly after my mother died, I got involved with a child-survivor support group. I was still ambivalent about whether I should deal with the past or not. Did I need to? What was the point? On the other hand, I must have had a feeling that with my mother gone, it was up to me now. With some misgivings at first, I joined Nicole David and the small group planning the Hidden Child Gathering. It was a very grass-roots effort. Our first big boost was a two-thousand-dollar grant from Judith Kestenberg, a Long Island psychiatrist and activist for Holocaust survivors. Kestenberg also lent us a small apartment in Manhattan to use as an office.

"Next we placed announcements of the gathering-to-come in a couple of Jewish publications. We didn't even have a phone! At my daughter Diane's urging we did get ourselves an answering service. As I retrieved the first twenty or thirty calls, I noticed that most of the callers were very ambivalent. They were reaching out, making contact, but they weren't sure they wanted to come to the gathering. I could relate to that! I was still feeling torn myself. Each person I convinced to come felt like a personal victory.

"In the fall of 1990 we approached *New York* magazine, in the hope that an article about us would be good publicity for the event. It worked, far better than we'd imagined. When the article in *New York* came out, the volume of calls from former hidden children grew suddenly and dramatically. Each night I stayed up as late as I could reasonably call people back. I urged them to come, I begged them to come. I was passionate! There was one man I spoke to who said he would be out of the country. Something made me feel that he just needed someone to ask him to come. I said to him, 'If you don't like it, you don't have to stay.' Well, he came, and of course he did stay.

"There were hundreds like this who needed encouragement and reassurance. Some of these were people coming out for the first time, which is very scary. By that time we had hired Rochel Berman, a publicist–social worker, to coordinate the gathering. She was doing an excellent job getting us funding and now even more publicity all over the country and beyond. Still, the committee felt that only hidden children should handle these phone calls.

"The calls kept coming! Originally we'd hoped to have two or three hundred people at the gathering, but it was growing faster than we could keep up with. Clearly in need of some beefed-up resources, we asked the Anti-Defamation League for help. They were very interested in what we were doing, and they invited us to set up in their offices in New York City. At last we had the space and facilities we needed.

"All this time my husband, Sidney, was extraordinarily patient. I was spending all my time at the ADL offices or on the phone. I wasn't doing anything at home, no cooking, nothing! I believe that Sidney had just about reached the end of his patience with me, but he was very good about it. He understood that I was connecting with people who were asking me to share the most painful and most private experiences of their lives. Sidney agreed that this was no time to worry about taking care of the house.

"The last day—the day before the conference—we got three hundred calls we couldn't answer; we had a recording telling people to come. I hope they came! I felt so guilty that I couldn't talk to each one of them personally and if necessary coax them out of hiding. I had already come out. The article in *New York* magazine had been the big push. Up to that point I hadn't been at all sure that I wanted my story appearing in print. Even Sidney had been skeptical. He'd said, 'It's a long time ago. Why bring up all those things?' In fact I was tempted to say no, but my daughter kept at me, insisting I'd be sorry if I didn't do it.

"I had wanted to help publicize the gathering, that was the main thing. Still, I was so scared of the exposure, I considered using a fake name. I had all kinds of rationalizations for doing it halfway or not doing it at all. Mainly I was scared that in telling my story I would have to relive all the horrors I had so carefully contrived to forget.

"In the end I went through with it. I cried buckets during the interview; the mascara was running down my cheeks, but I did agree to the use of my name and even my picture. I was still very nervous. I had many sleepless nights, wondering if I'd done the right thing. When the article came out, it was a holiday weekend, President's Day. Because of that they didn't have the magazine in my local store yet, so I didn't see it. Ava Landy, who was also in the article, called me to tell me that my picture was a full page. She started reading the article. I felt naked. I thought I would die.

"That was the real start of my new life out of hiding. That same afternoon I was getting out of my car to buy some fish, when a strange woman came up to me. She said, 'Aren't you the one in *New York* magazine?' I said yes. She touched my arm gently, and said, 'I'm glad you're here.' I was touched. That was just the first such encounter. It got to the point where I couldn't go out without people coming up to me. So many people told me they were moved by my story, and not just strangers! Fellow artists I'd worked with in the studio for twenty years were moved—and astonished. They said, 'It's amazing how you can know somebody and never really know them.'

"The conference itself was a most profound experience. There was so much energy flying around as we all went back in time, becoming little children again, but carefree, the way we should have been. We talked, we looked intently at every face, every name tag. Naturally each one of us was hoping to see someone from the past. I found not one but two beloved friends! We embraced, held hands, and clung to each other, laughing. Who but we, the hidden children of the Holocaust, could feel such deep empathy for one another? Finally it was time to say good-bye: a moment of sadness, but full of love and hope. We promised we would all meet again. We had become brothers and sisters. At the end we held hands and shared a wish for a better future for ourselves and our children.

"Now it's been more than a year since the gathering. I'm out of hiding for good! I've spoken out, I've been on television many times. In fact I'm so well known in my town now, Sidney likes to go around telling people, 'I am *Mr.* Ann Shore.' I think he's proud of me. It's funny—before, I was afraid that I would be regarded as a freak or that people would look at me with curiosity. As I've come to understand myself better, I've lost my nervousness about that. I feel so calm! I don't even have my old nightmares anymore. I think that's because I can finally talk about how frightening it was instead of keeping it inside. I've integrated the wounded child inside me with the adult—and I'm just astonished by the new freedom that has given me.

"Now I feel my healing continuing with exhilarating speed. This year I even made a point of seeing Genia, that woman from Zabno who lives ten minutes away from me. I realized that the last time I had seen her was when she came to my son Les's bar mitzvah—twenty years ago! Since my life was now unfolding in a new way, I wanted to call her. I procrastinated, but then finally I left a message. When I got home the next day, there was a message on my machine. The message was in Polish: my mother's language! What really blew my mind was that Genia addressed me as Hania, which was my name when I was a child.

"I said to myself, 'Is this me? Is this me she's calling?' As I listened to that message, I felt like I was embracing a lost part of myself. How curious to find in this simple call a 'me' that was part of another world before the war! I was so pleased. I listened to the message tape over and over. A week or so after that I went to see this lady, Genia. We had a lovely time! As a result, now I've started taking Polish books out of the library. I feel an insatiable need to speak Polish. It's as if I've reconnected. In essence, I'm saying to myself, 'Hi there, where were you all these years?'

"I know that other hidden children's lives have changed just as dramatically. Simply knowing that we're not alone has been so healing! If we hadn't acted to have the gathering, so many people would have gone on suffering in isolation, many of them not even knowing that there were others like themselves.

"Is our joy in coming out of the closet enough? Not for me. I feel that we owe something to the next generation. That's why I'm still here at the Hidden Child Foundation office every day. In a way it makes no sense for me to keep coming in here. I'm a painter, and I should be in my studio, painting, but it's as if a part of myself is saying, You must do it!

"This is the reason: In our own families we may have suffered in silence, but we were not in a vacuum. Inevitably our childhood experiences surely affected our children. Some of our children grew up feeling lonely, shut out of a secret. One young man who was in yesterday told me that his mother, a former hidden child, never told him about her experience. He was so angry at her. She thought she was protecting him, but her secrecy and her refusal to explain why she felt and behaved in certain ways had left him angry, guilty, and confused.

"Some of these young men and women suffered because

their parents had no experience with family life and therefore no skills. When you've had little or no family life yourself, you may not know how to act. That's caused pain too. Yesterday I chaired a meeting for the second generation. Lots of young people came. Most of them were asking for help in understanding and communicating better with their parents. We *need* to keep talking: to heal and to help our children heal.

"We also need to talk for the sake of history, so that even when we're gone, our voices won't be lost. Lately I've been speaking to groups of schoolchildren. Some of them are twelve-year-olds, which gives me goose pimples because that was how old I was when I was hiding. I start out by showing them a big blown-up photograph of my twelfth birthday party. They see nice-looking children, dressed up. This sets the scene, showing them quite graphically, instead of just in words, that there was a time before the Holocaust, when life was normal.

"Then I tell my story. They sit there riveted, astonished. They say things like, 'My gosh, *we* take so much for granted in our lives.' And 'How can people be so cruel to want to kill you just because you're different?' One girl was irate. She had just heard someone on TV claim that the Holocaust had never happened. 'If anyone dares to say that to me, I'll call them a liar,' she promised. So many of the children have thanked me for speaking. They acknowledge how difficult and painful it must be to talk and have to relive the experience.

" 'You're right, it is hard,' I say. 'I'm doing it for you.' I tell them how a lot of us hidden children chose to leave it all behind us, trying to forget the horrors that we lived through. 'But now,' I tell them, 'I have to speak out so that you will know what happened.' A couple of weeks ago I gave a talk at Finley Junior High School in Huntington, Long Island. At the end one student asked me, 'What would you do if there was another Holocaust?' I looked at him, and I said, 'You know what? It will have to be your job to see that it never happens again. That's why I'm here in your school today. We survivors can tell our stories of the past. What will happen in the future is up to you.' "

A HISTORICAL PERSPECTIVE: TRACING THE HISTORY OF THE HIDDEN-CHILD EXPERIENCE*

by Nechama Tec, Ph.D.

In Nazi-occupied Europe the presence of hidden children signaled an opposition to the German policies of Jewish annihilation. These children tried to shed their Jewish identity by living illegally in the forbidden Christian world. Defying Nazi orders, some of them went into hiding, while others passed for Christians; still others, probably a majority, had to switch back and forth between the two.

In 1933, when Hitler came to power, he initiated the policies that led to the destruction of European Jewry. Starting with legal definitions of Jews, these laws soon deprived the Jewish population of their German citizenship.

Next came the confiscation of Jewish property and the removal of Jews from gainful employment. This was followed by

---

*A list of references for this chapter, including more than forty citations, is available on written request of the author at: University of Connecticut, Scofieldtown Road, Stamford, Connecticut 06903.

a series of steps, all designed to isolate the Jews from the rest of the population. These efforts to isolate them were expressed in a variety of ways. Some Jews were incarcerated in concentration camps. Others were forced into specially designated housing. Still others were outright murdered.

In conjunction with these changes, Jews were also being pressured into leaving the country. The Germans wanted to make Germany free of Jews.

Defining the Jewish presence as a problem, the Nazis were willing at first to settle for mass emigration. But as the momentum for forced departures was building up, barriers against emigration appeared from several directions. In part as a gesture of goodwill toward the Arabs, the British had curtailed the Jewish influx into Palestine. Also, by 1924 the United States' traditional receptiveness to immigrants underwent a drastic change, making it the last year for open immigration. Apart from these developments the economic depression resulted in an overall reluctance to accept immigrants.

Despite these restrictions, from 1933 until 1939, the population of German Jews shrank from 500,000 to 220,000. Of the 220,000 who stayed on, only 10 percent had survived the war.

Nazi military successes, including the 1939 occupation of Poland, sharply increased the Jewish population under German control. The victors became concerned about the "excess" Jews. Most historians agree that the actual plan for Jewish annihilation, the so-called Final Solution, became crystallized after the start of the German-Russian war in June 1941. The 1941 capture of Russian-held territories coincided with the mass murder of Jews, most of which was accomplished by the specially trained SS troops, the Einsatzgruppen.

With German military expansion came a proliferation of

anti-Jewish measures. These destructive policies were introduced in different countries at different times, with varying degrees of ruthlessness. For Polish Jews who survived the initial
onslaught, the last quarter of 1941 signaled the beginning of
the end. On October 15, 1941, the Germans introduced a law
that made the protection of Jews a crime punishable by death.
Poles who had harbored Jews were executed, often with their
families, including children.

In contrast, only in 1943 did the Nazis decide to move
against the Danish Jews, ordering their deportations to concentration camps. Moreover, the non-Jewish population in
Denmark was treated very differently than the one in Poland.
Danes who had committed the "crime" of protecting Jews
were dealt with more leniently than Poles who tried to rescue
Jews. If discovered, only very rarely were Danes sent to concentration camps.

Though the process of Jewish annihilation varied with time,
place, and degree of ruthlessness, the basic steps in the overall
plan were the same. In all European countries under the Nazi
rule the mass murder of Jews was preceded by a carefully or-
chestrated sequence of violation of rights. In the first phase laws
were introduced defining who was and who was not a Jew and
requiring the identification of all those who were now defined as
Jewish. This was followed by the expropriation of Jewish property and a denial of gainful employment.

The next phase began with the removal of Jews from
their homes to specially designated areas, usually sealed ghettos or transitory camps, out of sight of Christian populations.
Isolation of the Jews before moving them to the death camps
was a rigidly enforced part of the master plan in virtually all
countries under the Nazi direct control. This was followed by
the final mass annihilation.

While exact numbers of those killed are elusive, and existing estimates are to be viewed with caution, they do point to an unprecedented human destruction. According to the figures from the 1945 Nuremberg trials, out of a prewar European Jewish population of a little less than 9 million, 5.7 million had perished during World War II. More recent estimates fluctuate between five and six million Jews killed, with most sources citing the six million figure.

In Nazi-occupied Europe the prewar Jewish child population came to about 1.6 million. During the war an estimated 1.5 million Jewish children were killed, leaving only 6 to 7 percent of them alive at the end of the war.

Clearly the survival rate of children (7 percent) lags behind the survival rate of Jews in general, which is 33 percent. Such differences are not surprising. In the German plans of Jewish annihilation children became special targets.

In line with these policies, upon reaching a concentration camp, practically all Jewish children were immediately sent to their death. On rare occasions a healthy-looking teenager or younger child slipped through the system. To illustrate, from a French police roundup of Jews in July 1942, nine thousand people were shipped off to Poland to the concentration camp Auschwitz. In this transport of nine thousand there were four thousand children. Of the entire group only thirty people came back after the war. None were children.

German preoccupation with the destruction of Jewish children suggests that most of the child survivors were hidden children. Efforts to protect Jewish children were born out of a battle between those who wanted to kill and those who wanted to save. It was an uneven fight, a fight that left many victims and very few survivors.

Still the German determination to destroy the Jews yielded different results in different countries. A basic condition, largely responsible for these differences, was the degree to which the occupying forces gained power over the governmental machinery. Where the Nazis were in virtual control, they were prepared to do whatever was necessary to annihilate the Jews and would tolerate no interference from any individual or group in regard to the carrying out of their policies.

Influencing their decision about how much direct control to exert was the Germans' attitude toward a country's Christian population. In the world of Nazi-occupied Europe policies and controls depended on racial affinities. For example the Nazis defined all Slavs and those who lived in the Baltic countries as subhuman, only slightly above the racial value of Jews. In contrast the highest social rank was reserved for the Scandinavians, who bore a close resemblance to the "Aryan" prototype valued by the Nazis. The rest of the European countries fell somewhere between these two extremes.

The Germans, however, were not always consistent in translating these racial principles into action. Moreover a particular kind of policy and control, in a particular locality, could and did change with time.

Another condition affecting the ability to withstand the persecution and death was the level of anti-Semitism within a given country. No doubt in an environment with a strong anti-Semitic tradition, denunciations of Jews were pervasive. In addition, in a society hostile to Jews, Jewish rescue by Christians was likely to invite disapproval, if not outright censure, from local countrymen. Moreover in areas of extensive anti-Semitism even some of those who were engaged in saving Jews had to cope with their own negative attitudes toward the Jews.

Aside from these cultural patterns, the sheer number of Jews within a particular country and the degree to which they were assimilated must have also affected their chances of rescue. It is easier to hide and protect a smaller number of people.

Besides, the easier it was for Jews to blend into their environment, the less dangerous it was for others to shield them.

In terms of these cultural differences among countries, Denmark represents a very special case. Conditions for the collective rescue of Jews were favorable in virtually every regard, and the Danes took full advantage of them. First, Danish Jews numbered only eight thousand, making up 0.2 percent of Denmark's population. Second, this small group was highly assimilated. Third, the Nazis defined the Danes as a superior "Aryan" race. Partly because of this definition they were left in charge of their own political destiny, retaining the prewar government. Of all European countries under Nazi domination, Denmark enjoyed the most favorable position, becoming Hitler's model protectorate state, which functioned relatively undisturbed until 1943.

In sharp contrast Poland had the least favorable conditions for Jewish rescue. Quite early the Germans designated Poland as the center of Jewish destruction. Jews from different European countries were forcibly brought to Poland to die. As the center of Jewish annihilation Poland provides the key to an understanding of the Holocaust in general, and the fate of the hidden children in particular.

The stories of the hidden children included in this book by Jane Marks deal with Belgium, France, Holland, Germany, and areas that were a part of prewar Poland. Out of the twenty-three cases, ten are Polish Jews, showing how central Poland was for that historical period.

Poland's wartime centrality is connected to its prewar conditions. In 1939, of all the European countries, Poland had the highest concentration of Jews: 3.3 million, making up 10 percent of the country's population. As the largest community of Jews in Europe, Polish Jews were also the least assimilated. They looked, dressed, behaved and spoke differently than Polish Christians. Some of these differences between Jew and Christian can be traced directly to Jewish religious requirements, which called for special rituals and dress. Other differences were accentuated by the urban concentration of Jews. Over 75 percent lived in urban settings, while the same was true for only 25 percent of the Polish population in general.

Still other differences were reflected in familiarity with the Polish language. In an answer to a 1931 census inquiry, the overwhelming majority of Jews mentioned Yiddish as their native tongue (79 percent), and only 12 percent gave Polish as their first language. The rest chose Hebrew.

Jews and Poles lived in different worlds, and their diverse experiences made for easy identification. It has been estimated that more than 80 percent of the Polish Jews were easily recognizable, while less than 10 percent could be considered assimilated.

The history of Polish anti-Semitism is uneven. During the fourteenth century the relationship between Poles and Jews was relatively free of antagonism. The fourteenth-century Polish king, Kazimierz the Great, invited the Jews to settle in Poland. He felt that their presence would improve the country's economic and cultural conditions. However, in Poland, as in most countries, economic and social upheavals would signal a rise of anti-Semitism. This happened after 1935, after the death of Józef Pilsudski, the head of the Polish government. At that time Poland's semidictatorial regime was faced with grave social, political, and economic problems. The government decided to solve the country's difficulties by relying on anti-Semitic measures. As a result Jewish participation in economic, educational, and cultural spheres was severely curtailed.

Taking its cues from its Nazi neighbors, the Polish government began to search for a so-called Jewish solution. In 1937 Józef Beck, the foreign minister, speaking to the Polish parliament, insisted that the country had space only for half a million Jews. This meant that almost three million Jews had to leave.

When in 1939 the Germans had occupied Poland, the Nazis had behind them six years of experience with anti-Jewish policies. This experience added to their efficiency. Moreover Polish anti-Semitism, with its many established patterns, offered a receptive environment. More importantly still, in Poland the Nazi political machinery was in full control and eager to act. No doubt, too, the Nazi view of Poles as only slightly above the Jews on the scale of racial values gave the Germans a free hand to behave in any way they saw fit.

From the start the German invasion of Poland brought with it virulent anti-Semitic propaganda. The Polish mob reacted by instigating attacks against Jewish property and the Jews. These seemingly spontaneous outbursts were followed by a succession of Nazi directives. Special identity documents were issued to Jews, and they were required to wear the Star of David sewn onto their clothing or as arm bands. Jewish properties were confiscated, and Jews were removed from gainful employment. Restrictions on travel and restrictions on movement within the communities were also introduced.

Pointing to the initial turmoil of anti-Jewish violence, the Germans presented it as proof that Poles and Jews must be separated. Soon Jews were forcibly removed from their homes and brought to ghettos, which were located in the most dilapidated parts of urban centers. Isolated from the rest of the population and from other Jewish communities, ghetto inmates had to work hard for starvation wages, or no wages, in industries that supported the Nazi war machinery. In the ghettos overcrowding, hunger, disease, epidemics, and death were the order of the day.

The next and final stage consisted either of mass executions or forced removals to concentrations camps, where death was waiting for most of them. In the end out of a 3.3 million prewar population of Polish Jews, an estimated 50,000 to 100,000 survived in the country. Another 250,000 survived because they managed to escape. Most of them went to the USSR, and a minority to Palestine and Sweden. Those who stayed in Poland and survived and those who succeeded in leaving bring the estimated total of Polish Jewish survivors to 10 percent. Ninety percent of the Polish Jewry had perished.

Many of those killed were children. Prewar Poland had an estimated one million Jewish children. Of these children, from infancy to age fourteen, an estimated five thousand, or half of a percent, were alive at the end of the war. As in all European countries, in Poland the survival rate of children was much lower than that of the general Jewish population.

Just as in Poland, the Germans were in full and direct control of the government in Holland as well. They installed a civilian administration headed by the highly experienced Nazi official Artur Von Seyss-Inquart. As head of the government he wielded absolute power, which he applied ruthlessly to the implementation of anti-Jewish policies.

In 1941, as the initial anti-Jewish measures were being introduced, which included attacks by Dutch collaborators, the citizens of Amsterdam protested by calling for a general strike that lasted three days. The Germans reacted swiftly with severe reprisals against both Christians and Jews. Many arrests and deportations to concentration camps followed. In this confrontation the Nazis came out as definite winners.

In Holland in 1942, after a series of preliminary anti-Jewish measures, the Germans began to implement their annihilation plans. This involved placing most of the Jews in

special transitory camps from which they were moved to concentration camps in Poland, usually Auschwitz. To prevent any
interference, the Germans made it clear that they "considered
assistance to Jews as help to the enemy, which was punishable
by torture and deportation to concentration camps." In reality
the Germans were reluctant to inflict the heavy penalties on
the Dutch for shielding Jews. They tried to avoid confronta-
tions with the local population. For example a farmer was
caught hiding Jewish children on his farm three times. Only after the third time was he sent to a concentration camp, where
he died.

After the 1941 strike well-organized Dutch opposition to
the Nazis did not resume until 1943. At that time the Dutch
underground equated aid to Jews with the opposition to the
occupying forces. But Jewish deportations to camps started in
1942, whereas the underground did not become effective until
1943.

The Jews made up 1.6 percent of Holland's population,
which amounted to 140,000 individuals. They were relatively
well integrated into the society. As for the degree of Dutch
anti-Semitism, there are some differences of opinion. The
Dutch are thought by some to be free of anti-Semitism. Some
Dutch Jews, however, disagree with this assessment.

Of the 140,000 Dutch Jews, an estimated 75 percent had
perished. Among the 35,000 survivors, 3,500 were children.

In contrast to Poland and Holland, the German Army
was in charge in Belgium, and for them Jewish annihilation
was not a top priority. Still, the military complied with the
Nazi plans, and by May 1942 they began transporting Belgium
Jews to concentration camps in Poland.

At the end of the war, of the 65,000 Belgium Jews, about
40 percent had survived. Among them were 3,000 children.

The Germans divided France into an occupied and an un-

occupied zone. The unoccupied section had a French government, known as the Vichy government. Not directly under
German control, this Vichy government was unusual. Of all
the Western European countries, it alone, on its own, had initiated and adopted anti-Semitic policies.

In the occupied part of France the French police were
very active in rounding up Jews. The French police took the
initiative in allocating Jewish children to convoys that were
leaving for the concentration camp Auschwitz.

Out of 350,000 French Jews, an estimated 90,000 had
been killed. Figures for child survivors range from 5,000 to
15,000, with most of them identified as orphans.

The eagerness with which the Vichy government partici-
pated in Jewish annihilation and the relatively high rate of
Jewish survival, 74 percent, look like a contradiction. Histori-
ans Michael Marrus and Robert Paxton explain that since the
French Jews were dispersed all over the country and protected
by the local populations, they were hard to find. These histo-
rians further suggest that time played an important part in
Jewish survival. For France the war had ended early. The
Vichy government had intended to give all the Jews over to the
Germans, but simply had no time to do so.

Despite the differences that had existed between some
countries, all Jewish children in wartime Europe were confronted by overpowering and destructive forces. In Poland I
was one of these children. For three years, protected by Christian Poles, I lived under an assumed name, pretending to be
Catholic. I survived because Christians were willing to risk
their lives to protect me. In 1945, when it was over, I resumed
my Jewish identity, determined to forget. I wanted to forget
the conditions that forced me to become someone else. I
wanted to forget the person I had so desperately tried to become. I even wanted to forget the Christian Poles who helped

me survive. And so I stayed away from everything that had to do with the war. And when, as it sometimes happened, the subject did come up in the form of a question, I refused to deal with it. I would retreat instead into my self-imposed silence.

For years my wartime experiences and my professional life remained totally unconnected. The books and articles I wrote were based on research on gambling, adolescent drug usage, and family deviance. But then, by 1975, for unexplained reasons my childhood memories began to stir, demanding attention. When these demands became a compulsion, I decided to revisit my past by writing an autobiography, *Dry Tears: The Story of a Lost Childhood.*

As I was recapturing my wartime experiences, the same few questions kept recurring. What was it like for other Jews who had tried to pass for Christians? Who were they? How did they survive? Who were the Christian Poles who defied all dangers and risked their lives for Jews, who were traditionally defined as "Christ killers"? These and many more questions led to my study of compassion, altruism, rescue, and survival during World War II. The fate of the hidden children was a part of my research. While as hidden children each of us had a unique story, all of us had shared similar experiences and characteristics.

Unlike the children who come to the attention of the courts or different health professionals, hidden children were neither physically nor psychologically handicapped. We were not what is being identified as abused children. Hidden children were special. After all, unlike the majority of the Jewish children, we were selected to be rescued.

For most of us the road to becoming a hidden child began with parents or guardians. Only very few, from age ten on, had by themselves decided to move to the forbidden Christian world. Whereas the decision to become a hidden child held out the promise of life, it also involved many hardships. Initially these hardships had to do with the pain of separation, experienced by both parents and children.

Only rarely could an entire family make an illegal move into the Christian world. Usually some family members lacked the necessary physical and verbal attributes for staying in the forbidden world. Others had no possibility of finding refuge. Still others lacked the will and determination to try.

Once the hurdles of separation were overcome, we had to rely on the protection of Christian rescuers. All Nazi-occupied countries had some Christian rescuers. The very presence of these protectors, just as the presence of the hidden children, reflected an opposition to the Nazi measures of Jewish annihilation. Such risky help came from private individuals or from people connected to organizations. Private aid from and through friends and acquaintances was more common than organizational help.

Most countries, among them Belgium, Holland, and Poland, had special sections of the underground that were devoted to saving Jewish children. Frequently these sections were run jointly by Jews and Christians. Convents, monasteries, and orphanages were also involved in saving Jewish children. Some of these religious institutions were connected to an underground, while others acted independently.

When taking a step into the Christian world the destinies of the Jewish children were influenced by their appearance and the extent to which it conformed to the stereotypical "Jewish look." How well we could blend socially into the new environment also made a difference. From the very beginning some children would go into hiding, some would pass as Christians, but most had to change from hiding to passing and back again.

Documents that identified the Jewish children as Christians offered some safety. Several kinds of identification were used. Some were manufactured illegally, bearing fictitious names. Others were duplicates of documents belonging to real people. Some papers were purchased on the black market. Others were offered free of charge by different illegal organizations. Special sections of the underground manufactured, collected, and distributed false papers. Parish priests were allowed to issue duplicate birth certificates, and some of them did offer such documents to Jews. However, not all Jews who stayed on the Christian side had false papers.

Those who had obtained new documents had to learn many new facts to support their new identities: names, dates, places regarding not only themselves but also their fictitious relatives. Inconsistency could arouse suspicion; one slip could mean disaster.

Becoming well acquainted with one's new identity was only a small part of what a passing child had to do. Familiarity with a Christian religion was another important prerequisite for the new life. Often those suspected of being Jewish were subjected to rigorous cross-examination. Failure to pass such tests often led to death.

Boys were in special jeopardy because in Europe only Jewish males were circumcised at birth. A casual examination could easily reveal a male's identity. For this reason alone, passing was more dangerous for Jewish boys than girls.

Except for infants, from an early age on, hidden children had to give up their childhood. I remember my father trying to impress upon me that childhood was a luxury Jewish children could not afford. While growing up fast, we also had to be flexible. An important part of this flexibility was being good and obedient. We were not supposed to cry. We did not, at least not in front of others.

Our daily existence was tied to two closely connected requirements: giving up our Jewish identity and silence. Giving up our identity meant playing a part, becoming someone else. The better we played the role, the safer we were. Sometimes we were so caught up in the new part that we actually forgot who we really were. Though helpful, this temporary forgetfulness was emotionally costly. For many of us, giving up our true identity created an emotional void and made us feel anxious, worried that we would never recapture our past. We also felt ashamed for giving up what had been cherished by our parents, by those we loved.

As we played our new roles, we were totally enveloped by silence. We had to be silent about our past, present, and future. Often we had to listen to anti-Semitic remarks. No matter how much this might have hurt us, we could not object. Breaking the silence could mean death. Silence became deeply ingrained in all hidden children.

Keeping silent and giving up our Jewishness, even temporarily, implied not only a rejection of our past but also a rejection of our religion. And even though most hidden children came from secular homes, religion assumed an important part in our lives. We knew that being Jewish had deprived us of the right to live. Being Jewish meant something bad, something for which one could be killed.

Being Christian could save us. Being Christian meant being protected. The difference between being Christian and being Jewish hinged on religion, on different kinds of gods. Invariably questions came up about the difference between the two kinds of gods. A God that could not even protect its children did not seem very trustworthy. Undoubtedly the extent to which hidden children had followed this kind of reasoning depended on many factors: age and contact with parents, other Jews, and Christian protectors.

Religion figured prominently in the lives of the hidden children, and it had a double edge. We were disappointed in our God. We felt abandoned by Him. Yet we needed the consolation from God. We were ready for a new God. In fact we were comforted by a new God that promised acceptance and safety. By saving us, this new God was protecting us from evil, and we equated this new God with goodness.

Of the different religions Catholicism was particularly influential in the lives of the hidden children, through both the Church's official and unofficial position. Throughout the war Pope Pius XII had never directly condemned the Nazi extermination of Jews. This historical fact is surrounded by much controversy. Up until now the Vatican had denied free access to its wartime archives.

But the pope's silence did not keep some Catholic clergymen from speaking out against the Nazi atrocities and from participating in the rescue of Jews. Some Catholic clergy expressed their opposition to the German occupation by saving Jewish children.

Most hidden children in Poland stayed in convents, monasteries, and orphanages. Children who could talk but were not old enough to grasp what was happening were in a particularly precarious situation. They had to be convinced that they were in fact Christian. This could be achieved in part through intensive religious instructions and baptism. From the perspective of many of these Jewish children, baptism and Catholicism were positive forces. Each had shielded them from danger. Each had offered them a feeling of security and comfort.

But conversion of Jewish children led to accusations and counteraccusations. Admitting that the Catholic church was active in rescuing children, the historian Emmanuel Ringelblum had questioned the reasons for this help. Citing the convent in Częstochowa, Poland, that accepted children only under the age of six, he concluded that this age restriction meant that the Church was concerned with the saving of souls, not with the saving of Jewish lives.

It is true that most children who survived in convents and monasteries were baptized. It is true that the Catholic church welcomes converts. Still, from these two facts it does not necessarily follow that Catholics saved children because they wanted converts. There are many cases on record showing reluctance to baptize these children without the permission of their Jewish guardians.

In this connection two important but often neglected facts ought to be considered. First, clergy and lay Catholics as rescuers were prompted by a variety of motivations, not all of which were conscious. The possibility that some of these motivations grew out of the desire to convert ought not to distract us from a basic and more important consideration: Pious rescuers, like all others, were risking their lives. Indeed it is the selfless, self-sacrificing, and lifesaving aspects of their actions that deserve special attention and not the questionable secondary gains that might have resulted from the acquisition of converts.

Inevitably the influence of religion spilled over into the postwar lives of the hidden children. For many the return to Judaism was a drawn-out process. Some never returned. Some hidden children were exposed to kidnapping and postwar sufferings.

In Holland an estimated 3,500 children had survived the war, with 1,941 orphans among them. Some orthodox Christian families, which had sheltered Jewish children, were reluctant to hand them over to their biological parents and to the Jewish community. Some of these wartime protectors felt that the request to give up these children showed an ingratitude for their past sacrifices. Moreover some of the rescuers were convinced that their wartime difficulties entitled them to keep these children. In support of this claim Holland passed a law that required Jewish parents who came back for their children to prove that they would be fit parents. Inevitably this law led to many hardships and many conflicts.

While in France the situation seemed less drastic, the French Jewish community also met with strong opposition when trying to reclaim Jewish orphans. Usually those who refused to hand over the children had the support of some church leaders.

In all countries attempts to reclaim Jewish children led to complicated and often painful reactions. Jewish parents, when faced with a reluctant and hostile child, suffered, as did adoptive parents when they had to part with the youngsters.

For the children these postwar changes were also painful. The very survival of these children was proof that they had adjusted well to their roles as Christians. But at the end of the war they were asked to switch their roles again. For many hidden children their parents were strangers, often unwelcome strangers. When parents came to claim them, it created ambivalent feelings at best.

Acceptance, hostility, ambivalence, resentment, shame, and regret were only some of the emotions we hidden children had. Some of us may still continue to have such feelings about our Jewishness, about our religion. At times mixed together, appearing and disappearing, these emotions are not surprising.

After all, we children could not easily give up that which helped us survive. If being Jewish meant danger, disapproval, something one could be killed for, why would a child want to take it back? Most hidden children were conflicted about these issues. For a while we were suspended between two worlds: the Christian and the Jewish. Some of us could not reconcile the two. Still others had taken a definite step toward Christianity or Judaism.

Has becoming a part of two different worlds given us, the hidden children, a broader, less prejudiced perspective on life, on people?

Perhaps.

Nechama Tec, a Professor of Sociology at the University of Connecticut, is the author of six books and numerous articles. Dr. Tec has been lecturing extensively both in the United States and abroad. Since 1977 she has been conducting research about compassion, altruism, resistance to evil, and the rescue of Jews during World War II.

Professor Tec's most recent book, Defiance: The Bielski Partisans, *was published by Oxford University Press in 1993 and was awarded the 1994 Anne Frank Special Recognition Prize.* Defiance *was supported by a 1991–1992 Littauer Foundation Grant and a 1992–1993 Memorial Foundation for Jewish Culture Grant.*

THE PSYCHOLOGY BEHIND
BEING A HIDDEN CHILD

by Eva Fogelman, Ph.D.

The concept of the hidden child is as ancient as the biblical story of Moses.

Moses was hidden by his mother and sister in a basket in the reeds of the Nile River when Pharaoh ordered that all new-born Jewish male children must be killed. One day the princess, the daughter of Pharaoh, who was walking by the Nile, heard the cries of an infant. The Bible tells us that from the child's tears she understood that he was a Hebrew baby. Still, the princess disobeyed her father to save Moses' life. She was the first rescuer. Through her rescue of a Jewish child she received a new name, Batya, "daughter of God."

Centuries later Hitler, like Pharaoh, made the Jewish children his principal target in order to deprive the Jewish people of a future.

For most of us Anne Frank has been the quintessential hidden child. Along with her immediate family and acquaintances Anne hid in an attic above her father's spice business in

Amsterdam. They were protected by the father's workers, who continued to run the business and care for the daily needs and emotional well-being of the family, until the day came when the family was denounced and sent first to Auschwitz and then to Bergen-Belsen.

This hiding experience was the exception rather than the norm. More often families were separated to ensure the safety of their members. Children were hidden by others ("passive hiding"), or they hid themselves, or they passed as Christians ("active hiding"). A warm and comfortable bed and food every day was rarely the hidden child's experience. For the most part they lived in hunger, under constant terror of discovery.

Whatever the hiding ordeal, few hidden children were spared encounters with violent death. Death imagery is indelibly etched in child survivors' memory. They witnessed naked men, women, and children—among them their own relatives—lined up and machine-gunned in town squares and in the outskirts of cities. The ghettos were littered with dead bodies. A few children saw or heard their rescuer(s) being shot for helping Jews. Those who hid themselves among the partisans were eyewitnesses to the murder of their comrades by the Germans. In the woods body parts were strewn everywhere after bombings.

The imminence of their own deaths was pervasive. Children had guns pointed at their heads by Germans who asked them if anybody was hiding in the attic. They were warned that if somebody was found they would be killed.

Deborah Dwork, a Yale historian, categorizes children as visible or invisible during their hiding years, although some were both. One would be invisible if he was actually hiding in cabinets, caves, pigsties, attics, cellars, or sewers.

Children such as Kristine Keren, who lived with her family in a sewer, and Kim Fendrick, who hid in a variety of places, from a rain barrel to a car-sized bunker beneath a barn, would be considered invisible. Rosa Sirota, who lived hidden with a Ukrainian peasant family, and Renee Roth-Hano, who survived by living in a convent, are examples of children who were visible.

In order to ensure their survival, visible hidden children were forced to lead double lives. To be visible meant to be constantly reminded of one's new identity. Children had to rehearse their stories: "Your family was bombed out, and you are living with cousins." Or, "you are from the city and came to work on a farm, where there is more food." And so on.

Hiding one's true identity enhanced the chances of security. Yet slip-ups could happen, and role-playing was not always so simple. Jewish children had to learn Christian ritual in order to "pass" at a church service, at the dinner table, in a convent, school, or orphanage. Renee Roth-Hano, Clem Loew, and Rosa Sirota, for example, experienced feigning Catholicism firsthand. Not knowing how to go to confession could cost a child his or her life. Those who were old enough to remember their Jewish past felt Jewish on the inside but at the same time had to act like Christians on the outside. Children such as Ava Landy could not risk forgetting her new Christian name and made-up family history. What child could not control a spontaneous humming of a Yiddish or Hebrew melody or saying something in his or her sleep?

In rare cases a hidden child had a double identity by masquerading as the opposite sex. A boy had to be taught how to walk and talk like a girl, as is so poignantly described by Richard Rozen. In Polish certain words are different when said by a man or by a woman. Most difficult of course was going to the bathroom. Jewish boys in particular had to make sure that no one saw their circumcised penises, as only Jewish males were circumcised in those days. At times hidden children, such as Lola Kaufman, played the role of a mute child, to keep the neighbors from suspecting that they were not one of them.

Unless they were infants, hidden children lost their childhoods. They had to grow up overnight and assume the adult responsibilities of caring for themselves, for younger siblings, or for parents who had lost their ability to be caretakers. A child had to know how to act, how to size up situations, and always had to be on the lookout for the next piece of bread. Hide-and-seek was reality, not a game. At any moment a hidden child could be confronted with life-and-death decisions. As a result the basic trust that a child develops in an ordinary childhood is absent among hidden children.

Feelings of abandonment are pervasive among child survivors who were abandoned by their own parents—who placed their children either in convents, monasteries, orphanages, boarding schools, or Christian families; or set them free to fend for themselves because parents thought that that was their children's only chance for survival. Those whose parents were killed were also abandoned, with the child left to take care of himself. After liberation children such as Joseph Vles, who was hidden as an infant, felt abandoned by their rescuing parents, who returned them to their natural parents.

Jewish children in hiding learned by necessity a host of survival strategies to cope with fears, imminence of death, starvation, freezing weather, illness, being invisible or maintaining a low profile, and loneliness. Most important was not to express any opinions or feelings and to remain silent. One had always to be a "good child," which meant not being seen or heard or making any trouble. Such strategies became second nature.

Continual distrust of the outside world, of new acquaintances, and of new situations actually protected the child in extreme danger. But what impact does this habit of distrusting the external world have on the everyday life of a person after liberation? While suspicion, extra precautions, and lack of basic trust were adaptive strategies in wartime, these strategies can be detrimental in adjusting to peacetime life and relationships.

Many hidden children, such as Nicole David and Carla Lessing, survived by complying with the demands of others and not expressing their own needs. The will to live gave them the strength not to allow themselves to succumb to infection, hunger, exhaustion, and freezing temperature. This same determination to survive enabled Annette Baslaw-Finger to cross the Pyrenees in freezing weather in light clothing and with literally nothing to eat.

For most homeless and stateless survivors the years immediately following liberation did not bring immediate relief and were fraught with many other hardships.

In Eastern Europe, surviving Jews were traumatized once again by the reception they got from their neighbors. Richard Rozen and Lola Kaufman had doors slammed in their faces. As an afterthought some people threw bread out the window or advised them to beg. Former neighbors told the survivors that all the Jews were supposed to be dead. Jews were informed that their houses and jobs were taken over. Ava Landy saw her father's prayer shawl used as a tablecloth on a neighbor's dining-room table while the neighbor denied knowing anything about the survivor's possessions. New occupants in Jewish survivors' old homes would not even return their pictures. They were told, "go away, or we'll call the police."

The ultimate in "welcoming" responses was to kill the returning Jews. In Kielce, Poland, forty-two Jews were murdered on July 4, 1946. Twenty-five miles away from Kielce in Radom there were incidents in which Jews were killed. Christian rescuers had to let out their Jewish charges in a clandestine manner because their lives were at stake as well.

Christian children in Eastern Europe were even more vicious to surviving Jewish children than adults were. Kristine Keren and Kim Fendrick were taunted by other children with anti-Semitic tirades and physical abuse, such as having lighted matches thrown at them. Some continued to hide their identity as Jews; others escaped the torment as best they could; in Kim's case it meant dropping out of school.

Separation from rescuing parents was a traumatic event. The trauma of hidden infant children, spared the immediate burden of identity problems, began when total strangers—either their own parents whom they never knew, a relative, or a representative from some Jewish organization—came to pick them up. They often felt that they had been abandoned by their rescuing parents. Many children had trouble accepting their new identities as Jews, feeling that they were being disloyal to both their foster parents and their adopted religion.

In many cases the rescuing parents did not want to give back children whom they had raised as their own for several years. Because of the strong attachment between the rescuing parent and the hidden child, some survivor parents completely severed their relationships with their natural children.

There were rescuers who handled the matter differently. For example, some thought it best for the children to develop a loving relationship with their natural parents, and deliberately severed contact with them, not realizing that the children felt abandoned and did not understand the genuine motivations of the rescuers.

After years of malnutrition, exposure to infectious diseases, and unbearable weather conditions, many child and adult survivors suffered physical illnesses. But they needed to recover their emotional health as well. Adult survivors who returned from the concentration camps were ill equipped to be able to care for young children. Therefore some hidden-child survivors, such as Marie-Claire Rakowski, were picked up by personnel from a Jewish organization and sent from one foster home to another. Some were reunited with family members who survived elsewhere. These reunions were not always pleasant. Hidden children who were sheltered during the war were resented by family members who were incarcerated in concentration camps or had other unfortunate survival experiences.

Conditions were not much better in the United States. Foster families or blood relatives were often unwilling to care for child survivors of the Holocaust. They wanted to protect their own children from hearing about the atrocities and demanded that the child survivors remain silent about their past.

Once they were in America hidden children had to make up for lost years. Josie Martin, Annette Baslaw-Finger, and Ruth Rubenstein learned English and other languages quickly and often graduated near the top of their American high school classes and even attended top competitive colleges. It is most striking that many child survivors completed college and graduate school and became successful professionals, despite the loss of their early education; perhaps it was through the same strength and determination that had helped them to survive. For Annette Baslaw-Finger the motivation to advance was a powerful driving force to make up for other losses.

Nietzsche says, "One cannot live without forgetting." And perhaps what has enabled hidden children to cope is not dwelling on the years of trauma. However, this has also meant that many have not properly or sufficiently mourned the death of family members.

In my psychotherapy with hidden-child survivors who today are middle-aged, I find that they are at various stages of the mourning process for losses incurred years before. Some still have not begun mourning because they cannot accept that a loved one will never come back. During the war years, when a child said good-bye to a parent, he or she did not understand that it could be for the last time. Some hidden children have not mourned their parents to this day; you cannot mourn a person you hope deep down to meet again. When traveling to a new city, hidden children take the opportunity to review phone books to search for lost relatives. Clem Loew, for instance, admits he still posts his father's name on the bulletin board of missing people at Holocaust-survivor meetings.

The mourning process starts with the breaking down of denial. In recent years hidden children whose parents were deported to concentration camps found their parents' names—and fates—on lists prepared by Serge Klarsfeld, a hidden child himself. Seeing in black and white the fate of one's parents has sometimes allowed the mourning process to begin. Other hidden children begin to confront the reality of their parents' never coming back as they themselves adapt to their own grown children leaving home or getting married. An immediate separation that evokes feelings of loss inevitably stirs up prior losses, many of which have not been mourned. The hidden children themselves are getting older, and this reality arouses thoughts of their own mortality and of unresolved previous losses.

A leading expert on child survivors of the Nazi Holocaust, psychoanalyst Judith Kestenberg, has observed that among the child survivors, depression in middle age is a sign of incomplete mourning and unacknowledged anger. This depression ought not be compared to clinical depression in other populations. Kestenberg further adds that to be angry, depressed, and anxious is a normal reaction to the persecution experience.

Despite the resilience of hidden children, the years of being hidden or hiding oneself have their residual effects. Until recently many hidden children did not necessarily link their war trauma to their present daily lives and coping mechanisms. The consequences may not be apparent to an observer, but they are more visible in intimate relationships and to the hidden children themselves.

Certain feelings have lingered in some hidden children's current lives. A predominant fear is that of abandonment, which inevitably affects intimate relationships. I have observed child survivors who develop a series of relationships in which they are abandoned for other lovers. Child survivors are often confused as to whether they are doing things in order to send people away as a way of coping with fear of abandonment. The irony is that for many hidden children the connection to earlier abandonment is not realized until they engage in a therapeutic process of recounting their life experiences chronologically beginning with their family and personal history before the years of persecution.

Feeling as if one does not belong and not knowing where one does belong are other pervasive experiences in the adult lives of many hidden children. Some hidden children still go to great lengths to hide their Jewishness for fear of being too visible in case of a future threat of genocide of the Jews. This fear keeps them isolated and alienated from the Jewish community. On the other hand some feel anxious with strangers, especially non-Jews, and therefore are hesitant to reveal themselves too much in fear of being mistreated.

Hidden-child survivors harbor many irrational fears: fear of the sound of a doorbell, of someone knocking, of hearing a plane overhead, of seeing a policeman in a uniform, and of being caught without food. Such everyday signals evoke a flashback to a traumatic period. Since they were raised with the belief that the outer world is dangerous—a place to fear—the feeling continues to linger in their present environment.

Threats of annihilation are intensified by such events as the Cuban Missile Crisis, the Gulf War, and the threat of nuclear war.

Some coping mechanisms that hidden children exploited during the years of persecution continue to be helpful: the ability to put on "a good act," determination to succeed at all costs, taking care of others, and learning to be cared for. Hidden children who were active in their own survival learned to size up dangerous situations and to know what to do. In later life this ability has helped them to outsmart people who placed obstacles in their way.

The secret to surviving as a hidden child was to remain silent, not to feel or express any needs or desires, to be as invisible as possible. Feelings such as aggression and assertiveness were certainly taboo. For survivors who are today professionals, as exemplified by Ruth Rubenstein, this self-effacing practice has often hindered their ability to promote themselves in the work world. When they do become successful, some child survivors fear being too visible or losing the person who has become a caretaker.

Hidden-child survivors who hid in several dozen places are still looking for another hiding place and do not enjoy a sense of belonging. For Joe Steiner this takes the form of always looking for a new job or fearing that he will lose his job.

When hidden children become parents, they are reminded of their own fears in childhood, and they may take extra precautions to ensure the safety of their children. When Annette Baslaw-Finger's children were young, she had to get out of bed many times to reassure herself that her children were actually tucked into a real bed in a real room. Youngsters also remind survivors of the loss of their own childhood.

Remaining silent, which was a coping strategy that saved many children, is not a realistic practice for life after the Holocaust. By not speaking up, child survivors deprive themselves of having their needs fulfilled and of allowing others to know who they are and what they think and feel. What most hidden-child survivors resist is sharing their suffering and losses with their children. Survivors tend to avoid letting their own off-spring know details of their survival because a parent is reluctant to show a child the depth of his or her humiliation, degradation, and vulnerability. Parents want to appear to their children as having some power and control in the world in order to protect their youngsters and make them feel safe.

The communication problem was compounded for younger survivors because parents, as in Josie Martin's family, discouraged them from recalling their past. While the official (adult) survivors set up social gatherings and organizations to reminisce and mourn, the child survivors were excluded. This resulted in the continuing isolation of hidden children after the war years. There were no organizations for hidden children as there were for survivors of the Warsaw ghetto (WAGRO), Bergen-Belsen (Federation of Bergen-Belsen World Federation), and the partisans (American Federation of Jewish Fighters, Camp Inmates, and Nazi Victims).

Furthermore, for many years after the war only survivors of ghettos and concentration camps were considered "legitimate" Holocaust survivors. Hidden children therefore did not identify themselves as such, nor did others perceive them as Holocaust survivors. Noted psychoanalyst Erik Erikson believes that individuals need to be recognized by their community for the crucial development of identity formation. Denial of the significance of the Holocaust for hidden children resulted in unresolved "identity confusion" and difficulty in developing true and mutual intimacies with another person.

In the mid-seventies I developed the first support groups in which hidden children participated. By meeting with other hidden children from diverse backgrounds and by sharing experiences, their past was validated. Children who were hidden when they were older helped fill in the gaps for those survivors who were too young at the time to remember. By hearing others and filling in missing images, a child survivor could begin to feel connected to his or her past and integrate it into his or her current self.

Many parents of the hidden children believe that their offspring do not remember, so "what's the point of talking to them anyway?" Yet dialogue between the generations about the past not only brings them together but also opens up new understanding about the self.

Hidden children whose parents and other relatives are still alive find that talking about the past and asking questions brings healing. Similarly, meeting others who were hidden in the same convent or orphanage can be a powerful healing experience. Seeing photographs of oneself gives tangible proof that one existed in a place and at a time that one could not remember. It is an exhilarating experience to learn what the child survivor looked like when he or she was young. While repressing painful memories was a coping mechanism in the immediate years following persecution, as hidden children are aging they are working on integration of past and present.

The mourning process can be facilitated by the recovery of memory, attests Flora Hogman, a psychologist and hidden child herself. In her research Hogman has found that whether the memories are real or are invented, they can become vehicles for recapturing lost feelings at a time when memories are elusive.

While many hidden children coped by numbing themselves, which lessened their pain, this ultimately does not allow psychological and emotional healing. Memories can be recaptured through the process of giving a testimony—an opportunity at integrating a fragmented life. Judith Kestenberg has developed methods for facilitating child survivors' memories from a preverbal stage. An interview about one's life before, during, and after the Holocaust sheds new understanding; it clarifies the relationship between adaptation to life after liberation and survival techniques during the war. The verbal reenactment of the trauma is healing.

Psychoanalyst George Pollock has theorized that from mourning comes creativity. As more hidden children confront the murder of their loved ones and their own lost childhoods, we witness a proliferation of the writing of personal memoirs, poetry, art, films, theatrical productions, novels, and research. These other forms of reenactment enable a hidden child to come out of hiding and to get affirmation from others. Renee Roth-Hano, author of *Touch Wood*, was honored in the town of Flers, where she was rescued. She reacted with "how strange and wonderful to be rewarded for the very thing I once was made to feel ashamed of." After liberation she felt ashamed of being Jewish and told people she was Catholic. She is now reaccepting herself as a Jew.

Returning to one's hometown or to hiding places are other routes toward integration and development of a sense of continuity in the self. By visiting places that were the source of trauma, danger, and helplessness, a renewed sense of mastery is gained. Nightmares may disappear or become less frequent. Meeting people who knew the survivor as a child offers a child survivor the validation that he or she existed and fills the gap of some missing information about the self.

Most important, the experience of reuniting with one's rescuer and being able to thank the rescuer or his or her children is a gratifying experience. Again, the helpless child can gain some mastery over prior helplessness. The rescuer or his or her children are a source of information that can confirm the hidden child's past, which has influenced the child's present, whether or not the child remembers his or her trauma.

When child survivors share their life stories with their children and with other close relatives, the child survivors experience a tremendous relief in not having to hide anymore. By openly talking about the past, others can get to know the real person, his or her pains and fears, as well as his or her joys and dreams.

When a group becomes identifiable—in this case hidden children during Nazi-occupied Europe—there is a tendency to want to compare symptoms of members of the group with those of other traumatized children from, for example, Cambodia and Vietnam or war-torn Lebanon, or of starving children in Africa, or of sexually and physically abused children in our midst. However, the abuse of the hidden children was unique in several ways. First, they were persecuted merely because they were Jews. Their core identity therefore had to be concealed from others for several years. How does one afterward establish a positive self-image as a Jew, when it meant being degraded, spat on, called "pig," "vermin," and the like, and was ultimately equated with death? How does one overcome the shame of being Jewish and feel pride instead?

Younger child survivors, such as Stan Turecki, did not even know what it meant to be Jewish. During the war years they learned that the Jews killed Jesus and they heard anti-Semitic sentiments expressed all around them. How could they gain a sense of belonging to a group with whom they do not share symbols, traditions, and values? Other traumatized groups, such as victims of incest, torture victims, and victims of racial bigotry, do not have this kind of identity conflict.

Second, the relationship between the abuser and the victim is different for hidden children from that of physically or sexually abused children. According to Flora Hogman, for those who survived the Holocaust the abuser is a more abstract force than it is when someone is abused by his or her parent or by another close relative. Children who are physically or sexually abused by a relative have a different psychological adjustment than those who suffered from Nazi persecution. Children who were physically and sexually abused suffer more guilt and shame about doing something wrong in order to deserve such treatment. Very young hidden children who did not have a loving hiding experience also experience self-blame for their suffering.

What we learn from hidden children is that abuse does not have to breed abuse in future generations.

The resilience of hidden children attests to the endurance of the human spirit. The loving homes that most Jewish children experienced prior to the Nazi era, or in some cases loving rescuers, is what has made a difference in their recovery.

Survivor guilt, a feeling that haunts many survivors, has also been an inspiration to give meaning to survivors' lives. To transform guilt feelings into an adaptive mechanism gives meaning to their survival and prevents them from dwelling on the pain and suffering. Some try to live in the name of those who did not survive; others do a few good things for other people and continue to live the Jewish life that was destroyed.

The First International Gathering of Children Hidden During World War II, on Memorial Day weekend 1991, which united more than 1,600 hidden-child survivors and an equal number who responded but were not ready to attend, was of monumental significance in starting the process of healing wounds by reducing a sense of isolation and alienation. The communal confrontation with a traumatic past provided a supportive environment in which participants felt understood and validated for their pain. For many this was the first time they met others from a similar background. They reminisced and cried together, mourned their dead family members and lost childhoods. And with this experience emerged an unconscious desire to "do something." The more fortunate survivors, such as Ed Lessing, began helping those who were left with nothing. The mental-health professionals among them formed groups to facilitate healing for themselves and for others. New immigrants are being helped by those who were once in the same position. Anti-Semitism and other forms of racism are being denounced and counteracted by those who themselves were once victimized by such attitudes and expressions.

Healing cannot be done in isolation. A communal tragedy can only be healed by collective mourning. The consolation of community gives a sense of belonging and the strength to be honest and open about oneself, as well as to confront the moral responsibility of a survivor to the continuity of the Jewish people and to a more humane society.

Eva Fogelman, Ph.D., is a social psychologist and psychotherapist in private practice. She is senior research fellow at the Center for Social Research, Graduate Center, City University of New York. Dr. Fogelman is founding director of Jewish Foundation for Christian Rescuers, ADL, and codirector of the Training Program for Psychotherapy with Generations of the Holocaust and Related Traumas, Training Institute for Mental Health. She is the writer and coproducer of the award-winning documentary Breaking the Silence: The Generation After the Holocaust *and the author of* Doing Moral Good: Courage During the Holocaust, *forthcoming from Doubleday.*

ABOUT THE AUTHOR

Jane Marks writes the monthly family-therapy column "Our Problem" in *Parents* magazine. A collection of the columns, *We Have a Problem: A Parent's Sourcebook*, was published by American Psychiatric Press in 1992. A free-lance writer specializing in problems of children and families, Ms. Marks has written three nonfiction books for teenagers and hundreds of articles and columns for magazines such as *Seventeen*, *Ladies' Home Journal*, *Glamour*, *Mademoiselle*, *Woman's Day*, *Family Circle*, *New York* magazine, and *Town & Country*. Ms. Marks won a National Easter Seal Society Communication Award for outstanding media coverage in 1986 and a first-place Clarion Award in 1991.